SUSTAINABLE TOURISM

SUSTAINABLE TOURISM

B.S. Badan
Harish Bhatt

Commonwealth

[*The responsibility for the facts stated, conclusions reached and plagiarism, if any, in this book is entirely that of the Author. And the Publisher bears no responsibility for them, whatsoever.*]

Sustainable Tourism

First Published : 2007

ISBN 81-311-0074-X

Published by :

Ajay Verma
For COMMONWEALTH PUBLISHERS
4831/24, Prahlad Street,
Ansari Road, Darya Ganj,
New Delhi - 110002
Ph. : 23272541, 23257835
Fax : 91- 011- 23257835
e-mail : campusbooks@hotmail.com

Printed at :
Roshan Offset Printers
Delhi

Preface

Tourism can be defined as the act of travel for the purpose of recreation, and the provision of services for this act. It is a service industry, comprising a number of tangible and intangible components. The tangible elements include transportation systems—air, rail, road, water and now, space; hospitality services, accommodation, foods and beverages, tours, souvenirs; and related services such as banking, insurance and safety and security. The intangible elements include: rest and relaxation, culture, escape, adventure, new and different experiences.

Travel and tourism is a major industry in the world and is at the top of the league of invisible earners of foreign currency. Many sovereignties, along with their respective countries and states, depend heavily upon travel expenditures by foreigners as a source of taxation and income for the enterprises that sell services to these travellers. Consequently the development of tourism is often a strategy employed either by a non-governmental organization or a governmental agency to promote a particular region for the purpose of increasing commerce through exporting goods and services to non-locals.

During recent years the tourism industry has witnessed unprecedented growth. Increasing consumer demand for educational and participatory travel experiences has resulted in a variety of specialty niche markets such as ecotourism, cultural-heritage tourism, and agritourism. New paradigms link strategic tourism planning with sustainable development.

The leisure and tourism industry is one of the leading global economic activities, a multi-billion-dollar industry with

700 million international travellers per year around the world. Tourism is a motor for employment and income creation and, especially in poor countries, a vehicle for development. But today it is not sufficient to simply create employment without regard for the quality of jobs and the social and environmental effects of tourism in vulnerable areas. A growing number of organizations, including the tourism industry leadership, are increasingly conscious of the risks and are adopting a more responsible attitude.

The present publication provides an authoritative look at how to manage travel and tourism industry in a better way. It introduces the complexities of the tourism system so that they will be better positioned to eventually assume the managerial challenges and responsibilities in a diverse and challenging industry. The latest advancements in tourism theory and thinking, retaining the thoroughness of content, diversity of applications, regional and international issues, economic significance, tourism operators and the role of technology in the tourism industry etc. are also described elaborately. Numerous regional and global case studies and examples are included to provide an appropriately broad geographic context. This work will be highly informative and useful to students, researchers, policy makers, managers and working groups of travel and tourism industry.

B.S. Badan
Harish Bhatt

CONTENTS

Preface (v)

Chapter *Pages*

1. Aspects of Sustainable Tourism 1
2. Tourism's Sustainability 28
3. Sustainable Wildlife Tourism 41
4. Travel Ecology 54
5. Accreditation for Tourism 71
6. Tourism and Programme for Raising Environmental Awareness 108
7. Tourism Certification Programme in Europe's National Parks 124
8. Perspectives on Sustainable Tourism in the South Pacific 146
9. Mekong Tourism 173
10. Examples from the UK Coast 201
11. Towards Sustainability Monitoring 219
12. Environmental Impacts of Leisure and Tourism 240
13. Sustainability and 'Green' Leisure and Tourism 264
14. Integrated Case Studies 290

1 Aspects of Sustainable Tourism

Introduction

As with other industrial sectors and fields of academic study, tourism research has also responded to the popularization of the concept of sustainable development in the wake of the World Commission on Environment and Development's Report, *Our Common Future* (WCED, 1987). Hence a growing proportion of the academic and policy oriented tourism literature is now devoted to examining the theory and practice of 'sustainable tourism' (ST). Indeed, 1993 saw the first edition of a journal entirely devoted to the topic the *Journal of Sustainable Tourism.* Although not ignoring the importance of theoretical developments in ST, it is interesting to note the emphasis placed on practical implementation in the editorial which introduced this new journal :

> *It is easy to discuss sustainability. Implementation in the problem. The time has now come 'to walk the talk'.* (Bramwell and Lane, 1993 : 4)

However this chapter is based on the belief that tourism researchers have, in general, not discussed theoretical aspects of ST enough (even allowing for developments in the subject area since 1993); a view shared by some other tourism researchers such as Milne (1998) and Sharpley (2000). Admittedly, it is easy to tire of sustainability rhetoric, but this should not discourage in-depth analyses of the theoretical underpinnings of the concept of ST. It is argued that too many studies appear to lack a clear vision of ST, and that without such clarity rather too many 'walks' (continuing with Bramwell and Lane's analogy) may meander aimlessly for too long, or even head in the wrong direction altogether. A key theme of this chapter is that much ST research is open to a charge of intellectual introversion, and that the clarity required to better understand interpretations of ST, and mechanism of implementation, is to be found in the wider sustainable development (SD) and environmental management literature. Detailed discussion of sustainability is not easy, but it is necessary in order to better understand the different perceptions of ST that are now emerging, and to make some informed choices about that future development of tourism at destination areas.

The chapter begins with a section which argues for the need to look outwards in formulating perceptions of ST, beyond the immediate concerns of tourism and the restrictive confine of much current tourism research. This is followed by the formulation to two broad, and simplified, variants of ST, as informed by an overview of different interpretations of the general concept of SD. Where possible, studies from the academic tourism literature used to illustrate divergent opinion on the meaning of ST. The reader should also note that throughout this chapter sustainability is examined from a natural environment perspective. I, therefore, acknowledge that a comprehensive overview of the SD / ST debate is not provided.

Sectoral Parochialism

It would appear that every conceivable sector or discipline or interest grouping has now attempted to translate aspects of the general concept of SD to its own, more familiar, disciplinary or intellectual frame of reference. For example, I have come across works addressing sustainability in the context of architecture, agriculture, business, cities, economy, forestry, heritage, industry, land use, planning, rural development, society, and water resources. A sceptic might suggest that all this endeavour has more to do with academics recognizing a publication's 'gift horse' than with the altruistic pursuit of knowledge. However, let us assume that genuine intellectual curiosity is at work, perhaps combined with what Wilbanks (1994) describes as the power of the phrase 'sustainable development' to capture a widespread sense of impending global eco-disaster and the need for change in the way societies utilize natural resources. Also, given the current dominance of the western, scientific-reductionist approach to understanding to the world (*e.g.*, Carley and Christie, 1992), it is not surprising that so much effort has been expended on interpreting SD in piecemeal, highly focused and sector-specific manner.

Clearly, sector-specific analysis of SD are required. Academics and practitioners from different backgrounds must bring their own expertise to the issues involved, focusing on those of most immediate relevance. However, this does not mean that they need necessarily lose sight of the implications of their own works for other sectors or disciplines, of that they become detached from the ongoing debate on the meaning and implications of SD. One must at least be aware of the limitations and potential difficulties inherent in sector-specific approaches to understanding and implementing SD. This may be particularly true of tourism which, by its very nature, is a nebulous industry characterized by many direct and indirect connections with other sectors, interest and activities (*e.g.,* Cater, 1995). Recently, for example, the UK suffered a major outbreak of 'foot-and-mouth' disease, a highly contagious viral infection affecting cloven-hoofed animals including cattle, pigs and sheep. In an attempt to control the spread of this disease millions of farm animals were destroyed, and restriction placed upon access to the countryside in both infected and non-infected areas. The latter course of action greatly reduced tourism activity throughout rural areas of the UK, bringing hardship to many tourist businesses. Nothing could more clearly illustrate the linkage that exist between tourism activity and the health, or otherwise, of other sectors.

In all the discussion and debate about aspects of SD, such

as inter-and intragenerational equity, the issue of sectoral fragmentation would appear to have been largely forgotten. A reminder of the World Commission's View (WCED, 1987 : 63) is timely :

> *Intersectoral connections create patterns of economic and ecological interdependence rarely reflected in the ways in which policy is made. Sectoral organizations tend to pursue sectoral objectives and to treat their impacts on other sectors as side effects, taken into account only if compelled to do so . . . Many of the environment and development problem that confront us have their roots in this sectoral fragmentation of responsibility. Sustainable development requires that such fragmentation be overcome.*

Very often, it is the sectoral organization referred to above that are responsible for policy formulation and implementation, and they may take their lead from, or at least be informed by, the views of academic researchers. Unfortunately tourism researchers would appear to be as prone to intellectual introversions as colleagues in other fields of study. Despite the surely incontrovertible truth that the magnitude and nature of tourism development in almost any area will be affected by a wide range of other existing and planned development types, *e.g.*, housing, transport, retailing, health service provision, light industry, nature conservation and agriculture, the tourism literature brims with plans, strategies, models and frameworks constructed solely, or almost exclusively, from a tourism perspective. Yet, many of these have been published under the banner of sustainability and some even claim to be holistic, based upon attempts to integrate only two concerns : tourism development and nature conservation (Hunter, 1995). It is disappointing to find that even otherwise excellent recent studies, which seek to harmonize tourism activities with regional resource charactereristic, apparently see no need to explore, or even summarize, how the proposed tourism development planning frameworks might link in with the characteristic of, and development plans for, other sectors (*e.g.*, Priskin, 2001 ; Ahn *et al.*, 2002).

Worse still, while many 'sustainable' tourism studies simply ignore sectors, some studies have a distinctly confrontational tone, where the potential for competition between tourism and other sectors for access to natural resources is highlighted. If one perceives ST as the 'need' to constantly maintain and extend the tourism resource base and tourism activity in all areas (*i.e.*, exclusive self-interest), then it becomes possible to see (sustainable) tourism as under threat form SD policies (*e.g.*, McKercher, 1993a) ; surely a rather bizarre twist of logic. However, accepting that exclusive sectoral self-interest is not in keeping with the spirit of SD more broadly, then the integration of activities and interest becomes a key task. As McKercher (1993b : 14) also argues :

> *For sustainable tourism to occur, it must be closely integrated with all other activities that occur in the host region.*

This attitude exemplifies a more realistic, mature and holistic strand of thought on the nature of ST that correctly challenges the understandable tendency towards sectoral parochialism in sustainable tourism research. Thus, McKercher's view is echoed by Wall (1993) who criticizes single sector tourism development planning in Bali, and Aravot (1992) who concludes that tourism planning should be part of general development planning to allow better coordination of efforts and the 'interweaving of mutual influences' (p. 17). Relatedly, Lane (1994) warns of the over-reliance of rural areas on tourism, promoting policies which work towards a balanced, diverse rural economy and one, therefore, which is more resilient (sustainable) in the face of change. More recently, Collins (1999), in asking the question, 'deck chairs or ploughshares?', takes issue with the parochial attitude evident amongst many tourism researchers who fail to recognize a role for other sectors in the sustainable development of an area.

If a parochial of 'precious' (Hunter, 1995) view of tourism is apparent amongst some tourism researchers, then it is not surprising to find this attitude even more evident amongst tourism policymakers and trade organizations. In a report on tourism's economic impact, the World Travel and Tourism Council (WTTC, 1999), for example, describes as 'top performers' those countries with the greatest reliance on travel and tourism. Some twenty countries are described as 'leading the way' with regard to the proportion of employment dependent upon travel and tourism, with the 'top' four countries (Anguilla, British Virgin Islands, Bahamas and Saint Lucia) having more than 50 percent of employment in the travel and tourism trade. For many with more of an eye on the implications of general sustainable development, such a heavy reliance on any single sector would be seen as very worrying, perhaps particularly so if the sector in question is as fickle as the international tourism market. At best, the attitude of the WTTC is irresponsible. It is, however, apparently echoed by the World Tourism Organization (WTO) as the following observation by Lanfant and Graburn (1992 : 112) illustrates :

> *At Zakopane in August 1989, the members of the Academy (International Academy for the Study of Tourism) considered Alternative Tourism as a means to contribute to the 'sustainable development' of a society, whereas by October at the WTO meeting in Tamanrasset, Alternative Tourism had become co-opted as a way to ensure the sustainable development of tourism itself. That should give us something to think about.*

Surely, this sleight of hand by the WTO will eventually come to be seen (at least by the great majority of 'objective' academics) as indicative of an industry 'walking' in the wrong direction. Alternative tourism must also be sustainable tourism and, in the sense of retaining any philosophical link with its parental concept of SD, the notion of ST only really makes sense if it is used as shorthand for tourism's contribution to SD (*e.g.*, Hunter, 1995; Collins, 1999), irrespective of the type (mass, alternative, eco, nature-based, green soft, hart, etc., etc.) of tourism being considered.

Thus, at the most fundamental level, there is a dichotomy in ST thinking : should ST be concerned with attempting to create the conditions whereby tourism flourishes as an end in itself, or should ST thinking be directed at finding a role for tourism as part of a more holistic strategy encompassing the more general aims of SD? In his 'state-of-the-art' review of ST, Butler (1999) recognizes this dichotomy, not for the first time, by distinguishing between 'sustainable tourism' (as a descriptor of the former position) and 'development of tourism on the principles of sustainable development' (as a descriptor of the latter position). Butler, rightly, regards ambiguity in the use of the term 'sustainable tourism' as a major issue :

> *The key problem, in my mind, is the current inability to define to the satisfaction of all, or even most, of the stakeholders in tourism, exactly what is meant by 'sustainable tourism'.* (Butler, 1999 : 19).

Unfortunately, it is not clear at least to me, which of the interpretations of ST Butler prefers. Any suggestion that the term 'sustainable tourism' be reserved solely as a descriptor of the former position above is unlikely to be widely adopted given its historical use as shorthand for either position. The existence of these two fundamentally different interpretations of ST highlights the importance of providing clear theoretical guidance for tourism researchers and policymakers, hopefully encouraging better explanation of the particular position adopted. Although it is true to say that many of the lists of principles of ST that have been derived over recent years are very similar in character to the key concerns of SD (Sharpley, 2000), this does not necessarily mean that ST policy and practice will follow what has been described as an 'extra-parochial' paradigm (Hunter, 1995) where the primary goal is for tourism to contribute to the wider goals of SD.

Ambiguity in the use of the term 'sustainable tourism' may also arise because SD is a contested concept. Despite claiming to examine the meaning of SD in the context of tourism, Butler (1999), as with many other authors, fails to provide any real detail of the SD debate : for example, the desired degree of substitution between natural capital (resources) and human-made capital, or the meaning of human needs and wants. Enhanced understanding of the concept of ST cannot await the (impossible) dream of a unifying definition, but rather must emerge through the more clearly articulated description, but rather must emerge through the more clearly articulated description of alternatives, and with an ongoing debate amongst those willing to defend alternative positions. I believe in a vision of ST dedicated to tourism's wider contribution to SD. Logically, adherence to this alternative requires ST researchers (followed, hopefully, by policymakers) to engage with the debate on the meaning of SD, and to address key aspects of the arguments that have emerged since the publication of the World Commission's report (WCED, 1987). The following section provides a very brief overview of key aspects of the SD debate. Fuller accounts can be found in the ST literature (*e.g.,* Hunter, 1997; Holden, 1999), with the most detailed of these (from a natural resources perspective) provided by Collins (1999).

Interpretations of Sustainable Development

It is now widely accepted that any quest for a universally applicable definition of sustainable development (SD) is not likely to be successful, and in recent years sustainability theory has advanced through the articulation of a range of possible interpretations of SD and their applicability under a variety of circumstances (*e.g.,* Mitlin, 1992; Turner *et.al.,* 1994; Wilbanks, 1994 ; Hanley, 2000). In exploring the details of the concept of SD, many issues have emerged as points of controversy and departure for adherents to different visions of environmentalism and the meaning of 'development'; Sharpley (2000) provides a useful analysis of development theory in the context of ST. Debate has revolved around such inter-related issues as : the role of economic growth in promoting human well-being; the substitutability of natural resource capital with human-made capital created through economic growth and technological innovation; the criticality of various components of the natural resource base and the potential for substitution; the ability of technologies and environmental management methods to decouple economic growth and environmental degradation; the meaning of the value attributed to the natural world and the rights of non-human species ; and the degree to which a systems perspective should be adopted entailing a primary concern for maintaining the functional integrity of ecosystems.

These issues have become interwoven in a complex debate on how best to achieve, or strive to achieve, equity in the nature of opportunities to access natural resources which create human well-being, and in the distribution of the costs and benefits (social, economic and environmental) that ensue from the utilization of resources (*e.g.*, Fox, 1994). Equity implies attempting to meet *all* basic human needs and, perhaps, the satisfaction of human wants, both now (intragenerational equity) and in the future (intergenerational equity). That is, the avoidance of development and the concomitant utilization of natural resources which maintains, creates or widens spatial or temporal differences in human well-being. Of course, interpretations of human needs and wants vary, and the use of these terms constitutes an important part of the SD debate. Furthermore, under some interpretations of SD, equity also applies across species barriers, in particular the inherent right of non-humans to exist above and beyond any utilitarian value imposed by humans (Williams, 1994). Hughes (2001) provides an interesting account of how an animal rights perspective brought about a structural change in tourism provision in the UK with reference to the viewing of dolphins.

Thus, the concept of SD can be shaped to fit a spectrum of world views, encompassing different ethical stances and management strategies (Owens, 1994). Interpretations of sustainable development can be classified as ranging from 'very strong' to 'very weak' (Turner *et al., 1994*). Rather than detail here all the characteristics of different visions of SD, the reader is referred to Table 1.1 which summarizes four major SD positions. Frequently, the very weak (traditional resource exploitative) and very strong (extreme resource preservationist) interpretations of sustainability are disregarded by many commentators as being rather too extreme. For example, the former lacks an environmental stewardship ethic and concern for the intragenerational distribution of development costs and benefits, while the anti-growth ethos of the latter may also contravene the intragenerational principle by denying the poorest people enhanced quality of life through economic growth. Most debate, therefore, has focused on the distinction between weak and strong interpretations (Collins, 1999; Table 1.1).

Table 1.1

A Simplified Description of the Sustainable of the Sustainable Development Spectrum

Sustainability position	*Defining characteristics*
1	2
Very weak	anthropocentric and utilitarian ; growth oriented and resource exploitive; natural resources utilized at economically optimal rates through unfettered free markets operating to satisfy individual consumer choice; infinite substitution possible between natural and human made capital; continued well-being assured through economic growth and technical innovation.
Weak	anthropocentric and utilitarian resource conservationist ; growth is managed and modified ; concern for distribution of development costs and benefits through intra-and intergenerational equity; rejection of infinite substitution between natural and human-made capitals with recognition of some aspects of the natural world as critical capital (*e.g.*, ozone, some natural ecosystems); human-made plus natural capital constant or rising through time; decoupling of negative environmental impacts from economic growth.

(Contd.)

(Contd.)

1	2
Strong	(eco)systems perspective; resource preservationist; recognizes primary values of maintaining the functional integrity of ecosystems over and above secondary value through resource utilization; interests of the collective given more weight than those of the individual consumer; adherence to intra- and intergenerational equity; decoupling important but alongside a belief in a steady state economy as a consequence of following the constant natural assets rule; zero economic and human population growth.
Very Strong	bioethical and eco-centric; resource preservationist to the point where utilization of natural resources is minimized ; nature's rights or intrinsic value in nature encompassing non-human living organism and even abiotic elements under a literal interpretation of Gaianism; anti-economic growth and for reduced human population.

Source : Hunter (1997), adapted from Turner *et al. (1994).*

There can be little doubt that weak interpretations dominate the thinking behind the great majority of governmental and other policy statements on SD ; for example, the 'need' for continued economic growth is never apparently questioned. Certainly, the World Commission (WCED, 1987) recognized the importance of economic growth in poverty-stricken areas of the Third World in order to meet basic needs, and there was no preclusion to continued economic growth developed countries. However, amongst academic commentators the question of whether or not continued economic growth can be justified in developed countries where basic needs are already met and greater well-being largely equates to the satisfaction of wants (*e.g.*, more vacation opportunities), has become a contentious one.

Frequently, however, visions of SD (and ST) are merely couched in the language of 'balance', *i.e.,* finding the right balance between the need for development and the need for environmental protection (the *degree* of protection is usually not made clear). Apart from the likelihood that one person's balance is another's imbalance, the language of balance can be misleading, being used to mask the reality that economic growth is generally the primary concern (Healey and Shaw, 1994). As pointed out by Cater (1995), with specific reference to ST, economic growth via tourism development will often conflict with environmental protection. What Cater describes as 'win / win' situations (where tourism development results in both wealth creation and environmental betterment) are, in my view, relatively rare, although examples, such as that of the Cape Byron Headland Reserve in Australia (Brown and Essex, 1997), do appear to exist. Usually, therefore, difficult trade-off decisions under 'win / lose' conditions have to be made. Tosun (2001), based upon an analysis of ST in Turkey, argues that the complex socio-economic and environmental trade-off decisions that have to be made may be particularly difficult in developing countries. Although economic concerns may dominate in most situations, the outcome of the decision-making process will vary according to the background and training of decision makers and to the specific circumstances surrounding the development proposal.

Logically, if it is accepted that alternative interpretations of SD are inevitable and that ST should be about trying to contribute to the wider goals of SD, then it must surely be recognized that ST cannot be seen as a rigid code. Rather, ST should be seen as a flexible or adaptive paradigm, whereby different tourism development pathways may be appropriates according to local conditions (Hunter, 1997). Of course, this leaves one open to a charge of :

> *neatly side-stepping the need for a concise definition.* (Sharpley, 2000 : 1)

Some recent work, however, suggests that it may be useful to examine particular types of tourism, development using an adaptive conceptual framework for ST : see, for example, Holden's (1999) analysis of downhill skiing in the Cairngorms area of the Scottish Highlands. Also, there may be a link between an adaptive view of ST developed from a natural resources perspective and the recent construction of a dynamic notion of sustainability in cultural tourism put forward by Tucker (2001). Additionally, and as argued earlier, it is unreasonable to expect a universally acceptable and concise definition of ST to emerge, at least in the near future. A very widely accepted definition of ST would almost certainly need to be rather vague and couched in the language of balance, and thus 'side-step' the reality of difficult trade-off decisions. A concise (and precise) definition would need to recognize the primary importance of one of the key aspects of ST; *e.g.* environmental protection, or economic growth, a parallel process to choosing between weak or strong versions of SD. As I hope to demonstrate below, the prospect of all, or even a large majority of commentators agreeing on either a weak or strong model for ST appears rather remote. The work of Miller (2001) will serve for the moment in illustrating how far we appear to be away from agreement as to the meaning of ST. In trying to develop indicators for ST, Miller conducted a Delphi survey of academic experts who had recently published relevant journal papers. Miller found considerable disagreement over the meaning of sustainability and where the 'borders of the concept exist' (quoted from the paper's abstract). Certainly, without much more informed debate on its conceptual underpinnings, a widely accepted and detailed model of ST will never emerge.

For the time being, a clear, detailed and frank account of why a particular pathway or sustainability interpretation has been chosen and one which certainly avoids the banal rhetoric of balance, is more important than the search for a theoretical construct suitable as a vehicle for policy formation under all circumstances. Unfortunately, many studies in the tourism literature that incorporate an attempt to define ST do not venture beyond the rhetoric of balance and underlying rationale for policy formulation, and action therefore remains obscured (Hunter, 1997). Of course, obscurity may be a deliberate ploy where those with vested interests want the primacy of, say, economic growth to remain hidden, but most academic commentators should not have this excuse. The inevitability of trade-off in development decision-making cannot, however, be obscured. Thus, even where tourism studies published under the banner of sustainability fail to address its meaning, or limit discussion to talk of balance, individual preferences and sympathies frequently appear as the description of a particular 'sustainable' tourism development unfolds. By default, therefore, different ST pathways are already being described, but only in relatively few studies does this appear to be a self-conscious process.

The remainder of this chapter is devoted to an analysis of two interpretations of ST : a model building exercise using material from the tourism literature, and simplifies constructs based loosely on weak and strong perceptions of SD. However, rudimentary these may be, perhaps attempts like this will find some utility and encourage studies of ST to preface the 'walk' part with a short 'talk' explaining, or even justifying, the planned route.

Meanings of Sustainable Tourism

The categorization of interpretations means using labels, and labels are frequently long-winded (consider 'extreme resource preservationist', for example). For the sake of convenience, shortened descriptors / personifications are used below : 'light green' (LG) and 'dark green' (DG). Table 1.2 is an attempt to bring together a range of attitudinal tendencies with respect to tourism and the environment, thereby providing a summary of the two variants of ST. In general these variants are scale-independent and could apply at different levels, from the individual business up to a national tourism development plan or policy statement. The following paragraph consider some aspects of Table 1.2 in slightly more detail, and with reference to specific studies in the academic tourism literature, where possible.

Table 1.2

Simplified Description of Light Green and Dark Green Variants of Sustainable Tourism

Light green tendencies	*Dark green tendencies*
advocate and strongly proadaptancy	cautionary and knowledge-based
benefit of tourism assumed	benefits of tourisms must be demonstrated
precious view of tourism as a sector and sectoral self-interest dominates	tourism need not necessarily be a component of sustainable development in an area and sectoral integration required
maintain tourism activity in existing destinations and expand into new ones	widen economic base if high dependency on tourism and engage in full proactive assessment of new tourism development
tourism products must be maintained and evolve according to market need (nature is a commodity)	natural resources must be maintained and impacts reduced (preferably minimized) where possible with products tailored accordingly (nature has existence value)
environmental action only when required and beneficial (*i.e.*, legal obligation, to tackle specific problem, marketing benefit and cost saving)	environmental impacts always considered as a matter of routine
narrow scope and geographical scale of environmental concern	wide range of potential and actual impacts considered beyond immediate geographical setting (*e.g.*, hotel, complex, destination area)
disperse and dilute activity (spread)	focus and concentrate activity (confine)

(*Contd.*)

(Contd.)

industry self-regulation as dominant management approach	wide range of management approaches and instruments required
introspective focus on tourism research and management literature	(more likely to reinvent the wheel)
most likely to have a direct involvement in the industry	most likely to have training in an environment-type academic discipline

Perhaps with training in tourism (or one of the social sciences dominated by economic aspects of development) and, or with a direct professional interest in tourism, LG is a tourism enthusiast, most likely to be found speaking from Jafari's (1989) 'advocacy' platform. For LG, tourism is a intrinsically good and has an inherent right to expand. After all, people evolved through natural processes, are part of nature and, therefore, anything they do is 'natural'. If people want the world to be a playground, then this is nothing more than natural selection, with the terms of destination area characteristics. Growth is good and the key issue is how to maintain it in existing enclaves and foster it where tourism is as yet absent, or 'underdeveloped'. Hence, satisfying demand (as expressed by preferences of individual tourists or tourist types) through correctly tailored products is the fundamental task. LG may also be found speaking from Jafari's (1989) 'adaptancy' platform, in so far as ST is primarily about finding new strategies for tourism to maintain and increase measure of its economic activity (*e.g.*, visitor numbers and expenditure).

Typically, LG's environmental concern is limited to the maintenance of sufficient environmental quality at the destination (probably largely through industry self-regulation) to ensure the continued survival of existing tourism products locations. Where LG does make explicit reference to environmental issues these will tend to be very product-linked, greatly limiting scope and scale to those aspects of direct, immediate and tangible relevance to the survival and promotion of the product; for example, landscape and visual amenity, local ecosystem attributes, and elements of townscape. This amounts to little more than beautifying the environment for tourism (clean streets and palm trees), rather than a radical appraisal of the environmental functioning of a destination area, resort center, enclave or even individual hotel complex.

This highly product-focused, anthropocentric view often leads to relatively little attention being paid to natural resource demands, with the environmental side-effects of growth only tackled retrospectively if possible and / or economically viable (House, 1997; Stabler, 1997). Both Hughes (1996) and MacLellan (1998), for example, are critical of Scottish tourism policy for its over-riding focus on economic growth targets; with the banner of sustainability being used, it is argued, principally as a means of providing new opportunities to market nature-based tourism products, such as wildlife tourism. Relatedly, Klemm (1992), in a review of the sustainability of the tourism product offered by the French region of Languedoc-Roussillon, barely touches upon the environmental implications of tourism development, so acute is the focus on change made to the product in order to maintain its appeal to tourists.

Another exemplar of LG thinking is provided by Owen *et al.* (1993 : 470) in their description of 'Project Conwy' in Wales, put forward as a practical example of successful sustainable tourism development :

> *Major efforts of investment have taken place in Conwy in order to transform the town that was once a down-market beach resort holiday destination for the 'candy-floss-brigade' to an up-market, walled heritage town.*

Going up-market in Conwy yanorder to improve and sustain its appeal involved a number of actions. These included : construction of a town by pass (in the form of an estuarine tunnel) and the first phase of a marina : the instigation of a four year town lighting plan covering street lighting the lighting of key buildings and decorative lighting; the search for a private developer to establish a 'quality' caravan park close to the town; and the further extension of out of town parking facilities. Unfortunately, we are not told of the natural resource implications (energy use, habitat loss, water supply issues, etc.) of these 'sustainable' tourism primarily focused on visual amenity, and geographically very limited.

At its most extreme, the LG position may become so 'pale' as to represent little more than the traditional, resource-exploitative and economic-growth-driven paradigm of SD. Butcher (1997 : 31), for example, provides a scathing attack on the whole concept of sustainability, arguing that :

> *The denigration of human process embodied in the sustainability paradigm is likely to hold back humanity from facing up to and solving the problem of poverty and underdevelopment. It is hence a far bigger problem than some of the troublesome by-products of unplanned tourism development.*

This assertion is not one that would be met with much sympathy by many engaged in the SD / ST debate. Nonetheless, Butcher's position is clear and he does not shirk from engaging with the broader sustainability debate. This is surely preferable to misconception that the meaning and implications of 'sustainability' are somehow already widely understood and agreed ; an issue highlighted by Butler (1999) in his ST review.

In contrast to LG thinking, those who adhere to the DG variant of ST are, it is suggested, much more likely to have background training in disciplines such as ecology, geography and the environmental sciences, and are more likely to express views from cautionary or knowledge-based perspectives (Jafari, 1989). Advocates of DG thinking typically espouse the importance of the precautionary principle, the need for proactive or anticipatory tourism development planning (perhaps in a multi-sectoral sense), and the systematic monitoring of changes to the natural environment / capital stock of natural resources using a variety of environmental management techniques. Broadly speaking, the emphasis is on the protection of natural resources that support tourism rather than the promotion of tourism-related economic growth for its own sake or as an end in itself. Goodall and Stabler (1997 : 291), for example, argue that :

> *In the face of uncertainty, irreproducibility of natural resources end the possible irreversibility of decisions, it should be assumed that a tourist activity or development might damage the environment. Unless there is clear scientific evidence to the contrary, decision-making should err on the side of caution where uncertainty exists as to the long-term consequences of current tourism resources use.*

Likewise, Stabler (1997 : 16) suggests that environmental appraisal should be a prelude to development actions, and that tourism's reliance on the natural environment as its primary resource base 'must compel it to move in the direction of ecocentrism'. Similarly, Collins (1999) clearly argues the case for strong forms of sustainability conditions in the context of tourism development as being the most appropriate for preserving biodiversity. He equates a strong sustainability position with a non-declining stock of natural capital over time. At a practical level, this strong sustainability philosophy is embodied in the , albeit local, 'constant natural capital rule' adopted in the definition of ST derived for two World Heritage Areas in Australia by Driml and Common (1996). Although dating from the mid-1990s, the paper by Driml and Common is still, in my view, the best yet available at linking ST theory and practice : following a review of alternative potential interpretations of sustainability, a clear theoretical stance is adopted according to local conditions / requirements, and then implementation mechanisms are described. This is an excellent example of practice following theory, and is exactly what is needed as a matter of routine in ST research (Collins, 2001).

DG is also much more likely than LG to believe in concentrating and limiting tourist activity rather than spreading and 'diluting' it. For example, contrast the aim of the Scottish Tourist Board (STB) to spread tourist activity away from the center of Edinburgh and Glasgow (STB, 1994), with the view of Wheeler (1993 : 128) :

> *How can we argue that spreading the tourist load spatially is solving the problem when one of the problems is the spatial spread of tourism?*

Wherever tourism occurs the DG variant of ST is likely to entail a more widely scoped, geographically extensive and stronger degree of environmental concern and action than the LG variant. It is suggested that DG will tend to consider impacts upon a wider range of resources and throughout a wider geographical area, recognizing that it is important to understand impacts beyond the immediate tourist setting. By way of illustration, Gill and Williams (1994) stress the importance of regional planning to the successful management of tourism development at individual resort centres and beyond, arguing that too narrow a geographical focus for management initiatives may simply transfer problems from individual centres to surrounding areas. This attitude might be taken as illustrating the less parochial conceptualization of ST typical of the DG variant. The importance of sub-national, regional planning is relatively frequently recognized in the tourism literature (*e.g.*, Dowling, 1993 ; Wall, 1993 ; Hall and Wouters, 1994 ; Priskin, 2001 : Ahn *et al.*, 2002), perhaps particularly where access to some sites within a region is strictly controlled or prohibited on the grounds of exceptional ecological value.

It is also likely that DG will argue for systematic environmental monitoring as a matter of course as part of tourism development appraisal (*e.g.*, Butler, 1999) even if this has significant cost implications, whereas LG will tend to think and act on environmental issues only when required or there is some direct advantage involved. For example, a requirement of act might come in the form of a legal obligation, or where an environmental problem, such as sewage pollution of beaches, sufficient to affect the satisfaction of tourists emerges. Direct advantage might manifest itself in several ways, the most attractive being some form of direct financial saving. Environmental guidelines for those managing tourism business, for example, frequently stress the potential savings available by 'going green', through reduced energy costs and other actions (*e.g.* , English Tourist Board *et al.*, 1992). Similarly, Stabler and Goodall (1997) recently highlighted the much greater likelihood of tourism businessess incorporating environmental objective and practices if these brought lower costs and / or higher revenues, with reference to the hospitality sector in Guernsey. Another form of direct advantage might be where limited environmental betterment is linked to a new marketing strategy designed to kickstart a flagging (hence 'unsustainable') local industry. This approach is described by Morgan (1991) for Majorca in Spain.

Perhaps more controversially, other discriminators might be advanced to distinguish between LG and DG variants. In Table 1.2, mention is made of the willingness to learn from other academic disciplines and the broader environmental management literature. A number of studies in the tourism literature have stressed the importance of measuring the general environmental performance of tourism operations, or aspects thereof, and encouraging the use of waste-free and low-waste technologies (*e.g.*, Buckley, 1996 ; Lukashina *et al.*, 1996 ; Buckley and Araujo, 1997, Tabatchnaia-Tamirisa *et. al.*, 1997). Furthermore, there are also studies where a detailed examination of the meaning, and tensions, of ST already benefits from an appreciation of the wider sustainable development literature (*e.g.*, Henry and Jackson, 1996), and also where the range of environmental management policy approaches and implementation techniques is examined in the context of tourism (*e.g.*, Hjalager, 1996). More recently, Ko (2001) stresses the importance of utilizing and applying contributions from other disciplines in aiding the assessment of ST. Perhaps these efforts, of themselves, may be seen as heralding a recent move towards DG sustainable tourism thinking, as an ability to engage with the concepts to be found in the wider environmental management literature can be seen as a cornerstone of the DG variant, because, potentially, this encourages the use of a wider range of methods and tools in the analysis and management of tourism's impacts.

This type of engagement also lessens the chance of tourism researchers and practitioners 'reinventing the wheel'. In the comparison of a number of tools for the management of tourism and recreation conducted by Wight (1998), for example, one is struck by the similarities (rather than the differences) between Visitor Impact Management (VIM) and Visitor Experience and Resource Protection (VERP) systems, and the more widely known (and used) approach of Environmental Impact Assessment, and its variant Strategies Environmental Assessment (see, for example, Hunter and Green, 1995). Likewise, when Wight calls for systems such as VIM and VERP to be employed as ongoing iterative management tools, the similarity with Environmental Auditing, and Environmental Management Systems is all too evident (the reader is referred to Goodall, 1995 and Todd and Williams, 1996, for example of the use of these techniques in a tourism context).

Conclusions

The idea of SD appears to have caught the imagination of many tourism researchers and policymakers. Enthusiasm generates a real desire for change, and a rush to operationalize principles of ST. However, these principles are frequently little more than very general statements of intent, and often raise more questions than they answer. Many studies of ST fail to provide an in-depth analysis of precisely how the term is being used or interpreted. Obviously, any kind of improvement in the environmental functioning of tourism operations can be seen as beneficial, but environmental betterment comes in many forms and does not necessarily mean long-term sustainability.

Well over a decade after the publication of the World Commission's report, *Our Common Future* (WCED, 1987), there is still a need to clarify the theoretical underpinnings of ST, but relatively few studies in the literature have set about this task, particularly in the context of the ongoing SD debate. It is clear, however, that neither SD or ST are value-free concepts (Butler, 1999). Whereas debate on the meaning and implications of SD has been intense (Hanley, 2000), resulting in relatively clearly defined alternative interpretations, this has generally not permeated the ST literature to the same extent. Nonetheless, because use of the term 'sustainable tourism' brings with it the preconceptions and values of the user, distinctive variants of ST have emerged over the last decade or so, although usually not in a self-conscious manner. If we accept that, as with general SD, a unifying definition or conceptualization or ST is unlikely to emerge, then the study of ST must advance through enhanced awareness of and debate around, more clearly articulated alternatives. If these alternatives become better understood, then it should case the operationalization of ST as the 'ground-rules', or key questions, for decision-making become more apparent, irrespective of the particular label attached to the tourism product.

There have recently been signs of a more detailed consideration of theoretical aspects of ST. Some commentators have shown willingness to espouse and defend alternative interpretations, based upon issues raised in the broader SD literature. Unfortunately, the multidisciplinary nature of (sustainable) tourism research can mitigate against the proper understanding of arguments put forward. This would appear to be the case with, for example, Velikova's (2001) commentary on Collins (1999) (see also Collins, 2001, for the rejoinder). It is even the case that a theoretical examination of SD and ST can lead to the conclusion that, 'the concept of sustainable tourism development is . . . ' a red herring' (Sharpley, 2000 : 14). Sharpley reaches this conclusion based partly upon the idea that ST should, but effectively cannot contribute to the broader goals of SD (see below). Most commentators would, I suggest, disagree with Sharpley's conclusion, particularly as his work does not really examine the different meaning of SD. Nonetheless, it is important to question the basic assumptions underlying the concept of ST.

This said, and without wishing to sound glib, ST is a notion that if we did not have, then we would have to invent, and so in this chapter an attempt has been made to organize a range of views on key issues into two broad ST variants; 'light green' (LG) and 'dark green' (DG) (Table 1.2). Perhaps the most fundamental choice facing tourism researchers and policymakers lies in deciding upon the basic purpose of ST thinking : should this (indeed, can this) be directed at the tourism sector in isolation, or should ST thinking be more holistic (multi-sectoral) and directed primarily at attempting to meet the more general goals of SD? These interpretations can be seen as indicative of LG and DG thinking, respectively, and the case for DG alternative here is surely the stronger one, although strategic, coordinated and spatially extensive planning is a difficult task (Collins, 1999). Other discriminators between LG and DG variants can best be derived from the ongoing SD debate; for example, the degree of protection afforded to the natural environment, the extent to which the precautionary principle is employed, and the nature of environmental management mechanism used. Without a systematic analysis of the ST literature, it is very difficult to discern a trend towards either LG or DG thinking (at least as far as the academic literature is concerned), although a strong strand of DG opinion is evident, and it would appear that more researchers are engaging with the broader environmental management literature in the search for appropriate means of identifying and controlling the impacts of tourism.

Whether one tends towards LG or DG thinking, in whole or in part, it is important that tourism researchers and policymakers are aware of alternative interpretations of ST, including the different development pathways that these signal, and that they also make the effort to provide clear reasoning for the stance adopted. With a final apology to Bramwell and Lane (1993) for again referring to their quote given at the start of this chapter, we need to be able to 'talk' to other disciplines engaged in marked paths. Both of these require a more proactive engagement with the general SD debate and literature.

Acknowledgements

This chapter is based upon an earlier paper : Hunter, C. (2001).

Sustainable tourism theory : an overview from a natural resources perspective. *Environment Paper Series* **4(2)**,: 42-52

References

1. Ahn, B., Lee, B. and Shafer, C.S. (2002) : Operationalizing sustainability in regional tourism planning : an application of the limits of acceptable change framework, *Tourism Management*, : **23**, 1-15.
2. Aravot, I. (1992) : Local tourism in misgav region a different model? *Proceedings of an International Seminar on Architecture of Soft Tourism*, pp. 11-18. Istanbul : Yildiz University Faculty of Architecture Press.
3. Bramwell, B. and Lane, B. (1993) : Sustainable tourism : an evolving global approach, *Journal of Sustainable Tourism*, **1(1)** : 1-5.
4. Brown, G. and Essex, S. (1997) : Sustainable tourism management : lessons from the edge of Australia, *Journal of Sustainable Tourism*, **5(4)** : 294-305.
5. Buckley, R. (1996) : Sustainable tourism : technical issues and information needs, *Annals of Tourism Research*, **23(4)** : 925-8.
6. Buckley, R. and Araujo, G. (1997) : Environmental management performance in tourism accommodation, *Annals of Tourism Research*, **24(2)** : 465-9.
7. Butcher, J. (1997) : Sustainable development or development? In M. Stabler (ed.) *Tourism and Sustainability : Principles to Practice*, pp. 27-38. Wallingford : CAB International.
8. Butler, R. W. (1999) : Sustainable tourism : a state-of-the-art review, *Tourism Geographies*, **1(1)** : 7-25.
9. Carley, M. and Christin, I. (1992) : *Managing Sustainable Development*, London : Earthscan.
10. Cater, E. (1995) : Environmental contradictions in sustainable tourism, *The Geographical Journal*, **161(1)** : 21-8.
11. Collins, A. (1999) : Tourism development and natural capital, *Annals of Tourism Research*, **26(1)** : 98-109.

12. Collins, A. (2001) : Thinking economically about sustainable tourism, *Annals of Tourism Research,* **28(3)** : 809-11.

13. Dowling, R. (1993) : An environmentally-based planning model for regional tourism development, *Journal of Sustainable Tourism,* **1(1)** : 17-36.

14. Driml, S. and Commor M. (1996) : Ecological economics criteria for sustainable tourism : applications to the Great Barrier Reef and Wet Tropics World Heritage Areas, Australia, *Journal of Sustainable Tourism,* **4** : 3-16.

15. English Tourist Board, Countryside : Commission and rural development commission (1992) : *The Green Light : A Guide to Sustainable Tourism, London.* English Tourist Board.

16. Fox W. (1994) : Ecophilosophy and science. *The Environmentalist,* **14** : 207-13.

17. Gill, A. and Williams, P. (1994) : Managing growth in mountain tourism communities, *Tourist Management,* **15(3)** : 212-20.

18. Goodall, B. (1995) : Environmental auditing : a tool for assessing the environmental performance of tourism firms, *The Geographical Journal,* **161(1)** : 29-37.

19. Goodall, B. and Stabler, M. (1997) : Principles influencing the determination of environmental standards for sustainable tourism, In M. Stabler (ed.) *Tourism and Sustainability : Principles to Practice,* pp. 279-304. Wallingford : CAB International.

20. Hall, M. and Wouters, M. (1994) : Nature tourism in the sub Antarctic, *Annals of Tourism Research,* **21** : 355-74.

21. Hanley, N. (2000) : The concept of sustainable development an economic perspective, *Progress in Environmental Science,* **2(3)** : 181-203.

22. Healey, P. and Shaw, T. (1994) : Changing meanings of 'environment' in the British planning system, *Transactions of the Institute of British Geographers,* **19** : 425-38.

23. Henry, I. and Jackson, G. (1996) : Sustainability of management processes and tourism products and contexts, *Journal of Sustainable Tourism,* **4(1)** : 17-28.

Journal of Sustainable Tourism, **4(1)** : 17-28.

24. Hjalager, A. (1996) : Tourism and the environment : the innovation connection, *Journal of Sustainable Tourism,* **4(4)** : 201-16.
25. Holden, A. (1999) : High impact tourism : a suitable component of sustainable policy? The case of downhill skiing development at Cairngorm, Scotland. *Journal of Sustainable Tourism,* **7(2)** : 97-107.
26. House, J. (1997) : Redefining sustainability : a structural approach to sustainable tourism. In M. Stabler (ed.) ,*Tourism and Sustainability : Principles to Practice,* pp. 89-104. Wallingford : CAB International.
27. Hughes, J. (1996) : Tourism and the environment : a sustainable partnership? *Scottish Geographical Magazine,* **112 (2)** : 107-13.
28. Hughes, P. (2001) : Animals, values and tourism : structural shifts in UK dolphin tourism provision, *Tourism Management,* **22** : 321-9.
29. Hunter, C. (1995) : On the need to re-conceptualise sustainable tourism development, *Journal of Sustainable Tourism,* **3** : 155-65.
30. Hunter, C. (1997) : Sustainable tourism as an adaptive paradigm, *Annals of Tourism Research,* **24(4)** : 850-67.
31. Hunter, C. and Green, H. (1995) : *Tourism and the Environment: A Sustainable Relationship*? London : Routledge.
32. Jafari, J. (1989) : An English language literature review. In J. Bystrzanowski (ed.), *Tourism as a Factor of Change : A Socio-Cultural Study,* pp. 17-60, Vienna : Center for Research and Documentation in Social Sciences.
33. Ko, J. (2001) : Assessing progress of tourism sustainability, *Annals of Tourism Research,* **28 (3)** : 817-20.
34. Klemm, M. (1992) : Sustainable tourism development : Languedoc-Roussillon thirty years on, *Tourism Management* June, 169-80.
35. Lane, B. (1994) : Sustainable rural tourism strategies, a tool for development and conservation *Journal of Sustainable Tourism,* **2 (1&2)** : 102-11.

2 Tourism's Sustainability

Introduction

One does not have to be an optimist to believe that tourism will grow substantially over the next century. Apparently, however, one does have to be an optimist to regard this as a positive development. As tourism has burgeoned in the latter half of the twentieth century it has been accused of being many things : a despoiler of pristine natural environments, a destroyer of valued lifestyles and age-old cultures, and an exploiter of poor nations. Tourism, it is claimed ultimately degrades the attractive natural and cultural feature of a place and thus can neither sustain the basic resources on which it relies, nor rely on itself as an industry in the long term. If these changes are valid then tourism either should be severely restrained or will eventually burn itself out, but not before causing a great deal of damage. When looking into the future this scenario gives little cause for optimism about the long-term sustainability of tourism.

It is possible, however, to regard tourism's future growths as not only assured but also highly desirable. That is not to suggest that tourism has not and will not cause problems, but these are not insurmountable and are potentially outweighed by the opportunities for improving the human condition. Tourism as a mass international phenomenon is in its infancy, barely fifty years old, and it is possible to learn from past mistakes. The existence of this book, a vast body of literature on tourism's impact, and numerous prescriptive tomes on sustainability, demonstrate a willingness and ability to learn. The optimistic view could be taken that tourism will continue to grow, that the challenges consequently presented can be met, and that the ultimate outcome will be positive, depending on how well both the tourism industry and governments respond to those challenges.

Tourism's Growth : Patterns and Prospects

A glance into the recent past reveals a remarkable increase in international tourist arrivals from 25 million in 1950 to 664 million in 1999, an average annual growth rate of 7 perc ent (WTO, 2001a). By the year 2020 international arrivals are predicted to reach 1.18 billion, representing an average annual growth rate of 4.1 per cent. Long-haul travel is predicted to grow even faster (WTO, 2001b). Such forecasts seem reasonable given the likelihood that most of the forces driving past growth will continue for the foreseeable future : faster, larger aircrafts leading to lower real travel costs; more widespread affluence in a greater number of countries; reduction of barriers to travel imposed by nations on their own citizens and visitors; and the globalization of media raising people's awareness of the world outside their own domains and tweaking their interest in experiencing other places. The only significant uncertainty revolves around the long-term consequences of the attacks on the World Trade Centre on September 11, 2001. The maintenance of the relatively peaceful global conditions which had been experienced for the previous fifty years are certainly threatened by these events, compounded by fears about the security of air travel. However, there are signs that international travel is recovering from those traumatic events and the ongoing effects are likely to be regional rather than global (WTO, 2002). The most likely outcome is that travel plans may be delayed, or destinations and modes of travel that are perceived to be safer will be substituted. From a sustainability perspective the result may be that more pressure placed on domestic and shorthaul destinations for major markets.

Providing the current conflicts can be resolved or at least

contained, it is highly likely that over the next few decades vastly more people will travel more often and to a wider range of international destinations. The trends are already apparent. In 1950 the top fifteen receiving countries accounted for 97 per cent of all international arrivals, a share that had declined to 62 per cent by 1999 (WTO, 2001c). Over the next twenty years arrivals are predicted to grow fastest in the emerging destinations of the East Asia-Pacific region, followed by Africa, the Middle East and South Asia, albeit in some cases from fairly low bases (WTO, 2001b). Casting some doubt on the accuracy of some these predictions is the prospect that the events and consequences of September 11 are likely to have their most profound impact on travel to the Middle East and parts of South Asia. However, other destinations further from the conflict, such as Latin America and southern and eastern Africa, may benefit and grow more rapidly than predicted.

From 1985 to 1998 outbound travel growth from the rapidly developing countries of East Asia-Pacific averaged 8.5 per cent year compared to the global average of 5.3 percent (WTO, 2001d). Rising, and more widely distributed, affluence reduced the economic barriers to travel for citizens of those countries, and this was often accompanied by the extension of rights to paid holidays to travel. Based on this experience, a clear consequence of economic prosperity is a realization of the desire to travel, and as this extends to other regions throughout the twenty-first century a continued supply of new travellers is assured. With time, increasing affluence should enable international travel to change from being an aspiration to an expectation for many more people, as has occurred in the economically developed world in the later half of the twentieth century.

Concerns and Doubts Over Tourism's Growth

The events of September 11 aside, there are other reasons to believe that this future will not, or even should not, be realized. One of the greatest uncertainties lies in at least maintaining the current historically low cost of international travel. With plans well advanced for the introduction of larger and more fuel-efficient aircraft the medium-term outlook is promising, but looking further into the future there must be concerns about the increasing scarcity of oil. Maintaining low travel costs may be contingent on developing alternative power sources and continually improving technology. Given the scale of the international travel industry, however, an optimistic view would be that there is a substantial incentive to anticipate and counteract this problem.

Developments in computers and information technology, such as the Internet and virtual reality may, it has been suggested, reduce the need or desire to travel. This notion can be summarily dismissed by considering the nature of the tourism experience and what motivates it. Tourism, in essence, is sensual, emotive and driven by a desire to experience a different place in more than two dimensions. The sights, sounds, smells, tastes, ambience and people are integral to the experience, as is the actual presence of the tourist within this milieu. Vicarious experiences can simulate some aspects but not the totality. Moreover, they cannot provide the surprise discoveries, sense of adventure and chance encounters that actual travel affords. It is more likely that the greater awareness of other places engendered by information technology will stimulate a desire to authenticate by direct experience. In this regard the developments in information technology could be seen as an extension of the globalization of media, a factor that has contributed to the growth in tourism over recent decades.

Far more difficult to challenge is the claim that tourism is ultimately unsustainable because of its impacts on environments and cultures that then make destination less appealing. Large-scale tourism, both, international and domestic, is often portrayed as a juggernaut consuming one destination after another and then rolling on. Tourism could become self-limiting in that accommodating the anticipated growth over the next twenty years may create the conditions for a subsequent decline. Signs are emerging, however, that the tourism industry has learnt some valuable lessons on the downside of its 'success' and has taken steps to secure its own future. Codes of environmental ethics and accreditation schemes have burgeoned and environmental management initiatives have been developed in key industry sectors. While some of these efforts may be viewed as cynical exercises, designed to improve tourism's public image, they have, arguably, served to raise awareness that tourism can do potential harm, and placed sustainability firmly on the tourism agenda. The greater risk is that such standards may only be selectively applied to situations where there may be some political or commercial advantage in doing so, or where high environmental standards are already evident within regularity frameworks and the standards do little more than confirm compliance. With regard to achieving sustainability, there are differential challenges for destinations in the developed as opposed to the less developed world, and the following sections of the chapter will highlight these challenges.

Challenges for Developed Nations

While ostensibly the problems of coping with tourism's growth may appear to be most profound in less developed nations, given the projections discussed above, developed nations will experience the greatest increase in tourist numbers over the next twenty years. Their growth rates in tourist visitation may be lower but these are occurring from a much larger initial base. The projections also do not include domestic tourism, which in many developed nations involves for greater numbers than international tourism. If the events of September 11 are prolonged, destinations within developed nations may be placed under even more pressure because there is likely to be a shift from international to domestic travel. A number of significant challenges emerge from this scenario.

The first is to determine whether the best way to cope with this growth is to allow further development of existing destinations, or to open up new destinations for tourism. The problem with the first option is that many destinations will have reached the point where they have lost their appeal for substantial portions of the tourist market and may, in fact, be in absolute decline. The second option involves an expansion of the tourism frontier and intensification in existing low-key destinations. The danger of this strategy is that it could entrench an ongoing process of invasion and succession, as the tourists with a preference for the more low-key destinations, and the industry that caters for their needs, continually move on in search of new experiences and opportunities. As this process occurs it is likely to create a situation where tourism increasingly threatens other values such as biodiversity and habitat protection. In the light of these probabilities there would seem to be a strong case for focusing considerable attention on the revitalization of existing destinations. Rather than accepting that such destinations have reached or exceeded their capacities, effort may need to be put into enhancing their capacity as a way of taking pressure off hitherto less developed places.

The second challenge is for developed nations to make more effective use of the tools for achieving sustainable tourism development that they have at their disposal. Developed nations are generally well equipped to handle the anticipated growth in tourism over the next few decades in ways that do not compromise sustainable development objectives. With respect to controlling the impacts of tourism, which is at the heart of sustainable tourism development, there is a substantial and growing knowledge base, particularly in relation to ecological impacts. Moreover there is the technical know-how to deal effectively with many such impacts. Most importantly, though, is the fact that there are long-standing legislative frameworks that enable many negative consequences of tourism to be controlled or prevented.

Virtually all developed nations have environmental or land use-planning systems in place, which incorporate both forward planning and environmental impact assessment procedures and requirements. All development, tourism included, is controlled through such mechanisms, with the regulations and laws associated with providing a means of effective enforcement. The precise details and mechanisms differ from system to system, but the fact remains that such regulations and laws exist and are a well-accepted part of the development scene in their respective nations. However, the problem in using these laws to enhance the sustainability of tourism often lies in their practical application and in the complexity of the concept of sustainability itself. Most environmental planning systems involve some degree of judgment and discretion on the part of political decision-makers. Trade-offs are often made involving the acceptance of some costs ; for example, environmental or social, in return for, say, economic benefits. It can be argued that such a trade-off is not inconsistent with sustainable development principles given that the concept is multidimensional and it is open to interpretations with regard to what is in the best long-term interests of a particular community. When faced with a choice decision-makers may, moreover, opt for the alternative that is geared to viewing the 'long term' as ending at the next election. Thus the problem becomes one of lacking not the means but rather the political will to appropriately enforce the means.

Challenges for Less Developed Nations

The emerging destinations of the less developed world are less likely to have their long-term interests protected as tourism develops. Less developed nations are particularly vulnerable for a number of reasons. They possess environmental and cultural features that tourists from the developed world wish to experience, given the right health, safety and security conditions. Given their existing low material standards of living, they also possess a powerful economic incentive to develop tourism rapidly and with as few constraints as possible. If sustainable development is open to interpretation and in a multidimensional concept incorporating economic, sociocultural and ecological consideration, then less developed nations are understandably likely to place higher priority on the economic dimension. I recently had the experience of teaching a course on environmental management for tourism in Cambodia. It was difficult to talk persuasively about culturally sensitive architecture and the need for travel and tourism business to reduce greenhouse gas emission in a country where there is no ready access to clean drinking water and in which the basic infrastructure has been dismantled and ravaged by decades of war. Understandably, the perceived need for economic development was paramount. It becomes even more difficult when the United States, the wealthiest and arguably the greatest contributor to a number of environmental problems, fails to demonstrate its willingness to make sacrifices in return for enhanced global sustainability by refusing to ratify the Kyoto Protocol on greenhouse gas emissions. If the United States is unwilling to compromise its material well-being, why should Cambodia?

The irony is that to achieve economic development through tourism, many less developed countries have felt it necessary to take steps that may reduce the long-term benefits they receive. Less developed nations lack capital to initiate tourism and provide the necessary supporting infrastructure. Consequently, they have frequently ceded control of tourism development to foreign interests. To attract capital they have offered a variety of concessions, such as tax breaks, liberal access to land and low environmental standards that may reduce establishment and operating costs. The result can be a failure to capture much of the income stream generated from tourism. There is no easy solution to this dilemma, but ironically it may lie in the growth of tourism itself. The combination of a growing market, increasing diversification in types of experiences and destinations sought, and rising levels of experience amongst tourists will likely lead to the industry constantly seeking out new destinations. Bargaining power under such a scenario, for so long in the hands of the multinational corporations, world shift in favour of destinations, although this is certainly not an immediate prospect and relying on this solution may require some patience.

In the interim, less developed nations must either rely on a genuine good intentions of the international tourism industry to act beyond the regulatory requirements that might be imposed upon them, or take some fairly limited steps to partially reduce the deleterious effects of tourism without deterring foreign investment. The former is likely to depend on the industry perceiving commercial advantage, either through cost savings or greater appeal to customers, in being more mindful of its impacts. The latter may rely on adopting measures that do not produce reverse effects for potential investors in terms of costs and consumer demand. Providing some degree of local participation in, and control over, tourism planning and development decisions is one potential method that could be adopted. It is, after all, a fairly standard feature of regulatory frameworks in developed countries and in principle allows 'acceptable' tourism to be negotiated between developed interests and the host community. However, achieving this to practice may be far more problematic in that few less developed nations have political structures that have effectively developed power to local community level. Implementing this strategy may require fundamental political change in many less developed countries between. It is practicable on a large scale.

It is far more difficult to be optimistic about the prospects of tourism developing sustainably in less developed nations than in developed ones. The need for economic development is far more urgent, and the political and legal means for controlling tourism and its impacts far less evident. It may be that we in the developed world have to allow those nations more latitude with their interpretation of sustainability. The transfer of knowledge concerning the potential long-term consequences of tourism is important, however, as it allows those nations to make informed choices. It can only be hoped that the sometimes less-than-democratic regimes that govern such countries will make those choice based on the best interests of their current and future generations. Just as has occurred with tourism in the developed world as well, less developed nations must, perhaps, be given the opportunity to learn from their own experiences, which may reveal to them the value of focusing on the long term and the means of developing tourism sustainably.

Quality or Quantity?

The discussion thus far has been based on the premise that the growth of tourism is inevitable and that countries, and destinations within them, will have to learn to cope with that growth and / or make more effective use of the means at their disposal. In this regard developed nations are in a better position. A general alternative, however, for all nations where the lifestyle, culture and natural environment are felt to be under threat, may be to focus on quality rather than quantity. This oft-promoted solution aims to reduce tourism's harmful effects without sacrificing economic benefits. The approach typically advocated is to provide high quality facilities and services and thereby attract high spending tourists, selective restraint operating through price. If adopted broadly it could constrain the growth of tourism below predicted levels, but will it be effective in achieving its aims, and is it socially desirable? In relation to the first question there must be doubts. High expenditure does not mean high yield, given that there are greater costs associated with providing higher quality. Given the greater capital commitment required this might also exacerbate less developed nations' reliance on foreign capital. Its desirability depend on how the social benefits of travelling are perceived. The mere fact that tourism has grown so rapidly and that new countries have emerged as major markets as soon as their citizens have the economic means and freedom to travel implies that individuals perceive great benefits. In the twenty-first century do we wish to reverse a significant trend of the twentieth century and revert to the conditions of the nineteenth century when only the most privileged could travel internationally?

If the answer to this question is in the negative then other solutions must be sought to more directly mitigate the impacts of tourism without unduly constraining growth. As discussed in relation to developed nations, there is a substantial, growing knowledge base about most of tourism's impacts, plus the technical means and legislative models to achieve this. A significant problem, however, remains in relation to one area of impact, that is, on culture.

The Vexed Question of Cultural Sustainability

The issues in relation to cultural sustainability are far more complex than in relation to, say biophysical impacts. A pessimistic view on tourism would suggest that its continued growth could dramatically transform cultures and create a homogenized world. Arguably, threats to cultures are more profound and seriously viewed in relation to less developed nations. This is so as the more developed nations provide, and will continue to generate, the vast bulk of tourists, and because they are likely, through the investment process, to maintain control over much of the tourism development in poorer nations. An optimistic, however, could retort that cultural change is inevitable and not necessarily undesirable; and moreover, that tourism could counteract other change agents and actually help maintain cultures, thus contributing to rather than threatening, sociocultural sustainability. Understanding this viewpoint, however, requires an examination of the nature of both culture and international tourism, and the relationship between them.

Simply conceived, culture represents a certain group of people's way of life, beliefs and values. Cultures evolve as mechanisms for survival, maintaining social cohesion and making sense of the world. Specific cultures are products of the environments where they are formed and are limited by knowledge, including that of other cultures. International tourism can change cultures in a variety of ways : it brings people from different cultures into direct contact thereby making them aware of different ways of lie, beliefs and values; it commodifies components of culture for tourist consumption thereby changing their meaning ; and it can lead to host cultures adopting aspects of the tourists' culture in order to accommodate them. Given the likely growth in tourism the potential for cultural transformation over the next few decades is profound.

Should we resist or embrace such change? The answer is probably mixed but can perhaps be best answered by posing a less equivocal question : should we deny people, both hosts and tourists, the opportunity to expand their horizons by experiencing other ways of life and of viewing the world? Cultures have evolved over the centuries through just such processes and the next century will be no different. Tourism will be one of many change agents, along with economic globalization, improved communication technology, migration and more widespread access to international media. If anything, international tourism could slow the pace of cultural change, trading as it does on cultural differences. It thereby provides an economic incentive for destinations to maintain their culture as a means of attracting tourists. The mere fact that tourist wish to experience a culture may create a sense of pride and reinforce a belief in its intrinsic worth. The real danger from tourism may be that it serves to preserve examples of picturesque poverty when a certain degree of cultural change is both desired and desirable. It is hard to argue for example, that the black township of Soweto should be preserved, and the way of life of its inhabitants maintained, so that the tour operator businesses based on this 'attraction' can be sustained. Quite clearly there are instances where maintaining a current way of life is not desirable. The concept of cultural sustainability must necessarily embrace a degree of change if future generations are to have a better life, which is a fundamental objective of sustainable development.

Conclusion

The ultimate optimistic perspective is that as we progress through the current century the world will become a closer, more harmonious place, partly because many more of its inhabitants will have experienced it more broadly through tourism. Both tourist and hosts can benefit from this process. Tourism represents an acknowledgement of the value of differences and the desire to experience them. The resulting social contact offers not only the potential to understand and ultimately respect those differences, but also to learn from them. If cultures consequently become more similar it may in fact engender a sense that the things that unite us as human beings are more profound then those that divide us. Restraining tourism may only serve the interests of elites who have been complaining about other tourist since Thomas Cook first escorted his 'hordes' to 'their' beauty spots. While the growth of tourism will inevitably present challenges over the next century, particularly in less developed nations, on balance there is little reason not to be reservedly optimistic about its ultimate sustainability.

References

1. World Tourism Organization (2001a) : 'Historical trend international tourist arrivals'. Available : http :// www.world-tourism.org/market_research/data/ historical_arrivals. html.
2. World Tourism Organization (2001b) : 'WTO Long-term forecast tourism 2020 vision'. Available : http :// www.world-tourism.org/market_research/data/ forecast.html.
3. World Tourism Organization (2001c) : Diversification of tourism'. Available : http ://www.world-tourism.org/ market_research/data/diversification.html.
4. World Tourism Organization (2001d) : 'Outbound tourism'. Available : http ://www.world-tourism.org/ market_research/data/outbound.html.
5. World Tourism Organization (2002) : 'Tourism Recovery Already Underway'. Available : http ://www.world-tourism.org/newsroom/Releases/more_releases/ march2002/berlin.html.

3 Sustainable Wildlife Tourism

Introduction

For the most part, tourism operators see interpretation as a means of adding value to wildlife tourism; while managers of protected areas appreciate its value in both managing on-site visitor behaviour and contributing to long-term wildlife conservation. Tourists, the primary target of interpretation, have a different perspective again on interpretation, seeing interpretative services as part of the overall experience that they have purchased. Whether delivered in the form of self-guided media (such as web sites, field guides, exhibits, brochures and audiovisual programmes) or face-to-face services (such as guided tours, overland excursions, talks, and demonstrations), such services have the potential to contribute both intellectual and emotional elements to a tourist's wildlife experience, it is the various roles that interpretation performs from the perspective of these three groups, and the link that such roles have to economic and ecological sustainability of wildlife tourism, that is the focus of this chapter. It begins by defining what we mean by *interpretation* and by *sustainability*. We then go on to outline how interpretation contributes to sustainability via four primary pathways.

Interpretation

What is meant by 'interpretation'? Originally defined by Tilden (1957), interpretation is an educational activity aimed at revealing meanings and relationships to people about the places they visit and the things they see and do there. As we have argued elsewhere (Weiler and Ham, 2000; Ham and Weiler, 2002), interpretation lies at the heart and soul of what any good tour guide can and should be doing, whether guiding visitors on land or on water; whether on foot, using non-motorized forms of travel (*e.g.*, canoe, raft, mountain bike or horseback), or vehicle-based tours (*e.g.*, bus, four-wheel drive, riverboat or sea-going vessels); and whether the company or tour is labeled as ecotourism or is part of an adventure, cultural, or heritage product attraction or resort programme.

While interpretive tour guiding is very important, interpretation is not just about face-to-face communication on guided tours. It also includes non-personal or 'static' interpretation such as printed materials, signs, exhibits, self-guided walks, and various electronic media (see Trapp *et al.*, 1991; Ham, 1992; Van Gameren, in press). Interpretation is used by tour operators as well as by resorts, lodges, attractions, theme parks, museums, parks, zoos, visitor centres, and so on. Many of these use interpretive media in an effort to enhance visitors' understanding and appreciation of the environments being visited and the various natural and cultural phenomena experienced.

Moscardo *et al.*'s (2000) literature review on wildlife tourism as well as Muloin *et al.'s* (2001) study of indigenous wildlife tourism in Australia identified guides as the interpretive service most frequently used in wildlife settings. Other popular media for wildlife tourism include interpretive signs, brouchures, guidebooks, animal shows and displays, audiovisual presentations and interactive computers. In our view, these media are more than just ways to transmit information to visitors. The premise of this chapter is that they constitute informational pathways to sustainable tourism.

Sustainability

The concept of sustainability first appeared on the public scene in the report put out by the World Commission on Environment and Development (better known as the Brusndtland commission) in 1987. The idea of sustainable development is that economic growth and environmental conservation are not only compatible, they are *necessary partners.* One cannot exist without the other.

Sustainable tourism is tourism that is developed and maintained in a manner, and at such a scale, that it remains economically viable over an indefinite period and does not undermine the physical and human environment that sustains and nurtures it. It needs to be *economically* sustainable, because if tourism is not profitable then it is a moot question to ask whether it is environmentally sustainable-tourism that is unprofitable and unviable will simply cease to exist.

So, while debate continues over the esoteric definition of sustainability (see, for example, Robinson and Bennett, 2000) for our purposes here it includes both ecologically and economically desirable outcomes. The remainder of this chapter looks at these two dimensions of sustainability, and how interpretation is central to each.

How Does Interpretation Contribute to Economic Sustainability?

Interpretation can facilitate *economic sustainability* in two main ways : first, by satisfying customer demand, and second, by creating local employment.

To what extent do *visitors demand* interpretation? According to the recent report by Fredline and Faulkner (2001), one out of every five international visitors surveyed by the Australian Bureau of Tourism Research in 2000 said that their decision to visit Australia was influenced by the opportunity to 'experience wildlife'. A key question here is what do visitors mean by '*experiencing* wildlife? For example, to what extent are learning and information seeking important motivations for tourists?

We know that learning and information seeking are important motivations for many nature-based tourists, including wildlife tourists (*e.g.*, Ballantyne *et al.*, 1998; Moscardo *et al.*,1998; Ham and Weiler, 2001; Armstrong and Weiler, 2002). What goes on inside a tourist's head strongly influences the on-site experience. There is evidence that visitors want accurate, timely and relevant information during their experience. In 'act, visitors seek information about the places they visit not only while they are *on-site*, but also *before* and *after* their visit. Indeed, they *expect* it, and they *demand* it as part of the experience for which they have paid.

In other words, wildlife tourists want to get the right information, in the right way, at the right time, and to the extent that they do this, their experience is more satisfying. Successful tourism businesses know this, and they concentrate as much on developing and delivering interpretive services as they do other aspects of their business. Wildlife tourism operators who provide interpretive services offer more than a physical experience : they offer an intellectual and emotional experience. It is this combination that creates satisfied customers, because of the connection that interpretation creates between people and the places they go to experience wildlife. To the extent that guided and self-guided interpretation helps wildlife tourists establish and intellectual and emotional connection with a place, the quality of their experiences will be enhanced. Providing quality interpretation is a primary means by which such links are established.

The 'connection' idea is important. Interpreting a place is not just a process of filling wildlife tourists' heads with endless facts and figures about animals and habitat. Something else must happen. We know from our own research on tourists' perceptions of quality guiding in Galapagos and Alaska that the best wildlife interpretation engages the visitor both intellectually and emotionally, and that it is personal, relevant and meaningful for them. Although visitors often mention the guide's factual 'knowledge' as being important to their experience, our research (Ham and Weiler, 2002) reveals that when visitors are asked to comment on the guide's personal contribution to their satisfaction, virtually none of them mention the sheer volume of facts given by their guides. They do, however, repeatedly allude to ways in which the guide's commentaries helped them to relate, connect, and care about the place and the wildlife that live there.

Enhancing visitor experiences through interpretation, whether guided or self-guided, makes business sense for the operator whose daily concern is economic sustainability. According to Conservation International, a Washington, DC-based environmental organization, high quality interpretation 'can also improve business by increasing the qualify of guests' experience, increasing repeat visitation and occupancy rates, providing unique marketing opportunities and allowing hotels to charge higher rates' (Sweeting *et al.*, 1999 : 27).

Researchers are finding increasing evidence that nature-based tourists expect not just raw factual information, but interpretation, as part of their experiences and that, for many, high quality interpretation is a major contributor to their satisfaction (*e.g.*, Pearce and Moscardo, 1998). In another study, Ham and Weiler (2000) found that guided and self-guided interpretive services contributed more to the satisfaction of nature-based tourists in Panama than did their use of most types of recreation facilities such as swimming and fishing areas, campgrounds, restrooms, and trails.

Is interpretation an integral part of all wildlife tourism? There is mounting evidence that interpretation enhances many wildlife tourism experiences, and that like most nature-based tourists, even very educated, well-travelled and highly experienced wildlife tourists seek out and appreciate quality interpretation. However, research is needed about how different market segments respond to interpretive options, whether interpretation affects visitors' choice of tours, and the extent to which tourists satisfaction varies with the type of interpretive offering. In general, though, the evidence to date certainly suggests that interpretation contributes to visitors satisfaction, and research on other forms of tourism has found that satisfied customers create positive word-of-mouth advertising and repeat visitation, all of which contribute to economic sustainability.

Interpretation facilitates economic sustainability not only by satisfying customers, but also by *creating jobs*. A conclusion of Muloin *et al.'s* (2001) study of indigenous wildlife tourism in Australia was that involvement of indigenous people as guides and interpreters adds an authentic element to a wildlife tourism experience that is valued by many tourists and adds depth to visitors' understanding of wildlife.

People with local knowledge, and with a passion for the place in which they have grown up and come to love, have the two essential ingredients that make the best interpretive guides : they are knowledgeable and they are passionate. Training and employing local people as guides and interpreters represents an important sustainable development strategy because it produces a type of employment that is based on, and even demands, an unspoiled environment (Weiler and Ham, 2001). For those employed in the industry, the economic value of protecting their very livelihoods is compelling. So training and employing locals as interpretive guides not only provides satisfied customers, it also provides satisfied locals, who become important allies in the protection of both the natural and the cultural environments that form the basis of the wildlife tourism industry (Weiler and Hamm, 2002).

How Does Interpretation Facilitate Ecological Sustainability?

In wildlife tourism, interpretation acts, firstly, as an on-site regulator of visitor behaviour—it is a key strategy for managing environmental impacts. Secondly, interpretation influences not only what people know and do on-site, but potentially what visitors believe about conservation generally. Interpretation can thus play a key role in long-term conservation.

What is the role of interpretation in *influencing and regulating visitor behaviour*? In attempting to develop a conceptual framework for wildlife tourism, Reynolds and Braithwaite (2001) discuss several strategies for controlling visitors, particularly in the context of tourist interactions with wildlife. Beyond the physical strategies (such as regulating group size and access) that have dominated management to date, they invoke the idea of 'intellectual control', which they describe as the use of a tour guide and other interpretive mechanisms to transmit knowledge and at the same time influence on-site visitor behaviour.

Interpretation has, of course, been employed for decades by agencies such as the Canadian Parks. Service and several land management agencies in the US, for precisely this purpose. More recently, the US National Park Service (Kohen and Sikoryak, 1999) has implemented a sophisticated interpretive planning process aimed at informing decisions (themes), with the specific purpose of influencing visitor experiences and often behaviour. in Australia, Parks Victoria is embarking on a very similar planning process.

These strategic interpretive planning strategies are underpinned by two related theories of human behaviour the theory of reasoned action (Fishbein and Ajzen, 1975) and the theory of planned behaviour (Ajzen, 1991). Twenty-five years of research based on these related theories have confirmed that much human behaviour, or at least behavioural intent, is *consistent with* our attitudes, and that these attitudes are consistent with our beliefs. Although relationships between beliefs, attitudes, behavioural intent and behaviour are more complex than this, the main implication is that if you want to influence how a person feels and acts toward a thing, you need to influence what they *believe* about it. As Ham and Krumpe (1996) have explained in detail, when interpretation is designed and delivered to influence a tourist's beliefs about an animal, an animal's habitat, or a concept such as 'respecting' or 'protecting' that animal or its habitat, it can potentially have profound impacts.

This is a different strategy than, say, just filling an allotted time period with facts and details about wildlife. It is more strategic and more purposeful, in the sense that it is aimed at a known desired outcome. This is thematic interpretation : the idea of communicating beliefs in an effort to strategically influence attitudes and ultimately behaviours. According to Ham and Krumpe (1996), a them expresses a belief about something. So whether it is a guide's commentary, an exhibit text, or a web site that is communicating to a visitor, the intent of thematic interpretation is to plant a seed that can become the foundation of a new belief related to a desired behavioural outcome. Of course, it must be done in a fun and entertaining way in order to be satisfying, but it is more strategic than just entertaining for entertainment's sake.

Around the world, protected area managers have put considerable resources into using interpretation as a way of influencing and regulating visitor behaviour, all in the interests of minimising negative impacts and facilitating sustainability (Ham 1992; Roggenbuck, 1992; Alder, 1996; Lackey and Ham, 2001; Lackey et al., 2002). The involvement of the commercial sector in controlling visitor behaviour has been more recent and much less strategic. However, park management agencies are well aware that interpretation has been largely taken out of their hands by government cut-backs and privatization, and are increasingly keen to 'use' the commercial sector for communicating minimal impact messages, managing visitor behaviour and role modelling appropriate practices at least while visiting protected areas.

Research by Armstrong and Weiler (2002), in cooperation with Parks Victoria in Australia, round that licensed tour operators in national parks could be doing much more in the way of delivering interpretive messages that act as a park management tool. Participant-observation and audiorecording of guide commentary on twenty guided tours found that seventeen of the guides delivered 107 messages related to Parks Victoria's goals. In relation to the length of the tours (many were full-day tours) and the amount of commentary, this is a very small number. The most frequently delivered messages were about minimizing impacts while on tour. Few messages imparted by the guides touched on the importance or difficulty of protected area management. The responsibility largely rests with the managers of protected areas being proactive in identifying and even requiring particular messages to be communicated by licensed tour operators, as a way of influencing on-site behaviour.

In addition to influencing what people know and do on-site, interpretation can play a role in *long-term conservation* by influencing what visitors come to believe about the area, about the importance of the resources being protected and about the strategies being used to protect them. Through the well-documented 'sleeper effect' process, it can be argued that a day spent observing or thinking about wildlife, whether free-roaming or captive, can theoretically turn into something much bigger in the form of new beliefs implanted in a tourist's psyche (see, for example, Hovland *et al.*, 1953; Guder *et al.*, 1978; Lariscy and Tinkham, 1999). As we will see shortly, that, of course, depends on the themes the tourist leaves with and the kind of reinforcement she or he experiences in the coming days and weeks, but it *can* happen.

However, evaluating the extent to which interpretation does this involves much more than just recording visitor's recall of ecological facts. The Parks Victoria study previously noted identified the kinds of messages delivered by operators and recalled by visitors, but did not go further in measuring whether these messages get translated into environmental attitudes, behavioural intentions and ultimately conservation behaviours. Longitudinal research of this type is difficult but necessary to determine how interpretation impacts on long-term conservation. Likewise, Lackey and Ham (2001) reported that Yosemite National Park (USA) visitors could remember some of the messages aimed at them regarding appropriate food storage behaviour in black bear country, yet improper food storage persists as a problem in the park. Guided by the theories outlined earlier, researchers believe that messages need to be redirected to target visitors' specific beliefs about storing food properly.

Direct evidence exists that high-quality thematic interpretation contributes to tourists' attitudes and behaviour in support of wildlife conservation. A theme-driven communication campaign developed for Lindblad Expeditions passenger in the Galapagos Islands (see Ham and O'Brien, 1998; Ham, 2001) directly resulted in significant increases in passenger donations to the Galapagos Conservation Fund

(GCF). Guided by the theories of reasoned action and planned behaviour, the GCF campaign consisted primarily of strategically developed messages that were developed and delivered to passengers via onboard interpretive panels, guide commentaries at various islands, in evening debriefings, and in pre-visit information sent to passengers prior to their departure. According to Solution Site Case Study (2001) :

> *The development of an organized communications strategy unquestionably resulted in consistent responses from our guests. This has translated into an average of about $4000 per week in steady support for Galapagos conservation.*
>
> (http://www.solutions-site.org/cat1-sol1116.htm)

Although demonstration of interpretation's success in achieving the ultimate goal of long-term conservation awaits further study, such results do suggest that thematic interpretation can indeed contribute in positive ways to how wildlife tourists think, feel, and behave with respect to wildlife conservation in a place like Galapagos.

Conclusion

Much remains to be learned about interpretation's role in sustainable wildlife tourism. However, the evidence presented in this chapter suggests that interpretation, strategically, packaged and creatively delivered, can contribute to sustainable wildlife tourism by : (1) satisfying customer demand, (2) creating opportunities for local employment, (3) influencing on-site visitor behaviour, and (4) promoting a conservation ethic in tourists that may extend well beyond their on-site experience. These are both the premise and promise of interpretation in sustainable wildlife tourism : done well, it enhances the wildlife experience of tourists, acts as a mechanism for job creation, serves as an on-site management tool, and acts as a strategic communication medium for long-term conservation.

References

1. Ajzen, I. (1991) : The Theory of Planned Behaviour. *Organizational Behaviour and Human Decision Processes* 50 :

179-211.

2. Alder, J. (1996) : Costs and Effectiveness of Education and Enforcement, Cairns Section of the Great Barrier Reef Marine Park. *Environmental Management* **20(4)**, 541-51.
3. Armstrong, K. and Weiler, B. (2002) : They said what to who?!'-Messages delivered on guided tours in Victorian protected areas. Presented to *Tour Guiding and Heritage Interpretation : Seminar on Research for the 21st Century*. Malbourne.
4. Ballantyne, R., Packer, J. and Beckmann, E. (1998) : Targeted interpretation : Exploring relationships among visitors' motivations, activities, information needs and preferences. *Journal of Tourism Studies* **9(2)** : 14-25.
5. Brundtland, H.G. (1987) : *Our Common Future : Report of the World Commission on Environment and Development*, UNESCO.
6. Fishbein, M. and Ajzen, I. (1975) : *Belief, Attitude, Intention and Behaviour : An Introduciton to Theory and Research*. Reading : Addison-Wesley.
7. Fredline, E. and Faulkner, W. (2001) : *International Market Analysis of Wildlife Tourism*. Wildlife Tourism Research report series, gold Coast, CRC for Sustainable Tourism.
8. Gruder, C., Cook, T., Hennigan, K., Flay; B., Alessis, C. and Halama, J. (1978) : Empirical tests of the absolute sleeper effect predicted form the discounting cue hypothesis. *Journal of Personality and Social Psychology* **36** : 1061-74.
9. Ham, S. (1992) : *Environmental Interpretation : A Practical Guide for People with Big Ideas and Small Budgets*. Golden, CO, USA : Fulcrum/North American Press.
10. Ham, S. (2001) : A Theory-based Approach to Campaign Planning for Traveler's Philanthropy. Invited address to Traveler's Philanthropy Summit hosted by Enterprises for Sustainable Tourism (BEST), Punta Cana Resort, Dominican Republic, Nov. 9-11.
11. Ham, S. and Krumpe, E. (1996) : Identifying Audiences and Messages for Nonformal Environmental Education : A Theoretical Framework for Interpreters. *Journal of Interpretation Research* **1(1)** : 11-23.

12. Ham, S. and O'Brier, T. (1998) : *The Galapagos Conservation Fund : A Case Study in Developing an Organized Communications Strategy for Conservation Fundraising*. New York : Lindblad Expeditions, Inc.

13. Ham, S. and Weiler, B. (2001) : 100,000 Beating Bird Hearts : Tourism, Wildlife and Interpretation. Keynote presentation at the First National Conferece on Wildlife Tourism in Australia. Hobard, Tasmania, Australia, October 28-30 (www.crctourism.com.au).

14. Ham, S. and Weiler, B. (2002) : Toward a Theory of Quality in Cruise-based Nature Guiding. *Journal of Interpretation Research* **6 (1)**, in press.

15. Hovland, C., Janis, I. and Kelley, H. (1953) : *Communication and Persuasion*. Yale University Press.

16. Kohen, R. and Sikoryak, K. (1999) : Comprehensive Interpretive Planning. *Legacy* **10(4)** : 25-30.

17. Lackey, B. and Ham, S. (2001) : Human-Bear Interaction Assessment. Yosemite National Park, California. Interim Research Report submitted to the National Park Service and the Yosemite Fund, November.

18. Lackey, B., Ham, S. Quigley, H. (2002) : *Message Catalog : Human-Bear Messages in Yosemite Valley*. Center for International Training and Outreach, Department of Resource Recreation and Tourism, University of Idaho.

19. Lariscy, R. and Tinkham, S. (1999) : The sleeper effect and negative political advertising. *Journal of Advertising* **28(4)** : 13-30.

20. Moscardo, G., Pearce, P. L. and Haxton, P. (1998) : Understanding rainforest tourist expectations and experiences. *1998 Australian Tourism and Hospitality Research Conference*. Bureau of Tourism Research, 295-308.

21. Moscardo, G. Woods, B. and Greenwood, T. (2000) : *Understanding Visitor Perspective on Wildlife Tourism*. Wildlife Tourism Research Report Series : No. 2, Gold Coast, CRC for Sustainable Tourism.

22. Muloin, S. Zeppel, H. and Higginbottom, K. (2001) : *Indigenous Wildlife Tourism in Australia*. Wildlife Tourism Research Report Series : No. 15, Gold Coast, CRC for

Sustainable Tourism.

23. Pearce, P.L. and Moscardo, G. (1998) : The role of interpretation in influencing visitor satisfaction : A rainforest case study. *1998 Australian Tourism and Hospitality Research Conference.* Bureau of Tourism Research. pp. 309-19.

24. Reynolds, P. and Braithwaite, D. (2001) : Towards a conceptual framework for wildlife tourism. *Tourism Management* **22** : 31-42.

25. Robinson, J. and Bennett. E. (2000) : *Hunting for Sustainability in Tropical Forests.* New York : Columbia University Press.

26. Roggenbuck, J. (1992) : Use of Persuasion to Reduce Resource Impacts and Visitor Conflicts. Chapter 7, in Manfred, M. (ed.), *Influencing Human Behaviour : Theory and Application in Recreation, Tourism and Natural Resources Management.* Champaign, Illinois, USA : Sagamore Publishing ; pp. 149-208.

27. Solutions Site Case Study (2001) : The Galapagos Conservation Fund (GCF). In Section V of web site http :// www.solutions-site.org/cat1_solll6.htm.

28. Sweeting. J.E.N., Bruner, A.G. and Rosenfeld, A.B. (1999) : *The Green Host Effect : An Integrated Approach to Sustainable Tourism and Resort Development.* Conservation International Policy Paper. Washington, DC : Conservation International.

29. Tilden, F. (1957) : *Interpreting Our Heritage.* Chapel Hill, NC, USA : University of North Carolina Press.

30. Trapp, S., Gross, M. and Zimmerman, R. (1991) : *Signs, Traits and Wayside Exhibits : Connecting People and Places.* Stevens Point, WI, USA : University of Wisconsin, Stevens Point Press, Inc.

4 Travel Ecology

Introduction

As development theories evolve, approaches to the use of tourism as a development tool need to be revisited to reflect these changes. A careful balance must be struck between new ideas and successful existing practices. This chapter presents a case study concerning how an innovative conceptual framework was integrated into a community tourism programme at Clemson University, USA. Over the last twenty years, the 'Developing Naturally' programme at Clemson has grown from serving local clients on a case-by-case basis to facilitating community development in eight-eight countries. While the efficacy of the programme has yet to be fully measured, the 150000 (electronic) requests for information that have been received, resulting international partnerships, and field experiences to date indicate that it has been well received. As the programme has evolved from being local to international in scope its basic framework has changed from one based on resource conservation, to one employing a sustainable development paradigm. In more recent times, a further development has occurred with a post-sustainable ethic termed 'travel ecology' being employed as the conceptual foundation for the Developing Naturally programme. This chapter overviews the development of this framework, placing emphasis on the coevolution of theory and practice.

Programme Evolution

In the early 1980s, the tourism extension programme at

Clemson University focused on the development of nature-based tourism in relation to recreational fisheries along the Southeastern US coast. Using resource conservation as a conceptual framework, this programme included the identification of natural resources (*e.g.*, fishery location and mapping), inventory of associated infrastructure (*e.g.*, guide, services, charter captains, and marinas), resource marketing including cooperative efforts in promotion and advertising (*e.g.*, printed guides, brochures, magazine ads, and trade shows), conservation education and other university supported public service programme (*e.g.*, charter captain workshops, special tournaments, television programmes, and newspaper articles).

While the fisheries programme was successful in increasing economic return for the recreational fisheries industry at the local level, and in the development of a conservation ethic within the recreational fisheries industry, the research team did not simultaneously address social, economic, and environmental concerns as called for in today's sustainable development programmes. The emphasis of the programme was essentially on industry development and conserving a natural resource for the benefit of specific local communities. Indeed, as with many similar programmes implemented at this time, the focus was very much on the development of tourism instead of developing communities for tourism although these efforts were still called 'community tourism development'.

By the late 1980s, the tourism extension programme began receiving requests for development assistance in Central Europe, a region struggling with severe economic development problems resulting from a disintegrating Soviet Bloc. Our first overseas tourism development projects was undertaken under the auspices of Volunteers in Overseas Cooperative Assistance (VOCA) and involved working within their Polish Agricultural Extension programme. The Polish experience provided unique insights into issues related to tourism and community development as this region underwent a radical social and economic transition from communism to democracy. The initial emphasis of the programme was to create new economic opportunities in the tourism area for farmers who had lost their traditional sources of income in the Soviet farm products market. The tourism infrastructure in these communities was, however, virtually non-existent. Villagers were striving to survive and had little faith in any plan for the future no matter how promising. During a local town meeting conducted by a Clemson University researcher concerning tourism development, a small farmer expressed his frustration and pessimism toward the future. When the researcher stated that tourism would offer some hope for bringing additional income to the community, the farmer responded by shouting, 'Hope! Hope! Hope is the Angel of Despair!'

In recognition of the context in which the programme was to operate, it was decided to focus on stimulating local entrepreneurship, within the context of sustainable agritourism, which included the development of Bed and Breakfast (B and B) enterprises. At the time, sustainable development was thought to be an appropriate paradigm for this type of tourism because it provided an alternative to mass tourism models. Smallscale bed and breakfast development was considered ideal for this situation, as it required little additional economic expenditures for the farm family, while at the same time bringing new income into the community. In 1995, a paper developed at Clemson University, *Beginning a Bed and Breakfast in South Carolina : Guidelines for Development* (www.strom.clemson.edu/publication/Potts/bb/bb1-3.pdf), was adapted and translated into Polish so it could be used as a resource for the programme. Over thirty bed and breakfast workshops were held in the country's rural communities. This effort resulted in the creation of several tourism associations and numerous farm-based bed and breakfast operations in Poland, hosting visitors from across Europe.

In one area with numerous small organic farms, the concept of a healthy bed and breakfast venue was developed, targeting the health-conscious German tourist. Meetings and workshops were also held with mayors and village officials featuring tourism development, based on a 'home town discovery' process (see later discussion) for community development tourism. However, while working in an area that lacked infrastructure and social capital, researchers began to realize that sustainable development had limitations in such contexts. Many of the case studies used in sustainable development programmes came from developed or semi-developed settings, and as such addressed few of the problems associated with 'starting from scratch'.

Conceptual Background

Up until the time that researchers began to question the efficacy of sustainable development in certain contexts, tourism extension programmes at Clemson closely reflected overall trends in the tourism research field. For example, marine fisheries project outlined earlier was influenced by environmental planning and policy dating back to Ian McHarg's *Design with nature* (1969), in that it utilized predetermined spatial attributes to locate fisheries in environmentally and commercially advantageous positions. The programme was also influenced by Gunn's *Vacationscape : defining tourism regions* (1972) in that it was expressly concerned with identifying and making use of regional tourism resources. Although these technical approaches fostered a new awareness of tourism as a development issue, they placed little emphasis on resident attitudes or citizen participation.

By 1979, Gunn, in *Tourism planning : basics, concepts, and cases,* called for a much broader approach to tourism development and importantly, more local participation throughout the planning process. Seekings (1980, p. 255) echoed this sentiment, stating, 'Tourism has become too important to be left to the experts.' Throughout the 1980s and 1990s, community-driven planning efforts were investigated by numerous researchers (Murphy, 1983, 1988, 1993 ; Blank, 1989; Keogh, 1990 ; Prentice, 1993 ; Jamal and Getz, 1995). In 1995, researchers at Clemson University published *Hometown*

Discovery : a development process for tourism (Amos and Potts, 1992). This publication was influenced by the books *An approach to assessing community tourism potential* (Harris *et al.*, 1989) and *Small town tourism development* (Howell, 1987). The purpose of *Hometown Discovery* was to allow residents to 'discover' their hometowns regarding tourism potential and plans for appropriate tourism development. This process would later be used as the basis for the Developing Naturally programme.

The *Hometown Discovery* publication provided residents with the opportunity to develop a customized tourism development plan for their area. Key headings in this book were :

- Is tourism for us?
- What will we need? (Maps, documents, etc.)
- What are our human resources? (Natural, built, etc.)
- Service and infrastructure
- Financing
- Market conditions
- Targeting customers
- Benchmarks (making a calendar)
- Communication inventory
- Visitation trends
- Competition analysis
- Comprehensive overview (putting in all together)
- Implementation (action steps).

The use of *Hometown Discovery* by communities involved the creation of a planning team. This team would act to rank and map resources, identify community assets and deficiencies, and develop a strategy for tourism development in their area. The *Hometown Discovery* publication was initially utilized by various communities throughout South Carolina. In more recent times, it has been translated by Polish and Russian organizations with an interest in community tourism development in their respective countries.

During the 1990s, sustainable development began to be incorporated into the tourism field and featured in Inskeep's *Tourism planning : an integrated and sustainable approach* (1991) and Gunn's 1994 edition of *Tourism planning*. By 1994, work began on a revision of the Hometown Discovery programme and the next year *Developing naturally : an exploratory process for nature-based community tourism* (Potts and Marsinko, 1995) was published. This publication built on the Hometown Discovery process with the addition of an analysis chapter dedicated to maintaining resource quality and a section on identifying potential nature visitors. At the time, the researchers identified nature-based tourism with sustainable development, only to the extent that they both shared a common environmental ideal. As a result of the researchers' Polish experience, they came to identify nature-based tourism with much larger issues embraced within the concept of sustainable development, such a politics and culture. As a result, the document *Developing Naturally* eventually became the centerpiece of a more comprehensive programme sponsored by Clemson University's Strom Thurmond Institute. The programme is today called 'Developing Naturally : enhancing communities' and is downloadable from the World Wide Web.

A Travel Ecology Approach

In 1996, we undertook a comprehensive review of the literature in the areas of sustainability, tourism, and community development. This effort was part of an overall plan to explain the barriers and associated social attitudes toward development we found in our Eastern European experience as well as trying to locate our experiences in the constellation of ideals that fall under the rubric 'sustainable tourism'. This review led to a presentation entitled *In search of a travel ecology paradigm* (Petts and Harrill, 1997) at the Travel and Tourism Research Associations national conference. This paper detailed the evolution of conservation, carrying capacity, eco-development, and sustainability, culminating in a travel ecology paradigm that challenged professionals to think beyond sustainability or 'sustainable tourism'. With a close affinity to the fields of cultural and political ecology, *travel ecology* implies that tourism planning and policy should help create communities that become resilient enough to survive a highly volatile political and economic environment and think beyond mere 'sustaining' tourism or some specific aspect of tourism development. Thus, we consider 'travel ecology' as theoretical shorthand for 'sustainable community tourism development', although in some respects improving on 'tourism sustainability' as a conceptual foundation by emphasizing a more holistic approach to community development and ecological enhancement. A subsequent presentation in 1998, *Developing Naturally : toward a travel ecology approach* (Potts and Harrill, 1998a), at the National Tourism Extension Conference, was used as an opportunity to engage in substantial dialogue regarding what we perceived as limitations relating to current approaches to sustainable tourism development and to further refine the 'travel ecology' concept. We felt that tourism planners and professionals, including ourselves, had, in general, historically focused narrowly on developing tourism. Although tourism professionals had engaged with the concept of sustainability, they had not appreciated the potential that tourism offered for long-term enhancement of communities and associated environments. Subsequently the opportunity through tourism to build environments where individuals could reach their potential had not been fully appreciated.

Today, the Developing Naturally programme, based on the conceptual foundation of travel ecology, calls for a restructuring of research and planning programmes in a direction that moves beyond sustainability and toward an investigation of how the relationship between community, ecology and travel can be used not only to sustain, but enhance human communities (Figure 4.1). The travel ecology approach is based on six principles with broad applicability to many types of 'communities', including local, regional, national, and international communities (Potts and Harrill, 1998b). We view

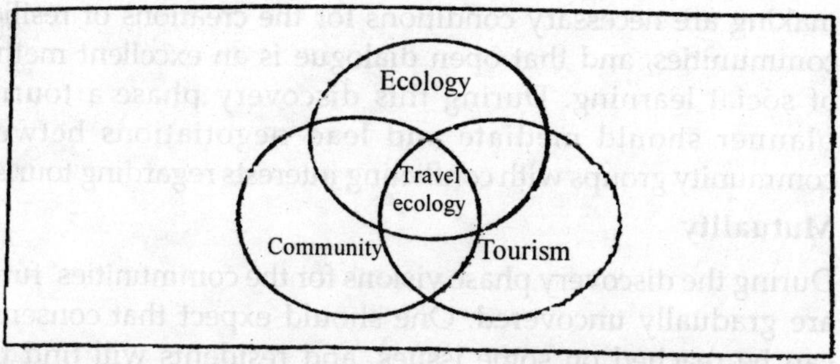

Fig. 4.1. Travel ecology model. *Travel ecology* differs from ecotourism, nature based and/ or 'sustainable' tourism models due to its emphasis on enhancement and focus on community.

these principles as contributing to tourism theory, rather than constituting a definitive model or process (Getz, 1986).

Discovery

The initial planning phase of 'discovery' is based upon the participation of all relevant stakeholders within a development area, for example citizens in a local village. A key to successful planning is the development of self-awareness within the community that occurs when residents inventory their own social, economic, and environmental resources. This inventory process allows the resident to discover sense of place' ; that combination of built and natural environment, history, and local culture that make a place unique. Through public discourse about the importance and value of these discovered resources individuals can address fears about potential changes and expectations for improvement. The original impetus behind Hometown Discovery and Developing Naturally was to design a process allowing residents to perceive their community's tourism resources from the perspective of an outsider-to 'discover' the community's tourism potential through collaborative, democratic forums. The process of discovery can at times be a turbulent phase in the tourism planning process, as conflicts in interest group values are gradually uncovered. The sustainable tourism literature places little emphasis on the potential conflicts arising over resource distribution and use. Conversely, the travel ecology approach recognizes that open public conflict and democratic decision-making are necessary conditions for the creations of resilient communities, and that open dialogue is an excellent method of social learning. During this discovery phase a tourism planner should mediate and lead negotiations between community groups with conflicting interests regarding tourism.

Mutuality

During the discovery phase visions for the communities' future are gradually uncovered. One should expect that consensus can be reached on some issues, and residents will find that they have common ground from which they can move toward an agreed goal of a better quality of life for community members. Mutuality means that citizens engage in a common language emphasizing shared values, ideas, and concerns while respecting one another's opinions. Healthy communities have a sense of mutuality that goes beyond the coordination of limited benefits, segmented goals or roles (Selznick, 1996 : 1998). The absence of mutuality that occurs during political transitions such as from communism to democracy can make tourism planning extremely difficult. Resource scarcity, political distrust, and the lack of social organization make tourism planning, much less sustainable tourism, extremely difficult to achieve in these contexts. Although infrequently emphasized, sustainable development is about relationship building : between generations, between social groups and institutions, and between individuals sharing nature's wealth on a local basis.

Locality

We are often asked to 'think globally' when we need to think and act locally. The travel ecology approach emphasizes 'backyard activism' or the 'geography of everywhere' : the recognition that all landscapes, no matter how mundane, contribute to the community tourism product. With tourism development in Central Europe, the researchers were pleased to find that residents had a very detailed 'cognitive map' of local places, a perspective rarely found in the homogenized West. Locality begins with the notion that environmental awareness toward environments such as rainforests or savannas begins with an awareness of commonplace environments. This is not to advocate an abandonment of 'endangered' environments, only that awareness of locality is critical to the development of 'sense of place' –often mentioned (Berry, 1993) as a component of community. The travel ecology approach is based upon the belief that the community is both a socially constructed and ecologically grounded place. Social networks and natural and built environments in which such networks evolve are mutually reinforcing elements of community. Environments may dictate both quality of life and economic resources opportunities. Individuals who recognize their relationship to the local environment more fully understand their neighbours and their common foundations.

Historicity

Historical knowledge is indispensable to the tourism planning process, despite the postmodern contention that 'history is dead' (Ritzer, 1993). As sustainable tourism models often emphasize 'best practices' management grounded in the present, a community's historical patterns of land and resource use are often neglected in sustainable development plans and policies. Tourism planners should become thoroughly familiar with oral and written traditions if they are to fully appreciate how residents interact with one another and their environment. In the Central European experience, it was found that there was some historical 'amnesia' due to Soviet efforts at cultural assimilation, while other traditions, particularly religious and fold, remained strong in the hearts of the people. The researchers realized that an awareness and appreciation of local history and culture on the part of the residents was important to developing an authentic and viable local tourism product. More importantly, however, this re-emphasis of their own history and culture resulted in a stronger sense of identity and self-esteem, which proved as valuable to long-term economic development as the recovery of some forgotten art form or cultural practice. Perhaps the greatest negative impact of long-term occupation was the loss of historical values relating to freedom. People had forgotten how to freely express themselves in public without fear of recrimination. They had lost the ability to govern themselves from the bottom up. This loss necessitates the development of discovery programme and projects that teach listening, sharing, and public entrepreneurship.

Potentiality

Whereas sustainable tourism tends to emphasize the integration of social, economic, and ecological concerns (Inskeep, 1991), the travel ecology approach emphasizes notions of growth and maturation along with integration. Thus, travel ecology is an integrative and developmental approach, whereas sustainable tourism is often conceived as simply integrative. It is not enough to consider disparate community characteristics holistically ; it is also important to consider these elements as they longitudinally change and transform the character and complexion of a community. This developmental perspective becomes critical in underdeveloped settings such as Central Europe in the same way that the first years of a child are considered critical to the development of a healthy, functional adult. A major tenet of Bookchin's (1996) philosophy of *social ecology* is that the relationship between society and nature are co-evolutionary and developmental, rather than only the sum of integrated parts. For example, a sustainable community may be seen as one that is whole, that has reached its potential in maintaining a high quality of life for all residents.

Enhancement

Sustainable tourism as we have practised it stresses the alleviation of negative impacts while obtaining maximum sustainable yield for the industry. For example, quantitative capacity is generally thought of as a tool for determining the number of visitors a resource can sustain without unacceptable degradation. We believe that carrying capacity can be enhanced through democratic dialogue and participation. How is carrying capacity related to a political idea like democracy? The management of the global common is intrinsically a political problem. Hardin (1968) in his famous essay *Tragedy of the commons* suggested that centralized authority would be necessary to prevent an ecological overshoot of the commons. Interestingly, under centralized Soviet rule many areas of Central Europe experienced severe negative impacts. Absentee owners are certainly not an essential component of wise stewardship. In reality, the local inhabitants of an area, due to their proximity to the resource base, their dependency, and their sense of place, have greater potential for making 'wise' choices. Sustainable development and local enhancement is possible through an active and democratic society that allocates scarce resources through participatory deliberation at home. The impetus for sustainability should become stronger if liberties and freedoms are nurtured. The Developing Naturally projects in Slovakia and Poland provided the basis for an understanding of the necessity of mutuality and locality, that public buy in and free expression is essential. Perhaps the project's greatest success was the facilitation of these attributes through the programme planning processes. It became evident that teaching tourism development through discovery actually taught citizens how to take charge and enhance their communities. In this respect, the need to establish tourism and democracy in Central Europe and other regions is related and is not treated as a separate issue under the travel ecology approach.

Operational Strategies

As previously discussed the principles of Discovery, Mutuality, Locality, Historicity, Potentiality, and Enhancement are the key components of travel ecology concept, which is the supporting foundation for the Developing Naturally programme. The overall goal of Developing Naturally is to enhance communities around the globe by developing and providing resource materials and workshops based upon these principles. Our experience and the influences of significant contributions of others in the field of tourism and community development suggest that the programme needed to be broader in scope than previous conservation and sustainable development approaches. In response to this call the following strategies guide the Developing Naturally programme :

- Enhancing communities' quality of life on a long-term basis.
- Improving destinations, rather than only 'developing' destinations.
- Creating community environments that nurture human potential.
- Building linkages between individual homes and neighbourhoods to national and international organizations.
- Facilitating public discovery process that promote democratic principles through participation and self-reliance.
- Addressing ecological change within the local community context.
- Preserving community cultures and heritage, inclusive of all groups and histories.

Programme Management

Although the Developing Naturally programme has the ambitious goal of enhancing communities throughout the world by developing and providing resource materials and workshops, the reality is that it is a physically small programme located at Clemson University's Strom Thurmond Institute of Government and Public Affairs. Due to recent technological advancements in computer capabilities and Internet access in 1998 Developing Naturally began to provide resource material available at no charge to the recipient on the World Wide Web. Resource manuals are developed and adapted for Internet distribution and made available at the web at http://www.developingnaturally.com/. One permanent director staffs the programme and a high value is placed on the creation of, and long-term use of, informal partnerships. It is the programme's philosophy that materials should be adapted for local communities and therefore international volunteer partnerships are used to identify programme needs, translate publications, and facilitate workshops in their prospective regions. Current international partners include : VOKA (VOCA)-Vidiecka Organizacia pre Komunitne Aktivity, Mateja Bela University in Slovakia, Rivne State Technical University, Ukraine, and Universidad de Ciencias Comerciales, Nicaragua. Programme activities have also been supported by the US Peace Corp-ACDI/VOCA, and the Fulbright Commission.

Products presently available include materials for community tourism planning, home-based business development of eco-tourism enterprises, and recycling. In 2001, government, educational private sector, and individuals in over eighty-eight countries downloaded over 40,000 of our documents.

Overall, the goal of the programme is to develop at least two partners on each continent in the near future. Marketing will be broadened through additional participation in international conferences. Fundraising will be undertaken to support an additional staff member with multiple language skills and to hold annual partnership meetings. New product development will be focused on guidelines for increasing public participation (listing projects), home-based business development (crafts), and enhancing community environments (urban forestry, small parks).

Conclusion

Social scientists often use worldviews or paradigms to frame their research efforts. These frameworks help researchers make sense of evidence, allow for continuity between research programmes, and contribute to disciplinary cohesion. Blindly following the lead of the top researcher in the dominant paradigm may advance an academic career, while challenging the popular paradigms is often an unwise career move. Practitioners often quote the dominant perspective or paradigm to make their efforts seem innovative although their actual practice may have change very little. However, researchers and practitioners alike must be aware of the constant evolution of concepts and ideas. The concept of sustainable development evolved form such precursors as conservation, preservation, carrying capacity, and eco-development, and continues to evolve. For the Developing Naturally programme, the researchers took a critical look at sustainable development form a paradigmatic perspective instead of attaching the term to their final product. We actively looked for differences between the practice and theory to improve both. In the end, we found enough differences to develop our own framework, 'travel ecology'. We encourage other researchers to help us develop this framework in an area of rapid global political, economic, and technological change.

It is our belief that tourism professionals are at an exciting crossroads in history in which they can make a positive difference in the quality of life around the world. By adopting a travel ecology type of approach, we believe the tourism industry can be proactive regarding the future and advance beyond sustainability, providing a form of tourism development that will encourage a more holistic form of community development. For the first time, through such tools as the Internet, we have the opportunity to build partnerships and educate on a global basis at an extremely low cost.

Since the Industrial Revolution, we have been saddled with a narrow ideology of development : development for economic sake alone, beginning with conventional or industrial development and now through a relatively narrow perspective toward 'sustainable' development. Through the evolution of concepts such as travel ecology, we are now provided with the opportunity to abandon the narrow traditional development paradigm altogether. The focus of the tourism researcher, planner, developer, etc., should transcend that of sustaining environments for future generations. The focus of tourism planners should be more than tourism projects that produce a maximum sustainable yield for that industry alone. The industry has the potential to improve the world, not just sustain itself. Properly planned can tourism enhance human communities on a scale compatible with their resources and infrastructure. By emphasizing the principles of discovery, mutuality, locality, historicity, potential, and enhancement, we think we can conceive a model for tourism that can help millions of individuals reach their potential in a global society.

References

1. Amos, C.J. and Potts. T.D. (1992) : *Hometown discovery : a development process for tourism* Clemson, SC : Clemson University Cooperative Extension Service.
2. Berry, W. (1993) : *Sex, economy, freedom and community*. New York. Cambridge University Press.
3. Blank, U. (1989) : *The community tourism industry imperative: the necessity, the opportunity, and its potential*. State College, PA : Venture Publishing.
4. Bookchin, M. (1996) : *The philosophy of social ecology*. New York : Black Rose Books.
5. Getz, D. (1986) : Models in tourism planning : Towards integration of theory and practice. *Tourism Management* 7 (2) : 21-32.
6. Getz, D. and Jamal, T.B. (1994) : The environmental-community symbiosis : A case for collaborative tourism planning. *Journal of Sustainable Tourism* **2(3)** : 152-73.
7. Gunn, C.A. (1972) : *Vacationscape : Designing tourism regions*. New York : Van Nostrand Reinhold.
8. Gunn C.A. (1979) : *Tourism planning : Basics, concepts, and cases,* New York : Crane, Russak.
9. Gunn C.A. (1994) : *Tourism planning : Basics, concepts, and cases.* 3rd edn. New York : Taylor and Francis.
10. Hardin, G. (1968) : The tragedy of commons. *Science* **162** : 1243-8.
11. Harris, C.C., Timko, S. E. and McLaughlin, W. J. (1989) : *An approach to assessing community tourism potential*. Moscow ID : Department of Wildland Recreation Management, College of Forestry, Wildlife and Range Sciences.
12. Howell, R.L. (1987) : *Small town tourism development*. Clemson, SC : Department of Parks, Recreation, and Tourism Management, College of forest and Recreation Resources.
13. Inskeep, E. (1991) : *Tourism planning : An integrated and sustainable approach,* New York : Van Nostrand Reinhold.
14. Jamal, T.B. and Getz, D. (1995) : Collaboration theory and community tourism planning. *Annals of Tourism Research* **22 (1)** : 186-204.

15. Keogh, B. (1990) : Public participation in community tourism planning. *Annals of Tourism Research* **17(3)** : 449-65.
16. McHarg, I.L. (1969) : *Design with Nature*. Garden City, NY : Doubleday Press.
17. Murphy, P.E. (1983) : Tourism as a community industry : An ecological model of tourism development, *Tourism Management* **4 (3)** : 180-93.
18. Murphy, P. E. (1988) : Community-driven tourism planning, *Tourism Management,* **9 (2)** : 96-104.
19. Murphy, P.E. (1993) : Community-driven tourism planning and residents' preferences. *Tourism Management* **14(3)** : 218-27.
20. Potts, T.D. and Harrill, R. (1997) : *In search of a travel ecology paradigm*. Presentation at the Travel and Tourism Research Association. Norfolk, VA.
21. Potts, T.D. and Harrill, R. (1998a) : *Developing naturally : Toward a travel ecology approach*. Presentation at the National Tourism Extension Conference, Hershey, PA.
22. Potts, T.D. and Harrill R. (1998b) : Enhancing communities for sustainability : A travel ecology approach. *Tourism Analysis* **3 (3,4)** : 133-42.
23. Potts, T. D. and Marsinko, A. (1995) : *Developing naturally : An exploratory process for nature-based community tourism*. Clemson, SC : Strom Thurmond Institute, Clemson University Cooperative Extension Service.
24. Prentice, R. (1993) : Community-driven tourism planning and residents' preferences. *Tourism Management* **14 (3)** : 218-27.
25. Ritzer, G. (1993) : *The mcdonaldization of society*. Thousand Oaks, CA : Pine Tree Press.
26. Seekings, J. (1980) : Pro bono publico : The case for a systematic system, in D. W. Hawking, Shafer, E. L. and Rovelstad, J. M. (eds), *Tourism planning and development issues,* pp. 251-70. Washington, DC : George Washington University.
27. Selznick, P. (1996) : In search of community, in Vitek, W. and Jackson, W. (eds), *Rooted in the land : Essays on community and place,* pp. 195-203. New York : John Wiley and Sons.

5 Accreditation for Tourism

Introduction

Making tourism more sustainable requires action on a number of fronts. Regulation by government can, for example, establish minimum standards of performance with regard to the generation of certain environmental impacts. Strategic environmental planning of tourism, supported by laws relating to land use and environmental impacts assessment, can anticipate a range of potential problems and establish protective measures to prevent them arising, or at least mitigate them to some extent. The degree and scope of government regulation required, however, may be determined by the tourism industry's willingness and ability to adopt sustainable environmental practices. At the same time there may be some matters that are difficult to regulate, or, where regulations are imposed, difficult to enforce effectively. Industry self-regulation may thus have a role in extending the scope of performance improvements with respect to sustainability.

At lest three issues have a bearing on whether tourism enterprises will adopt self-regulatory sustainable practices : (1) knowledge of appropriate practices and technologies to adopt in ascertain context; (2) the perception that some benefits will arise as a result of adopting such practices; and (3) the existence of effective sanctions to ensure that an appropriate level of environmental performance is maintained. Industry accreditation schemes are one form of self-regulation that have attempted to address these issues. They are generally based on operators achieving certain performance standards, in return for which the operator receives the right to use an identifiable logo or brand, which demonstrates their environmental credentials to other industry operators and customers. The scheme is often supported by advisory services that provide knowledge on the benefits of improving environmental performance and how best to achieve the standards. The sanction is typically the withdrawl of the right to use the logo and the consequent loss of any advantage that it confers, should the standards not be maintained.

One of the more comprehensive environmental accreditation schemes which has been developed in the last decade is Green Globe. Its scope is geographically global, it is designed to cover all sectors of the tourism industry, and it encompasses the accreditation of not only operators but also tourist destinations. It is supported by a research capacity and to set of advisory services, and arguably has gone further than most such schemes in terms of ensuring the credibility of its assessment of candidates and their ongoing adherence to the standards. Moreover, it is a multifaceted programme which seeks to encourage improvements in the environmental performance of the tourism industry in ways other than the formal accreditation process. This chapter describes the evolution of Green Globe and the programmes that it operates, with particular emphasis on the accreditation scheme. It reviews and discusses the effectiveness of the programme and the contribution it can potentially make to enhancing the sustainability of tourism.

AN OVERVIEW OF GREEN GLOBE

History

Green Globe was established by the World Thyel and Tourism Council (WTTC) with the aim of implementing the Agenda 21 principles defined at the 1992 Rio Earth Summit (Green Globe, 1997a). The WTTC executive approved its establishment in March 1994 and it became operational in July of that year (Dain

Simpson & Associates and Calkin & Associates, 1997). Originally it was a wholly owned subsidiary of the WTTC, with its chief executive also being president of WTTC. Since 1999, however, it has operated as an independent company limited by guarantee and overseen by and international advisory council, which comprises representatives from the tourism industry, non-government organizations and environmental consultancies around the world (Green Globe 21, 1999). This reorganization was accompanied by a renaming, to 'Green Globe 21', and a change in focus, from primarily an environmental education and awareness programme to a formal accreditation scheme, which had been initiated prior to the reorganization. It operates from a head office in the United Kingdom , which is also responsible for Europe and the Middle East. Regional offices have been established in Australia, covering the Asia/Pacific region, Puerto Rico, responsible for the Americas, and most recently an Africa office in South Africa. The regional offices operate through joint ventures with other organizations. In Australia, the programme is operated by the Cooperative Research Centre for Sustainable Tourism (CRC Tourism), while the Caribbean Alliance for Sustainable Tourism (CAST) and Green Seal operate the programme in the Americas.

Initially, membership of Green Globe was open to any travel and tourism business or destination organization willing to make a commitment to improving their environmental performance. To become a member, a company or organization was required to specify certain areas, to which it then became committed. This commitment had to be made at Chief Executive Officer level. To maintain membership the company then had to report annually on its success in achieving its targets. Green Globe undertook no formal monitoring process but simply reviewed its members' annual performance reports (Sisman, personal communication, 30 January 1998). Prior to the reorganization the vast majority of members, approximately 85 per cent, were relatively small businesses, with turnovers of less than USSI million. Large organizations with turnovers in excess of USS30 million comprised only about

5 per cent of the membership (Sisman, personal communication, 30 January 1998). An annual turnover-based fee was payable, in return for which the members received a variety of advisory publications, access to professional environmental expertise and training opportunities, the right to use the Green Globe logo, access to a range of promotional benefits, and automatic entry into the Green Globe annual awards that recognized members' achievements (Green Globe, 1997a).

Membership

Membership grew form less than 100 at the end of 1994 to 547 in 103 different countries in 1998. At the time, while there were members in all continents, there was far from an even global distribution. Western Europe contributed the largest proportion of members, over 40 per cent, although it share had progressively declined as membership increased in other parts of the world. In march 1997 Western Europe had accounted for about 55 per cent of members (see Table 5.1). The greatest growth occurred in the Caribbean where membership increased more than tenfold in 1997, largely due to a strategic alliance being formed between Green Globe and the Caribbean Hotel Association and the subsequent establishment of the Caribbean Alliance for Sustainable Tourism (Green Globe, 1997b). Membership also more than doubled in South Asia and China in 1997, although the numbers here were still relatively small. In most other regions membership continued to increase steadily until 1998, although declines were experienced in Latin and South America, North America and the Pacific. In 1998 the countries with the greatest number of members were the United Kingdom with seventy members. Germany with fifty-seven and the USA with twenty-seven. Few countries outside these three contributed more than a dozen members each.

From 1994 to 1998 there was an average annual resignation rate of about 10 per cent. The reasons for resignation varied but most commonly it was due to business failure or changes in management (Sisman, personal communication, 30 January 1998). Given the small scale of most members this was to be expected. Green Globe reserved the right not to renew a company's membership if it failed to maintain its active commitment or implementation of its agreed programme. According to the managing director at the time, however, this was never invoked and all resignations were voluntary (Sisman, personal communication, 30 January 1998).

Table 5.1

Green Globe Membership by Geographic Region, 1997/1998

Region	*Members (March 1997)*	*Members (February 1998)*	*Percentage Increase*
Africa	28	36	28.6
Australia/New Zealand/Japan	18	18	0.0
Caribbean	7	76	985.7
Eastern Europe	17	21	23.5
Latin and South America	38	36	-5.3
Middle East	27	32	18.5
North America	42	36	-14.3
Other East Asia	17	23	35.3
Pacific	3	2	-33.3
South Asia and China	12	33	175.0
Western Europe	256	234	-8.6
Total	465	547	17.6

Source : Green Globe Annual 1996/97 and Membership List Feburary.

In 1998, approximately three-quarters of members were accommodation establishments, ranging from international hotels and resorts to camps and youth hostels, although the Hotel Inter-continental chain alone accounted for nearly 10 per cent of membership. Tour operators were the second largest group, comprising a further 15 per cent. The remainder of members covered a wide range of organizations, including carriers, regional and national tourist organizations, tourism consultants, development and investment companies, local government bodies, museum authorities and even one educational establishment (Sisman, personal communication, 30 January 1998).

Table 5.2

Green Globe Members by Geographic Region, 2001

Region	*Number of members*	*Percentage of total members*
Africa	22	3.4
Australia/New Zealand/Japan	145	22.2
Caribbean	184	28.3
Eastern Europe	2	0.3
Latin and South America	20	3.7
Middle East	31	4.7
North America	13	2.0
Other East Asia	7	1.1
Pacific	1	0.2
South Asia and China	25	3.8
Western Europe	200	30.8
Total	651	100.0

Source : Green Globe Membership List. December 2001, Available : http://greenglobe 21.com and http://ggasiapacific.com.au.

Since 1999, 'membership' has been based on a three-tiered accreditation programme, which is described further later in this chapter. At the end of 2001 there were 516 companies or organizations that were members of Green Globe, with the vast majority having 'affiliate' status, the lowest level in the accreditation process. The geographic spread, although still involving all continents, had narrowed somewhat, with a total of seventy-three countries represented (see Table 5.2). The greatest proportion of members still came from Western Europe, even though the numbers declined after the reorganization. Membership in the Caribbean continued to grow to the point where it challenged Western Europe as the most prominent region. Together these two regions accounted for nearly three-quarters of all members. For all other regions membership numbers declined, particularly in Asia, North America and Eastern Europe.

Industry Partners

Green Globe also has industry links through its affiliation with a variety of what are termel 'industry partners'. At the time of writing Green Globe had the support of twenty-six such partners (see Table 5.3). These generally comprise national industry peak organizations, such as the New Zealand Tourism Industry Association, Africa Travel Association and the Hungarian Society of Tourism, broadly based international associations, such as Pacific Asia Travel Association, or sector-specific national and international associations, such as Airports Council International, European Tour Operators Association and the International Hotels Environmental Initiative. The partners work with Green Globe to promote membership of the programme amongst their members.

Goals

Green Globe's original primary objective was 'to provide low-cost, practical means for all Travel and Tourism companies to undertake improvements in environmental practice' (Green Globe, 1997b :) Its more specific goals were to :

- Increase environmental responsiveness throughout the Travel and Tourism industry—including suppliers and customers;
- Encourage global participation from tourism destinations and companies of all sizes and sectors.
- Ensure that the beneficial links between good environmental practice and good business practice are understood;
- Demonstrate, through the GREEN GLOBE logo, the commitment of the Travel and Tourism industry to improving environmental practices; and

- Highlight leading examples of best practice and outstanding progress through Achievement Awards.

Table 5.3
Green Globe Industry Partners, December, 2001

ACI	Airports Council International
AITO	Association of Independent Tour Operators
ATA	Africa Travel Association
ASATA	Association of South african Travel Agents
ATS	Adeventure Travel Society
BITOA	Bristish Incoming Tour Operators Association
EFCT	European Feoeraticn of Conference Towns
ETOA	Auropean Tour Operators Association
HCIMA	Hotel and Catering International Management Association
IACVB	International Association of Convention and Visitors Bureaus
IATA	International Air Transport Association
IFWTO	International Federation of Women's Travel Organizations
IH&RA	International Hotel & Restaurant Association
IHEI	International Hotels Environment Initiative
IIPT	International Institute for Peace through Tourism
MATUF	Hungarian Society of Tourism
NZTIA	New Zealand Tourism Industry Association
PATA	Pacific Asia Travel Association
RSA	Receptive Services Association
SATH	Society of the Advancement of Travellers with Handicaps
SITE	Society of Incentive Travel Executives
SPARC	South Pembrakeshire Programme for Action with Rural Communities

(Contd.)

(Contd.)

TIA	Travel Industry Association of America
TIANS	Travel Industry Association of Nova Scotia
TS	The Tourism Society
WATA	World Association of Travel Agencies

Source : Green Globe 21 (2001 Green Globe 21- Company Information Industry Partners. Available : http://www.greenglobe 21.com.

In its initial manifestation its prime *modus operandi* involved providing various services and information packages to its members, based on the following set of priority action areas derived from Agenda 21 :

- Waste minimization, reuse and recycling;
- Energy efficiency, conservation and management;
- Management of fresh water resources;
- Waste water management;
- Control of hazardous substances;
- Company transport and the environment;
- Land-use planning and management;
- Involvement of staff, customers and communities in environmental issues;
- Design for sustainability;
- Partnerships for sustainable development;
- Noise control; and
- Environmentally sensitive purchasing policy (Green Globe, 1998a : 2).

While maintaining its focus on the abovementioned priority areas, in its current form the goals have been simplified to reflect its emphasis on the accreditation programme. The stated goals are to :

- Encourage companies and communities off all sizes to join Green Globe 21 to show their commitment to sound environmental practice;

- Promote the simple fact that adopting good environmental practice makes good long-term business sense;
- Explain examples of industry best practice to Businesses and to Governments; and
- Sustain the quality of our holidays for our children—and our children's children (Green Globe 21, 2001a : 1).

Programmes

The main programme which Green Globe 21 operates in order to pursue its goal is an accreditation programme, or 'certification' as it is called. The programme applies to both tourism organizations and destinations. Both aspects of this programme were introduced prior to the reorganization but have been substantially developed since that time. Green Globe also operates a number of other, less significant programmes, including :

- Annual awards
- Projects, incorporating training and advisory services; and
- Consumer awareness activities.

Each of these minor programme areas will be described briefly, before a more complete review of the certification programmes is provided.

Annual Awards

Green Globe has been conducting its annual achievement awards programme since 1996. The stated aims of the programme are to : 'recognise outstanding achievement within the Green Globe programme; encourage further progress; serve as an example for other companies to follow; and demonstrate leadership of the Travel and Tourism industry on key environment issue' (Green Globe, 1997cm 1). The awards are open to all Green Globe members and judging is based primarily on the annual reports submitted by members on their own performance over the preceding year. Each company is assessed on its performance in relation to the priority action areas, defined earlier in this chapter. Based on these criteria, awards are made at two levels : Distinction awards for demonstrating outstanding achievement across all action areas, and Commendation Awards for demonstrating significant improvements in environmental performance (Green Globe, 1998a). In 2001 the programme was tied to the benchmarking and certification process and drew on outside advice in determining award winners (Green Globe 21, 2001b).

Table 5.4

Green Globe Award Winners, 2000
Distinction Awards
Turtle Island, Fiji
La Cabana All Suite Beach Resort, Aruba
Strattons Hotel, UK
Victoria Falls Safari Lodge, Zimbawe
Commendation Awards
Avis Europe, UK
Avis Rent a Car System Inc., USA
Bali Inter-Continental Resort, Indonesia
Boardmans, UK
Borneo Eco Tours, Malaysia
Explore Worldwide, UK
Hotel Inter-Continental, Singapore
Hotel Mocking Bird Hill, Jamaica
Inter-Continental Budapest, Hungary
Jeddah Conference Palace, Saudi Arabia
Jetwing Hotels, Sri Lanka
Maho Bay Camps, Virigin Islands
Merlia Bali Hotel, Indonesia
Presidente Inter-Continental Cancun, Mexico
Quetta Serena Hotel, Pakistan
Table Mountain Aerial Cableway, South Africa

(Contd.)

(*Contd.*)

Zomerlust Gastehuis, South Africa
Recognition Awards
The Orchid, India
Landsker Countrysides Holidays, Uk

Source : Green Globe 21 (2001) International Award Programme. Available : http://www.greenglobe21.com.

A new category, Recognition Awards, was added in 1997 to acknowledge achievements outside Green Globe membership. These are based on nominations of companies by individual Green Globe industry partners which, in the partner's view, have made the most significant environmental improvements over the preceding year (Green Globe, 1997d). Table 5.4 lists the 2000 award winners in each category. The award winners are fairly well spread geographically and to a lesser extent across industry sectors, with the predominance of hotels and resorts reflective of the composition of Green Globe membership.

Projects

Green Globe offers a range of services to both members and non-members for assistance on specific projects. Areas of project support include :

- The raising of environmental awareness in the local tourism industry;
- Training and education;
- Organization of conferences and seminars; and
- Specific consultancy support for environmental projects (Green Globe 21, 2001a).

One such project involved working with three French ski operators and an industry partner, the Association of Independent Tour Operators, on developing a scheme that would generate money from visitors for local environmental protection and conservation works. This was part of a larger Visitor Payback Project founded by the European Union

(Green Globe, 1997e). Other projects have included conducting an international training conference on risk assessment and crisis management, and undertaking an environmental review of the UK Marriott Hotel chain, with a view to implementing an environmental management system (Green Globe 21m 2001).

Consumer Awareness

There are two levels on which consumer awareness is relevant to Green Globe's operations : one is making tourists aware of their potential impacts and how they can contribute to more environmentally sustainable tourism; the other is awareness of the Green Globe 'brand' and what it might mean in terms of environmental management practices, which might in turn affect their destination and product choices. As regards the first level, Green Globe in its early days produced a leaflet entitled 'Tips for Travellers' which provided essentially behavioural advice for tourists on what to do before during and after a trip. Included in the advice was to 'try to travel with companies which are making a positive environmental statement by being members of GREEN GLOBE' (Green Flag International Ltd, 1995 : 1). Green Globe estimated that it distributed about 50 000 of these leaflets annually through its member companies (Green Globe, 1997b). More recently, Green Globe has introduced the concept of the 'Green Globe 21 Traveller', whereby consumers can register as 'supporters of sustainable tourism' and thereby receive information through the Internet, including special deals from members, join discussion forums and have access to travel planning advice (Green Globe 21, 2001c).

On the second level Green Globe clearly appreciates the significance of consumer recognition of the brand, stating in an early annual report that :

> In recent years brand images have become ever more important in marketing and product development and the world's public have come to expect differing levels of quality from different brands. GREEN GLOBE members

have to be confident in the GREEN GLOBE brand before they will use it. (Green Globe, 1997b : 7)

Indeed, since Green Globe's inception it has stressed the right to use the brand and the commercial benefits that will flow from it as a way of encouraging new membership (Green Globe, 1997a). However, until the introduction of the Green Globe Traveller concept little had been done to raise consumers' awareness of Green Globe, and limited research has been conducted on the current level of awareness. Limited consumer testing of the brand by some hotel members took place in the late 1990s (Sisman, personal communication, 30 January 1998). In its early days, Green Globe had no consumer advertising budget (Dain Simpson & Associates and Calkin & Associates, 1997) and effectively relied on the World Travel and Tourism Council for its general marketing (Sisman, personal communication, 30 January 1998). The introduction of the Traveller concept and the information flow this provides goes some way towards redressing this deficiency.

THE CERTIFICATION PROGRAMME

Overview

Green Globe's formal certification process was launched in November 1997. The general purpose of the programme is to provide members with an avenue for independent verification that they are meeting certain standards with respect to environmental performance. It thus represents a level of environmental accreditation beyond the commitment to the cause and largely self-administered performance evaluation embodied in the original membership scheme. The certification process is based on the 'Green Globe 21 Standard'. This document sets out the requirements needed to meet a level of environmental and socio-economic management performance which meets environmentally sustainable development outcomes sought by *Agenda 21*, incorporating the triple bottom line principles of economic, sociocultural and ecological sustainability. The original standards were those relating to Environmental Management Systems as defined by the International Organisation for Stadardisation (ISO) (Green Globe, 1997c). These are currently being adapted to reflect the World Tourism Organization (WTO), Global Code of Ethics and regional/national variants. Verification and subsequent certification are carried out by a number of contracted, independent companies, including *Societe Generale de Surveillance South Africa* (SGS), the world's largest testing, inspection and verification organization. Some degree of flexibility is allowed, with a company being required to reach a level deemed appropriate to its size, type and location (Green Globe, 1998b).

The certification programme is open to all travel and tourism industry sector, and all sizes and types of operations, including companies, communities and protected areas, referred to collectively as 'operations'. The incorporation of 'communities' into the process is an extension of an earlier programme that was designed to afford tourist destinations the opportunity to improve upon, and receive Green Globe acknowledgement for, their environmental management practices and performance. The destination programme pre-dated the introduction of the certification programme, with Jersey being the first destination to be awarded Green Globe status in November 1997, the same time that the certification programme was launched. 'Communities' in Green Globe terminology, are equivalent to destinations.

There are three levels of status within the programme : Affiliate, Benchmarked, and Certified (see figure 5.1). Affiliate status is typically the entry level and is roughly equivalent to the original membership status in that it reflects a commitment to the cause of sustainable tourism without any formal verification of environmental performance. It may serve as a one-year trial period before progressing to the next stage and confers the right to use the Green Globe Affiliate stamp, but not the logo. Benchmarked status involves the preparation of an environmental performance report and confers wider benefits on the operation, including the right to use the Green Globe logo and additional support from the Green Globe organization. Operations may choose to enter the programme at the Benchmarked level, or indeed the final Certified level, thereby foreshortening the process. Achieving Certified status requires submitting to a full, independent verification of environmental performance. Certified operations are then able to use the Green Globe logo with an added tick. The logo may only be used after the successful completion of the process. At this time a certificate is issued which has a unique serial number, is year dated and has an expiry date.

The Standard

The Green Globe 21 standard has evolved and improved through research, analysis and experience with its application

Fig. 5.1. Green Globe stamps and logos. (*Source* : Green Globe 21, 2001c).

over time. Initially it was based on an ISO style approach involving an environmental policy and a 'tick and box' checklist. This process-based system has been improved dramatically by adding performance outcomes. A process system alone can easily mean that a company might achieve all requirements of the Standard, but could still be failing to achieve sustainability outcomes. A more sophisticated but workable Standard has been developed. The latest Standard, introduced in April 2001, drives quantification of actual environmental performance through benchmarking.

The Standard is based on required performance criteria, organized into the following five sections :

- Environment and Social Sustainability Policy;
- Regulatory Framework;
- Environmental and Social Sustainability Performance;
- Environmental Management System; and
- Stakeholder Consultation and Communication.
- Each section of the Standard is briefly described below.

Environment and Social Sustainability Policy

This section is prescriptive and requires that applicant operations have a written Environment and Social Sustainability Policy that :

- is adopted and promoted at the highest managerial level in the operation;
- commits to year-on-year improvements in relevant sustainability performance indicators;
- commits to compliance with relevant environmental legislation and regulations;
- establishes a framework for regularly recording and measuring performance indicators, analyzing performance and setting targets;
- commits to give special consideration to employment of local persons and use of local products and services :
- is actively communicated to employees, customers and suppliers, and made available to all stakeholders :
- is reviewed annually; and
- demonstrates an understanding of the WTO Global Code of Ethics for Tourism and regional/national variants.

Regulatory Framework ***

This section reinforces the importance of a regulatory framework to the attainment of sustainability objectives by requiring operations to :

- maintain an up-to-date register of relevant legislation, regulations and other requirements and comply with all;
- maintain records of compliance, and where compliance was not maintained, records of remedial action taken; and
- comply with any special guide developed by Green Globe for a particular geographical location.

Environmental and Social Sustainability Performance

This section establishes the framework for benchmarking an operation's environmental and social performance by specifying that an operation shall :

- assess the significance of the positive and negative impacts of its activities, products and services in each of the key performance areas;
- annually benchmark environmental and socio-economic performance (in the key performance areas) against Green Globe Benchmarking Indicators and achieve a Green Globe Benchmarking Report above Green Globe Baseline performance for all indicators;
- establish targets to reduce negative/improve positive impacts in key performance areas;
- develop an improvement programme to implement performance objectives and targets; and
- monitor progress to ensure year-on-year improvement.

Environmental Management System ****

An environmental management system (EMS) is an integral part of the Green Globe standard, hence this section requires an operation to :

- Develop, implement and maintain a documented EMS, or in the case of communities or protected areas, an environmental management framework (EMF);
- Nominate a senior executive officer of the operation to be responsible for the implementation, ongoing performance and outcomes of the EMS;
- Provide, where necessary, training for all staff with key responsibilities for actions within the EMS;
- Take steps to correct situations not conforming with the Sustainability Policy and prevent their re-occurrence;

- Using the Green Globe Benchmarking Report, ensure that a minimum significant improvement is achieved in the relevant performance area(s);
- Retain records demonstrating conformance with requirements of the standard, and records of monitoring activity;
- Assess possible environmental impacts of planned, accidental and emergency situations and develop and implement minimization and mitigation plans; and
- Regularly undertake review of the EMS or EMF and the Sustainability Policy in fulfilling the requirements of the Standard.

Stakeholder Consultation and Communication

This section states that operations shall :

- Regularly communicate their environmental and social performance resulting from participation in the programme to customers and stakeholders;
- Determine the significance of its impact through consultation with stakeholders;
- Encourage and respond to feedback on the Sustainability Policy and targets;
- Encourage customers and suppliers to engage in their environmental and socio-economic programmes; and
- Inform customers about sensitive local custom, ways of life, natural areas, environmental issues and how best to contribute to the local economy.

Participating in Green Globe : Affiliates

Affiliate status is the introductory stage, where organizations are learning about sustainable tourism and the Green Globe path. Affiliates pay a fee, fixed for companies but variable for communities, in return for which they receive such benefits as listing on the Green Globe website; use of the Affiliate Stamp for marketing purposes; and web-based access to information on Benchmarking, Certification, the Standard, sector guides and performance indicators. They also have access to the list of Green Globe registered Environmental Management support consultants. Operations are encouraged to enrol in the Benchmarking or Certification process and to take practical steps towards improving their sustainability performance. As at the end of 2001, over 80 per cent of participants in Green Globe were at the Affiliate stage.

Participating in Green Globe : Benchmarking

Benchmarking was added to the programme in April 2001. Its very recent inclusion accounts for the very low numbers of participants, ten, which had achieved Benchmarked status by the end of 2001. However, it represents a significant development in sustainability accreditation for tourism by focusing on the measurement of real environmental and socio-economic performance of tourism operations. The process is applicable to operations worldwide and hence provides an internationally comparable performance standard. Benchmarking can either be undertaken as an end in itself or as an essential part of the Certification process. A variable fee, depending on the characteristics and size of the company or community, is paid for undergoing benchmarking. There is no compulsion for a Benchmarked operation to proceed to full certification.

Benchmarking targets major environmental concerns by measuring the environmental performance of companies and destinations in the following nine Key Performance Areas :

- greenhouse gas emissions;
- energy conservation and management;
- fresh water resource use;
- ambient air quality protection;
- waste water management;
- waste minimization, reuse, recycling (including hazardous substances)
- ecosystem conservation and management (including biodiversity impact, particularly on habitats);

- environmental and land use planning, particularly in areas of high social and environmental value; and
- local social, cultural and economic impact, in particular, respecting local culture and generating maximum local employment.

The benchmarking process involves operations collecting measures of indicators for Key Performance Areas on an annual basis, and the subsequent preparation of the Benchmarking Assessment Report. It is similar in logic to the generation of an annual financial performance report. Green Globe has researched and selected both the performance criteria, called Benchmarking Indicators, and their measures in order to ensure they are practical, easily measured and provide and accurate picture of an operation's performance. Green Globe will work with operations to choose the best measures for their situation. For example, the measurement of the overall energy consumption for a hotel uses the annual electricity, gas, diesel and other fuel bills as its source of information. The benchmarking process employs a common unit of measurement, *e.g.*, megajoules for energy, and assists with the conversion of the collected information to this unit. A compact disc is supplied to Benchmarking operation and, when energy bill data is entered, the CD automatically calculates the energy consumption in megajoules. This information is then converted to a ratio. When the energy usage is combined with the hotel's total annual number of guest nights, the result is a ratio of the hotel's total annual number of guest nights, the result is a ratio of the hotel's fossil energy use per guest night. Such ratios provide a basis for comparison and allow for differences in the scale of operations and for growth or contraction of operations over time. For a tourist railway or airline, a similar calculation could produce an energy figure. per passenger kilometre.

The information collected by an operation is dispatched to Green Globe, which evaluates the performance in each key area and calculates an aggregated Reporting Index. A Benchmarking Report is then produced for the operation, which indicates its current standing and provides advice as to where as to where appropriate and worthwhile improvements may be made. Green Globe has established Baseline and Best Practice levels of performance in order to illustrate where an operation is placed within its sector of the industry. It allows comparison with industry best practice, and for improvements in performance to be tracked annually. The Baseline level also takes into account variation between countries. Fig. 5.2 illustrates the Baseline and Best Practice concept.

To receive a Green Globe Benchmarked Certificate, the measures in all key Performance Areas must be above the Baseline level, and the operation must have a sustainability policy. Operations are subject to annual review and this level of performance must be maintained in order for an operation to retain its Benchmarked status. If an indicator's measure is above the Baseline, but below Best Practice, the operation is encouraged to make annual improvements for that indicator. Once Best Practice is achieved for all Key Performance Areas, operations are encouraged to maintain this level of performance and to select supplementary performance indicators to facilitate continuous improvements.

Whilst a key issue in defining sustainability performances benchmarks is that they must be credible by reflecting best practice, they must also be achievable by reflecting local conditions and the type of activity being certified (Fig. 5.2). The intention of Green Globe is not to discourage the industry by setting standards that only a few can achieve, but rather to encourage, through its services and support, widespread adoption of the principle of continuous improvement towards achieving sustainable tourism. The baseline level reflects performance indicators developed at the global, regional, national and even local levels, where applicable, and will evolve over time.

A Focus on Greenhouse Gases

The greenhouse gas issue, intimately linked to energy, encompasses both fixed and mobile assets, and transcends local and international boundaries. It provides the most high profile international sustainability performance currency by

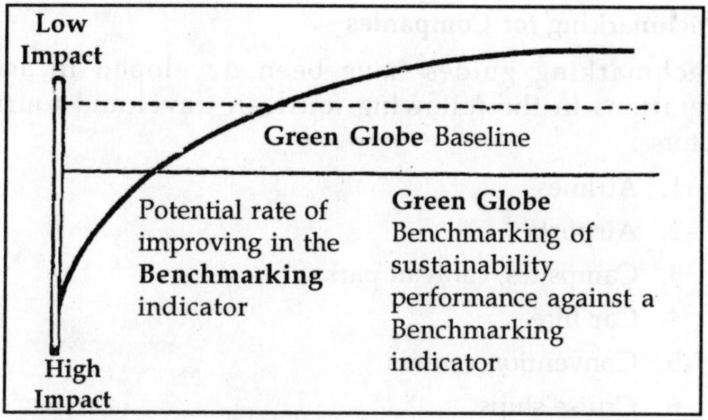

Fig. 5.2. Benchmarking of environment performance.

which to gauge and benchmark performance. The issue has particular relevance to the tourism industry, given that it consumes significant amounts of fossil fuels. Green Globe has consequently asked its participants to concentrate on this area for improvement, with the major focus being reduced energy use per customer, although the sequestration side of the equation is also taken into account. Thus greenhouse gas emission reductions can be measure collectively through reductions in energy use for all purposes and the primary consumption of raw materials, as well as the sequestration of carbon through habitat conservation. Green globe provides a means by which its participants can monitor and enhance their performance, primarily through energy savings, which translate directly into significant economic and environmental benefits. The Green Globe database of benchmarking and performance criteria also enables operations to benchmark their performance, not just locally, but internationally.

A key long-term function of Green Globe is to stimulate initiatives for tackling non-compliance in meeting emissions targets. There is a particular focus on capacity building in developing countries, such as the transfer of climate-friendly technologies, and establishing the Kyoto protocol's market-based mechanisms-emissions trading, carbon trading, joint implementation and a clean development mechanism.

Benchmarking for Companies

Benchmarking guides have been developed to assist operations in the following fourteen travel and tourism sectors :

1. Airlines
2. Airports
3. Campsites/caravan parks
4. Car hire
5. Convention centres
6. Cruise ships
7. Exhibition halls
8. Golf courses
9. Hotels
10. Marinas
11. Tour operators
12. Railways
13. Restaurants
14. Vineyards

At the time of writing, further guides were being developed. The guides assist operations to work through the steps to achieve Benchmarking. They recognize the key differences between travel and tourism operations through the inclusion of Key Performance Area indicators and measures specifically determined for each sector. An example of the Green Globe Sector Performance Indicators for Hotels is provided in the appendix at the end of the chapter.

Benchmarking For Communities (Destinations)

Green Globe's destination accreditation programme actually pre-dates the introduction of certification. The stated aim of the programme, when initiated, was to provide' a framework to guide tourist locations towards sustainable development based on the principles of Agenda 21' (Green Globe, 1998c :

2). To be considered, destinations first had to demonstrate that there were strong environmental issues or opportunities to be dealt with, that the local tourism industry would have a role in the process, and that there was strong support from all stakeholders (Sisman, personal communication, 30 January 1998). Destinations are an appropriate scale for considering sustainable tourism management, planning and development. Effective planning generally occurs at the destination level, usually through local government, and a new tourism product would be developed within a destination image and brand.

In November 1997 Jersey was the first destination to be award Green Globe status after an evaluation and accreditation process that took two years. Its involvement in the programme was seen to be a natural progression from a previous environmental review that had been conducted. Since that time another two destinations have been certified : Vilamoura in the Algarve region of Portugal and Cumbria in the United

Table 5.5
Examples of Communities Working Towards Green Globe Certification, 2001

Community	*Country*
Algarve	Portugal
Aviemore	United Kingdom
Bournemouth	United Kingdom
Camiguin Island	Philippines
Capetown	South Africa
Dominica	n/a
Douglas Shire	Australia
Geneva	Switzerland
Holy Trail	Jordan, Egypt and Israel
Ifuago Rice Teraces	Philippines
Koh Samui	Thailand

(Contd.)

(Contd.)

Redlands Shire	Australia
Scottish Borders	United Kingdom
Sri Lanka	n/a
Ulugan Bay	Philippines
Victoria Falls	Zimbabwe

Source : Green Globe 21 (2001) Community-Current Participants, Available : http://www.greenglobe 21.com.

Kingdom. A number of other destinations are currently going through the process. The range of applicants varies in scale form small resort towns, such as Aviemore in Scotland, to local government areas, regions and cities, and extends up to a national level. One case, the Holy Trail, even transcends national boundaries. Table 5.5 presents a list of some of the current applicants.

The accreditation process for communities is designed to be flexible enough to deal with a number of different scales of destination and may involve working with a variety of destination-based organizations to initiate and drive the process, from both the public and private sectors. In Jersey, the Phillippines and Dominica the programme was initiated and supported by government at the highest level, whereas in Vilamoura the initiator was a private resort developer and operator, Lusotur South Africa.

In keeping with the fundamental Green Globe principles, a destination is required to demonstrate environmental performance according to the principles of *Agenda 21*. Subsequent to certification, it must demonstrate continuous improvement. Beyond this, a destination must encourage cooperation between the tourism industry, governments, non-government organizations and communities at a local level. Local political, cultural and social conditions are considered in order to create a realistic, achievable programme of action that is flexible to suit a location's various attributes. A key intended result of destination certification is the increased involvement of the private sector in environmental action, which will create synergies through the application of a common framework and in turn provide the opportunity to heighten community and consumer awareness through the Green Globe destination brand. The implementation of a Green Globe destination programme also requires the presence of a lead organization that can deliver on both sustainable tourism development and environmental regulation.

The accreditation of Green Globe destinations requires detailed research on developing clear indicators, benchmarks and targets. Certification of community performance will also require new approaches from third party auditing companies. The Green Globe destination concept is a complex one, but it has enormous potential to harness market forces to drive the environmental sustainability of Communities and Protected Areas. At the time of writing pilot studies were being undertaken in Douglas and Redlands Shires in Queenland, Australia and Kaikoura in the South Island of New Zealand. Given the complexity of communities, the pilot studies were focusing especially on expanding the Benchmark criteria and developing Benchmarking indicators. In a similar vein a pilot resort project had commenced in Bournemouth (UK).

Green Globe is currently re-evaluating its approach to certifying entire communities as well as protected areas as sustainable tourism destinations, with a view to having an upgraded Certification programme for booth Communities and Protected areas in place by the end of 2001. This upgrading process reflects the desire by a number of Communities and Protected Areas for both acknowledgement of their environmental performance and a desire to improve such performance *via* a benchmarking process.

Participating in Green Globe : Certification

To achieve the Green Globe with distinctive tick, all operations are required to undergo independent third-party assessment against the Green Globe 21 Standard. Accredited companies and assessors undertake such certification assessments. Certified operations must undergo an annual review to maintain their certified status. Operations registering for certification automatically receive the same benefits as those registering for Benchmarking. Benchmarking is a necessary step before certification and, once they have been successfully benchmarked, an applicant is able to use the Green Globe logo without a tick. By the end of 2001, forty-one participants had been Certified.

As with benchmarking, an operation pays a variable fee for the certification process. Various advisory services and resources are available to assist applicants with the process. The operation initiates work on the requirements of the Green Globe 21 Standard in preparation for Certification Assessment. Environmental management professionals may provide guidance on the EMS as well as customizing performance criteria, and assessor companies may participate in a pre-assessment of environmental performance. The operation then undertakes a self-assessment against the Green Globe Checklist. Once it considers that it is ready, the operation requests Green Globe to organize a Certification Assessment. Green Globe then assigns the task to an accredited certification organization, which is provided with the Benchmarking Report. An assessment checklist is completed, on the basis of which Green Globe determines whether to approve Certification. Successful applicants are subject to annual Benchmarking and Certification Assessment to ensure continued compliance with performance standards.

An Evaluation of Green Globe

Green Globe is a relatively young organization with a rather ambitious set of objectives, and it may consequently be a little too early to fully evaluate its success. At the time of writing it had been operating for eight years, but only three in its current from. Its main programme, the certification scheme, had been operating for less than five years, with one of the main components, the benchmarking process, operational for only a year. What is probably its most ambitious programme, relating to the accreditation of destinations, has been going a little longer than most other programmes, but the sheer complexity of the task means that this takes a long period to implement and even longer to bear fruit. In principle, however, Green Globe represents possibly the most global, cross-sectoral approach to industry self-regulation thus far attempted.

There are at least two basic concerns with industry accreditation programmes such as Green Globe. The first is whether a significant proportion of the industry will embrace it. In the short term this depends very much on the perceived benefits of participating, and in the longer term on whether it can be demonstrated that those benefits have been realized. The second concern is whether such certification and ecolabel schemes achieve real environmental improvements. Amongst other things this would depend on the criteria on which the accreditation is based, the quality and objectivity of the assessment process, ongoing monitoring and enforcement procedures, and the effectiveness of sanctions that might be imposed for non-adherence to the required standards. The two concerns are interrelated, as whether a scheme achieves real improvement will influence its credibility and hence adoption by the industry, while the realization of benefits to participants will impact on the effectiveness of the strongest possible sanction, *i.e.*, the withdrawal of accreditation. The credibility of the scheme also impacts on the value placed on it by consumers, which affects the potential of the scheme to confer marketing advantage on the accredited operator. How effectively Green Globe has addressed these concerns is discussed below.

Will the Industry Participate?

Initially this depends on the perceived benefits. Green Globe promotes itself as : (1) offering a number of benefits to participants, including cost savings, (2) assisting in compliance with environmental legislation, (3) widening market appeal, and (4) improving the quality of the customer experience. The first two are relatively easy to demonstrate; the second two are more problematic and contentious.

Benchmarking and certification can directly contribute to improvements in the efficiency of operations through the use of fewer resources. Savings can be achieved through reduced energy consumption, reduced waste generation, reduced use of potable water and enhanced efficiency arising from treating such issues in an integrated, systematic manner. Such savings quickly become apparent and can be clearly articulated to prospective applicants. Being part of the accreditation process can also have considerable human resource benefits, including improved staff commitment and greater productivity linked to clear sustainability policies and programmes, and improved knowledge and awarness of sustainability issues through targeted environmental training and on-the-job implementation.

The Green Globe 21 Standard includes requirements relating to the regulatory framework and thereby encourages an understanding of and compliance with it. Inherent in many environmental planning regulatory frameworks, however are discretionary elements relating to broad matters of public interest and a host community's feelings about tourism in general or specific tourism developments. Hence improving the relations between tourism operations and their local communities can smooth the path for acceptance by regulatory. Again through the standard, operations are actively encouraged to work with local communities through transparent and participatory consultation and communication activities, as well as incorporation of 'buy local' and 'employ local' strategic where feasible and appropriate. Multi-stakeholder consultation is a requirement of the process and Green Globe provides a tried and tested system.

The extent to which a marketing advantage is conferred on an operation is debatable. There is a widely held perception at least, that the tourist market is becoming increasingly conscious or environmental issues and will prefer operators who can clearly demonstrate that they are behaving in an environmentally benign way. Certainly there is ample evidence of tourists being well intentioned in this regard. Various recent studies (Mori, 1995; Travel Industry of America, 1997; Mori, 1998; Tearfund, 2000) have shown that a majority of travellers express a preference for environmentally and socially responsible companies and a willingness to pay more for their services. Some doubts have been raised, however, about whether such good intentions actually translate into purchasing behaviour (Blamey, 1995, Blamey *et al.*, 1999).

Of course none of this debate at out tourists purchasing preferences means anything unless they are aware of what an environmental logo infers about the behaviour of the operator. Without this awareness the logo has no credibility. Hence for participants to realize this benefit there must be some effort put into increasing consumer awareness of the programme so that informed choices can be made. The introduction of the concept of the Green Globe Traveller goes some way towards addressing this issue, although there is no clear evidence about the effectiveness of this, or indeed the general level of consumer awareness about Green Globe at this stage. This may be only a temporary limitation, a function of the youth of Green Globe and in particular its benchmarking and certification programme, and could be resolved with time as membership increases and the use of the logo becomes more commonplace. Realistically, though, if Green Globe is to get significant participation from the millions of businesses involved in the tourism industry it will require a major marketing effort directed at the world's consumers. This effort will require a commitment of considerable financial resources by Green Globe and/or its partners and members.

In terms of actually attracting numbers of participants, Green Globe could be labelled as a moderate success. On the surface, achieving a membership of a little over 650 in eight years is hardly awe-inspiring in an industry the size of tourism, particularly as numbers have been static for the past four years. However, the fact that Green Globe has experienced a major reorientation in that period and is still into the process of fully developing its programmes provides a partial explanation for this. A strength of the organization, too, is that it has at least gained a foothold in a large number of countries, the global impact of which is somewhat lessened by its heavy concentration in two regions Western Europe and the Caribbean. The Caribbean and New Zealand experiences, however, show what can be achieved with effective promotion of the scheme to industry by a strategic partner. In regions where it has managed to gain a significant foothold, and is able to demonstrate achievement, it may well eventually prove to be influential, particularly if it can deliver the promised commercial benefits to its members. The incorporation of destinations into the certification programme also has the potential to strengthen the organization's regional presence and membership numbers by greater awareness. The number of destinations currently involved in the process is encouraging, as is the fact that some are at a national level.

Will it Achieve Real Environmental Improvements?

Green Globe was originally conceived as a membership-based programme whereby companies joined and implemented sustainable tourism practices based on *Agenda 21* principles. It achieved some degree of profile within the industry, and through its training and advisory services, heightened awareness of environmental and sustainability principles and practices. In its original form, Green Globe was very simple. It required a company to pay an annual fee and develop an environmental policy and checklist. In return, the company received advisory materials on environmental impacts and means to minimize them, and the right to use the Green Globe logo. The logo represented a statement of intent to undertake improvement.

In the late 1990s Green Globe moved into certification. The key to this was the introduction of independent verification of the achievements of an operation, thereby legitimizing its credentials for certification. A two-logo process was established, whereby the operation could use the logo without a tick during it path towards certification, which had to be undertaken within two years, and the logo with a tick once certified. Without certification Green Globe membership involved little more than a commitment to a voluntary code of practice which was rather informally enforced, although membership was at least likely to raise a company's awareness of certain environmental issues and how best to deal with them.

A report on tourism certification schemes published in 2000 criticized tourism ecolabel schemes as a 'greenwash' that allowed less-than-green companies to falsely market their products (WWF-UK, 2000). Although the report generally recognized Green Globe as the most serious approach of any global programme it was nevertheless argued that Green Globe had shortcomings. Companies joining Green Globe and paying the entrance fee could use the logo without any requirement that their claims of environmental and social responsibility be assessed and rated by independent experts. Concern was also expressed that the programme was focused on process rather than on the achievement of tangible improvements and outcomes. In addition, the programme was criticized for not taking into consideration the variations in tourism operations in terms of scale, nature, capital, location and sector.

In response to these criticisms Green Globe initiated improvements. In February 2000, Green Globe began to develop a new framework focusing on measurable outcomes as well as process. The decision was taken to introduce the concept of benchmarking sustainability performance, and thereby enable the measurement of real improvements. The key steps included the introduction of the educational Affiliate concept, and the strengthening of the Standard to include baseline benchmarking and quantification of environmental and socio-economic performance. The result was an improved certification system that married process with performance and gave scope for systematic progress towards fully verified accreditation. The use of the logo was subsequently limited to those operations which had been successfully benchmarked above a baseline level of performance in all Key Performance Areas, and Benchmarking was made a compulsory step in the certification process. The process now possesses rigour in the breadth and depth of assessment, precision in the measurement of sustainability performance, an appropriate focus on outcomes, independent verification by experts, and practical means of supporting operations in getting through it.

The programme also includes practical means of maintaining compliance with the performance standards, including an effective sanction for non-compliance and an apparent willingness to use it. In committing to maintaining the integrity of the brand, Green Globe has withdrawn the right to use the brand for matters of non-compliance or where the use of the brand has been abused. A dispute process has been instituted, bases on ISO Certification guides and involving independent assessment of the dispute. In the event of an incident of non-compliance, Green Globe requires rectification, which may involve both immediate and longer term corrective action before certification is restored.

Green Globe has also taken a number of steps to ensure that is maintains the quality of its assessment process. The organization's sales and marketing functions have been separated from its research and development activities. Ongoing research and development, now conducted by the Cooperative Research Centre for Sustainable Tourism in Australia, is vital to maintaining the quality and appropriateness of the Standard and the Sector Performance Indicators. Supplementing this, the International Advisory Council provides crucial peer revise of both the Standard and the Sector Performance Indicators. Experience gained through implementing the scheme, including feedback from customers and consumers, and feedback from the community, contributes to Green Globe's system of continuous improvement. Finally, there is a clear separation of functions between the certification assessors and the environmental management advisors/ consultants who may assist operations to prepare for benchmarking and certification. This helps to maintain the impartiality and integrity of the process.

Conclusion

Certainly in principle, Green Globe stands up well to scrutiny. It has all the essential elements of a credible accreditation and certification programme and has responded well to past constructive criticism of its operations. It clearly has the potential to deliver improvements in the sustainability performance of tourism firms and destinations. However, the true measure of its success, in delivering meaningful improvements will be the scale and level on which it operates; that is, its ability to attract participants from the tourism industry who are willing to pursue benchmarking and certification. At this early stage, very few companies or communities have pursued this path. If the bulk of participants remain at the Affiliate stage, its efficacy must be open to question. If there is a progression by most only to the Benchmarked stage some credibility questions might still remain, given that there is no independent verification of performance required. If, on the other hand, Green Globe can encourage a large number of tourism companies and destinations to achieve and maintain full Certification it is likely to make a substantial contribution to the cause of sustainability. This is a challenging task, given the time and expense for those involved in following this path, and to do so will require them to be convinced of the benefits that will arise. In the long term Green Globe will need to be able to demonstrate those benefits and to take steps, such as raising consumer awareness, to increase the prospects of the promised benefits being realized. For tourism businesses, even those with the best of ethical intentions, the emphasis is nonetheless likely to be on the commercial benefits of participation, such as cost savings and increased levels of demand.

The destination component of the certification programme is perhaps the one with the greatest potential to produce significant results. It expands the programme beyond reliance on commercial motivations, and has the ability to reach a large number of operators and stakeholders and encourage cooperative action. By generally incorporating governments as well as industry and by focusing on broad environmental protection and conservation, land use planning and infrastructure development, this component has the potential to improve environmental management practices beyond those sometimes marginal measures which an individual enterprise might employ simply to produce costs savings or gain a marketing advantage. Arguably it is in this realm of collective action that the greatest gains are likely to be made with respect to sustainable tourism development.

Acknowledgement

We wish to thank Mr. Dick Sisman, former Managing Director Green Globe.

References

1. Blamey, R. (1995) : *The Nature of Ecotourism,* Bureau of Tourism Research, Canberra.
2. Blamey, R., Bennett, J., Louviere, J. and Morrison, M. (1999) : *Validation of a Choice Model Involving Green Product Choice,* Choice Modelling Research Report No. 10, University of New South Wales, Canberra.
3. Dain Simpson & Associates and Calkin & Associates (1997) : *A Review of Green Globe.*, Unpublished report prepared for Tourism Council Australia's Environment Committee.
4. Green Flag International Ltd. (1995) : *Tips for Travellers,* prepared for Green Globe, Available : http://www.wttc.org.
5. Green Globe (1997a) : *What is Green Globe*? Available : http://www.wttc.org.
6. Green Globe (1997b) : *Annual Review* 1996/97, Available : http://www.wttc.org.
7. Green Globe (1997c) : *Green Globe Achievement Awards,* 1997. Available : http ://www.wttc.org.
8. Green Globe (1997d) : *Green Globe Rewards Environmental Excellence,* News Release, 10 March, Available : http://www.wttc.org.
9. Green Globe (1997e) : *New Environmental Standard Demonstrates Compliance with Agenda 21,* News Release, 19 November, Available : http ://www.wttc.org.
10. Green Globe (1997f) : *Green Globe Newsletter,* Issue, 6 January, Available : http ://www.wttc.org.

11. Green Globe (1997g) : *Green Globe Training Programmes,* Available : http ://www.wttc.org.
12. Green Globe (1998a) : *Green Globe Members List by Country—February 1998,* Available : http ://www.wttc.org.
13. Green Globe (1998b) : *Green Globe Certification,* Available : http ://www.wttc.org.
14. Green Globe (1998c) : *Green Globe Destinations,* Available : http://www.wttc.org.
15. Green Globe (1998d) : *Green Globe Industry AssociatesFebruary 1998.,* available : http://www.wttc.org.
16. Green Globe 21 (1999) : *New International Advisory Council for Green Globe 21,* News Release, 17 November. Available http://www.greenglobe21.com.
17. Green Globe 21 (2001a) : *Company Information—Current Projects,* Available : http ://www.greenglobe21.com.
18. Green Globe 21 (2001b) : *International Award Programme,* Available : http ://www.greenglobe21.com.
19. Green Globe 21 (2001c) : *Traveller Status,* Available : http :/ /www.greenglobe21.com.
20. MORI (1995) : *Business and the Environment,* MORI, London.
21. MORI (1998) : *Public Views on Travel and the Environment,* MORI, London.
22. Tearfund (2000) : *Tourism-An Ethical Issue, Market Research Report,* produced by IPSOS-RSL for Tearfund, Middlesex.
23. WWF-UK (2000) : *Tourism Certification : An Analysis of Green Globe 21 and Other Tourism Certification Programmes,* a report by Synergy for WWF-UK, London.

6 Tourism and Programme for Raising Environmental Awareness

Introduction

Over the last decade a number of schemes have been developed to raise environmental awareness and standards of behaviour in relation to tourism. This case study provides an overview of how one such scheme, the Blue Flag campaign for beaches in Slovenia, operates. The process of creating environmental awareness through this scheme is discussed, and the key elements of a successful Blue flag campaign are identified with the aid of an environmental responsibility model. Attention is also paid to the link between the Blue Flag campaign and the growth of environmental awareness in Slovenia's tourism industry, where the campaign is seen as both a tool for improving environmental quality and a means of promoting safe beaches. However, as the Blue Flag criteria become more demanding, a development welcomed by those concerned with integrated coastal management, there is potential for conflict with tourism industry interests, an issue discussed in the conclusion to this case study.

Development of the Blue Flag Campaign

The environmental quality of a destination is a key factor in making travel-related decisions (Pizam, 1991 : 79; Inskeep, 1991 : 339; Mieczkowski, 1995 : 11; Middleton, 1997 : 136; Font, 2001 : 2). There is some evidence that a growing segment of visitors turn away from what they consider to be polluted destinations, with tourists not willing to trade lower environmental quality for a lower price (OECD, 1992 : 8). This is especially true where health risks from air or water pollution are perceived as a problem (Middleton, 1997 : 138), as illustrated by the decline in western Mediterranean tourism in the early 1990s (Mieczkowski, 1995 : 210).

The Blue Flag logo, a white circle with a bottle floating on three wave crests, is a symbol used to denote a beach or marina that has met specific environmental criteria, and as such is meant to convey a message of personal health and safety to those using them. It originated in a pollution-traking campaign of the Foundation for Environmental Education in Europe (FEEE). This campaign involved the use of bottles containing messages that requested those finding them to contact FEEE, and was designed to track the spread of solid waste at sea (FEEE, 1990). The Blue Flag programme was first launched in France in 1985 and was, at that time, concerned only with the water quality of beaches. In that year, eleven French municipalities were awarded the Blue Flag for their bathing water quality and wastewater treatment. By 1986 that number had risen to forty-three. The following year the campaign broadened to encompass a further nine countries, as well as marinas, as an activity of the European Year of the Environment. Co-ordination of this expanded programme fell to FEEE and the Commission of the European Communities (FEEE, 1990). In subsequent years the Blue Flag campaign continued to grow (see Figure 6.1), under the umbrella of FEEE, and with the help of its national branches in each participating country. In 2001, Blue Flags were awarded to 2041 sea and inland water beaches and 713 marinas in twenty-one European countries :

Belgium	Finland	Italy	Slovenia
Bulgaria	France	Latvia	Spain
Croatia	Germany	The Netherlands	Sweden
Cyprus	Greece	Norway	Turkey
Denmark	Ireland	Portugal	United Kingdom
Estonia			

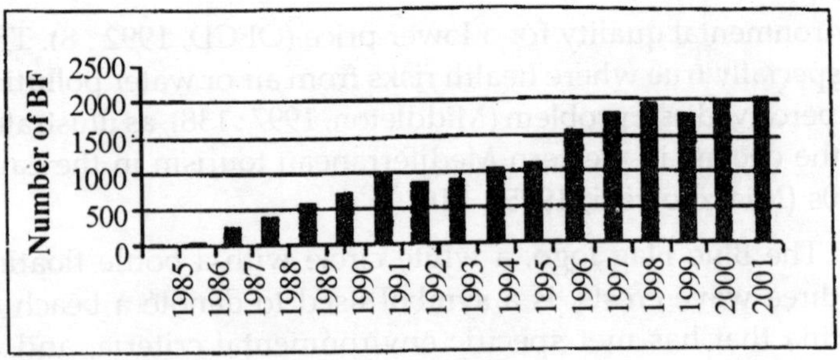

Fig. 6.1. Numbers of Blue Flag beaches in Europe, 1985-2001.

In 2001, for the first time, the campaign will travel beyond Europe to South Africa and the Caribbean (FEEE, 2001a). With the spreading of the campaign to non-European countries FEEE has now been renamed FEE (Foundation for Environmental Education), with the words 'In Europe' removed from its name.

The Blue Flag Campaign in Slovenia

Slovenia is a new transitional country that was established in 1991 when it separated from the former Yugoslavia. Geographically, it lies in the north-east corner of the Adriatic Sea, between the Italian and Croatian seasides, and has a 46-kilometre-long coastline with thirty-one public beaches. Tourism along this coastline is highly developed, with 1.6 million tourist nights being spent in its resort towns. This figure represents more than 25 per cent of total tourist nights in Slovenia (SORS, 2000).

In socialist Slovenia environmental issues were not high on the political agenda. Arguably, the first time concerns were raised concerning the environmental effects of tourism was at the Tourism Forum, a component of the Alpe Adria tourism fair in the capital Ljublljana in 1992 (Mihalic, 1992). At this time, however, there appeared to be little desire on behalf of the tourism industry to address environmental quality issues. Indeed, some Forum participants were concerned that to do so could damage the image of Slovenia's coastal tourism product. Given that at the year prior to the Forum, 52 per cent of Slovenian beaches, according to government tests, did not meet national standards for bathing water quality (see Figure 6.2), such a view is perhaps understandable.

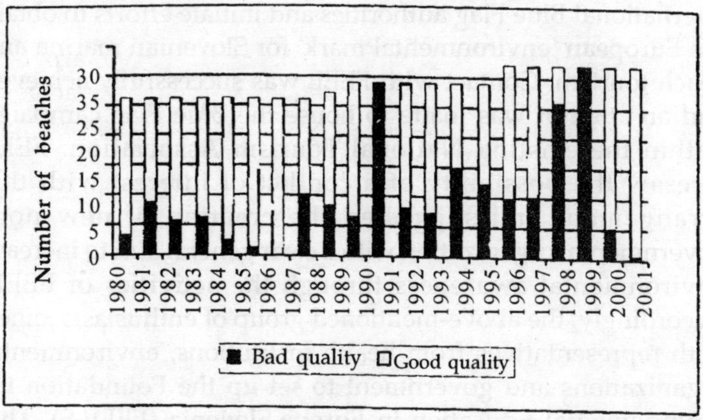

Fig. 6.2. Number of Slovenian beaches by bathing water quality (according to national legislation), 1994-2000.

After 1991 environmental awareness in Slovenia started to develop rapidly due to the increased flow of information from beyond the state's now open borders. Additionally, many foreign consultants from different fields were hired by the new democratically elected government, to advise it on various matters, including environmental management. It was in this atmosphere of change and the reappraisal of old practices and ideas, that the concept of sustainability became integrated into the national tourism development strategy (Sirse *et al.*, 1993). External pressures were also serving at this time to push beach tourism operators in the direction of being more environmentally aware. For example, international tour operators, especially the German tour operator. Turistic Union International (TUI), checked the environmental performance of its partners and identified Blue Flag beaches and marinas in its catalogues.

In 1993 the Ministry for Industry, then responsible for tourism, spurred on, in part, by a group comprising enlightened members of the tourism industry, institutions involved in tourism research, and several journalists with an interest in the environment, asked the Faculty of Economics at the University of Ljubljana to establish contact with the international Blue Flag authorities and initiate efforts to obtain the European 'environmental mark' for Slovenian marina and beach tourism. Contact with FEEE was successfully achieved and an attempt was made to house the Blue Flag campaign within the existing National Tourism Association. FEEE foresaw the possibility of a conflict of interest with this arrangement and suggested the creation of new non-governmental organization with a clear general aim to increase environmental awareness through the activities of FEEE. Accordingly, the above-mentioned group of enthusiasts joined with representatives from health institutions, environmental organizations and government to set up the Foundation for Environmental Education in Europe-Slovenia (FEEE-S). This body became a member of FEEE in 1994. In the role of 'a godparent', the Italian national FEEE operator worked closely with the Slovenian organization to help implement the Blue Flag campaign in Slovenia.

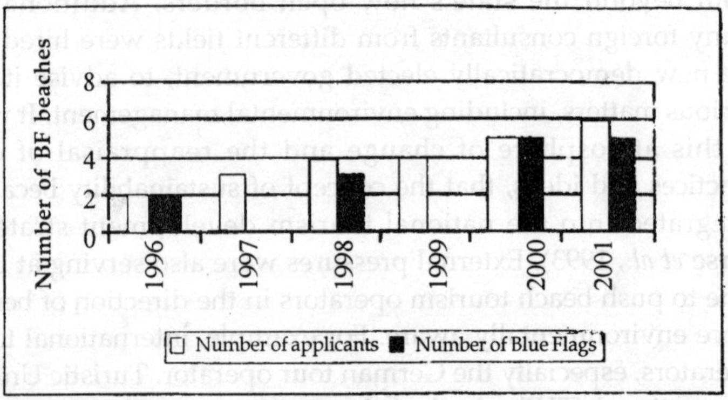

Fig. 6.3. Numbers of applicant and awarded Blue Flag beaches in Slovenia. 1996-2001.

In Slovenia the marina Blue Flag campaign started in 1995 and the beach campaign in 1996. In 1996 two beach applicants met all the standards and were awarded the blue logo; by 2001 this number had climbed to six (Figure 6.3). Over this same period (see Figure 6.3), a number of beaches were also rejected. Indeed, in 1997 and 1999 when no Slovenian beach was successful in gaining a Blue Flag award; media and public debate on water quality and broader issues relating to tourism and environmental quality increased dramatically.

Blue Flag Award Criteria

Criteria for being awarded a Blue Flag are pre-defined by the FEEE Blue Flag campaign and are merely implemented by each national operator. For the 2001 bathing season there were twenty-seven criteria for beaches that related to four key aspects (FEEE, 2001b). Some of the criteria relating to each of these four areas are given here for illustrative purposes.

Water quality. The criteria here state that there must be compliance with requirements and standards such as those of the EU's Bathing Water Directive. This directive prescribes the percentage of test results that must comply with guideline and imperative values for total and faecal colibacteria and faecal streptococci. There are also standards on colour, transparency, mineral oils, phenols content and other substances. Furthermore, no sewage discharges may affect the beach area, and the community must observe sewage treatment requirements of the EU's Urban Waste Water Directive. This directive sets exact standards for treatment and discharge of urban wastewater and requires that all the sewage discharged must be collected and treated. It sets different standards and implementation deadlines according to the type of area and size of the settlement (Hellenic Society for the Protection of Nature, 2001 : 9).

Environmental education and information. Information on flora and fauna must be publicly displayed, including advice on how to behave, to minimize impacts on these. Data on bathing water quality also needs to be displayed on the beach in the form of a table or figure that can be easily understood.

Environmental management and facilities. Example criteria are : rubbish bins in adequate numbers that are properly secured and regularly maintained and emptie; safe access paths to the beach; facilities for receiving recyclable materials; the presence of local land-use and development plans for the coastal zone; and the active promotion of sustainable transport to and along the beach area (*i.e.*, bicycling, walking or public transport).

Safely and services. Requirements relate to such matters as : the presence of beach guards; first aid services; provision of drinking water; access and facilities for people with disabilities; and general maintenance of buildings and equipment.

Some Blue Flag criteria are imperatives; like the water quality criteria or litter bins in adequate numbers, while others are merely guidelines, such as recycling waste materials. A beach that does not comply with one or more of the imperative criteria cannot be awarded a Blue Flag. Each year a number of guideline criteria become imperative and new criteria may be added. The same criteria apply for candidates from all states. Where national legislation is stricter on a particular issue, this must be complied with rather than the Blue Flag criterion. For example, the Slovenian nation standards on bathing water quality are stricter than those of the EU, which form the basis of the Blue Flag standards.

At the moment the Blue Flag beach campaign only relates to operated urban beaches. The beach operator (who is licensed by local government) can act directly to fulfil some criteria (*e.g.*, provision of beach access for people with disabilities), whereas the fulfillment of others (*e.g.*, the new EU Urban Waste Water Directive), may call for the engagement of the local community and other partners, even the national government.

Partners in the Blue Flag Campaign

The Blue Flag campaign works at three levels : local, national and international (see Figure 6.4).

Local Level

At the local level, the Slovenian campaign involves direct and indirect partners. According to the application procedure,

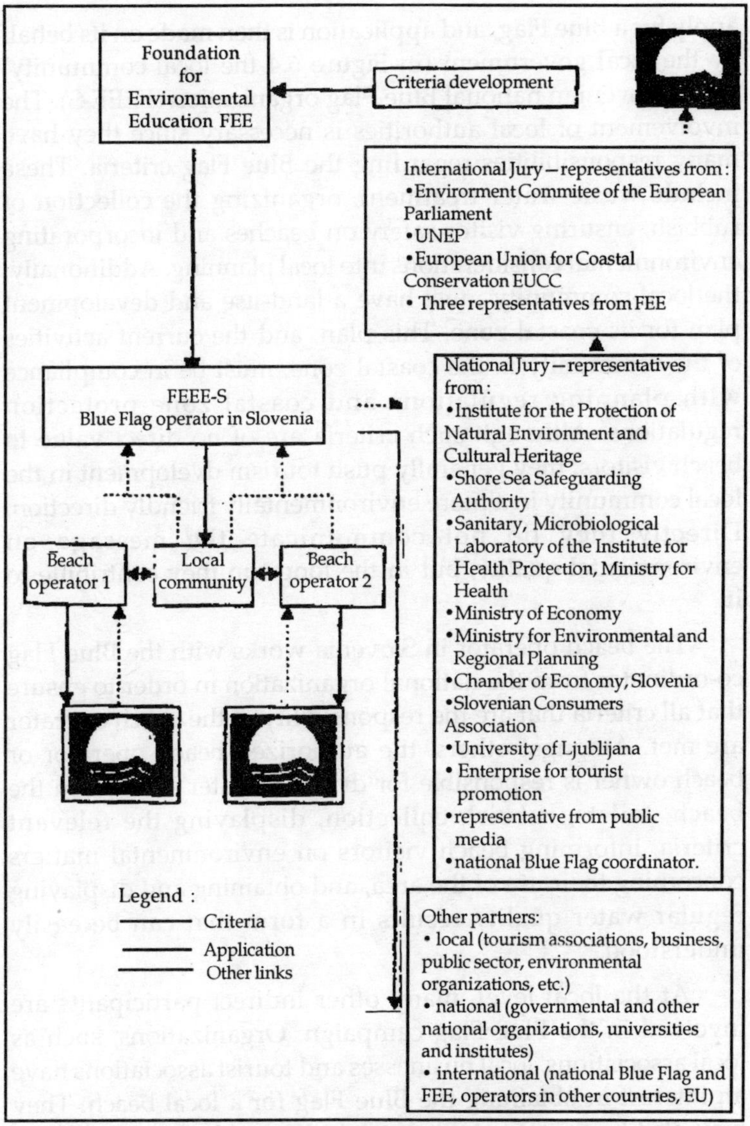

Fig. 6.4. Organizational chart of the Slovenian Blue Flag campaign : participants and application procedures.

direct partners are the beach operator and the local government. The beach operator makes the initial decision to apply for a Blue Flag, and application is then made on its behalf by the local government (in Figure 6.4 the local community) to the Slovenian national Blue Flag organization (FEEE-S). The involvement of local authorities is necessary since they have many responsibilities regarding the Blue Flag criteria. These include waste-water treatment, organizing the collection of rubbish, ensuring visitor safety on beaches and incorporating environmental considerations into local planning. Additionally, the local community must have a land-use and development plan for its coastal zone. This plan, and the current activities of the community in the coastal zone, must be in compliance with planning regulations and coastal zone protection regulations. Although such criteria are of no direct value to beach visitors, they generally push tourism dvelopment in the local community in a more environmentally friendly direction. Directly they do not communicate the message on environmental quality, but in the long run they contribute to it.

The beach operator in Slovenia works with the Blue Flag co-ordinator from the national organization in order to ensure that all criteria that are the responsibility of the beach operator are met. Amongst others, the authorized beach operator or beach owner is responsible for drinking water sources on the beach, toilets, rubbish collection, displaying the relevant criteria, informing beach visitors on environmental matters concerning their use of the area, and obtaining and displaying regular water quality results in a form that can be easily understood.

At the local level, many other indirect participants are involved in the Blue Flag campaign. Organizations, such as local associations, local businesses and tourist associations have an interest in obtaining the Blue Flag for a local beach. They may also have interests that are in line with the aims of the campaign and therefore they might act to co-operate in Blue Flag activities within their local community or with the national organization itself. As regards this last point, the Slovenian Blue Flag campaign has relationships with the Sanitary

Microbiological Laboratory, conservation organizations, environmental organizations, the Institute for protection of the Natural Environment and Cultural Heritage, as well as with other partners in the coastal community, as shown in Figure 6.4. Also, the local population has a vested interest in the success of the campaign, and it is therefore in their interests to support it in whatever ways they can.

National Level

The Blue Flag campaign within Slovenia is coordinated at the national level by the FEEE-S (Foundation for Environmental Education of Europe in Slovenia). This body is a voluntary, independent, non-profit, and non-governmental association. Its main aim is to raise environmental awareness in Slovenia. It acts to inform the public regarding matters associated with environmental protection; it organizes and manages various activities of the international organization FEE, of which it is a full member, and also represents Slovenia within this organization.

The FEEE-S, as the national Blue Flag co-ordinators, works with local communities and other parties interested in applying for Blue Flags. At the same time, it represents the Blue Flag campaign's interests vis-à-vis national authorities such as the Ministry for the Environment and Regional Planning, and Health Ministry and Ministry for Sport, Science and Education.

The Slovenian international jury (see Figure 6.4) meets once a year and selects applicants who are then sent before the International Jury of FEE.

International Level

As of 2001 the Blue Flag scheme involved twenty-one European and one non-European country (South Africa), which work under the international umbrella organization known as FEE (Foundation for Environmental Education).

FEE's primary role is to promote environmental education, and in doing this it offers its members four general environmental-awareness raising projects : Eco Schools, Young

Reporters for the Environment, Learning about Forests and the Blue Flag Campaign (FEE, 2001 : 1). These programmes are delivered/conducted through a network of national operators under common standards and criteria. FEE's headquarters are presently in England, and decisions regarding its activities and policies, etc., are made by its annual general assembly.

The Blue Flag, as one of the FEE's campaigns is run through the European Blue Flag secretariat in Copenhagen. Its activities include : organizing meetings for national operators to discuss common problems and future changes to Blue Flag criteria; facilitating the exchange of information and expertise among countries; the production of common European information and promotional materials; and the running of the European Jury (UNEP, 1996 : 10).

Contribution to Environmental Responsibility

The Blue Flag campaign for environmentally responsible beaches and marinas started out as a way of encouraging local authorities to provide clean and safe beaches and marinas

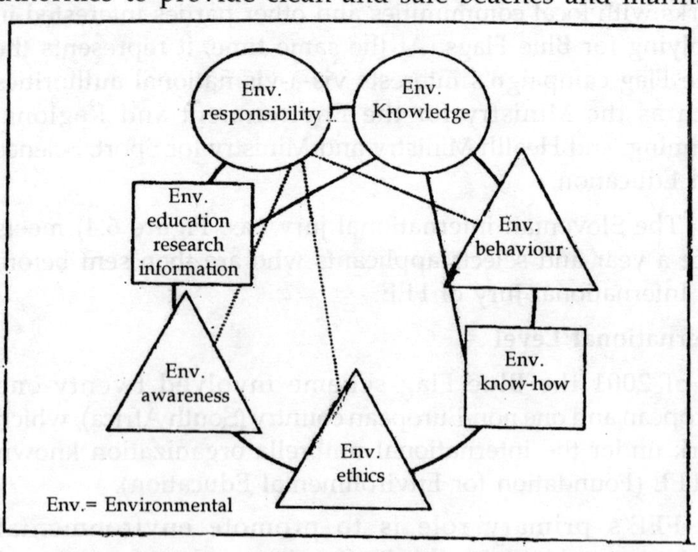

Fig. 6.5. Know-how as an essential of the environmental responsibility-knowledge model.

for tourists and local residents. But the campaign has been increasingly conducted within the much wider context of environmental management of the coastal area, and the criteria used in the campaign have been progressively broadened. The campaign's long-term objectives are to improve environmental awareness of the coastal environment and promote environmental behaviour, thereby developing environmental responsibility.

Environmental responsibility and environmental knowledge are two main foundation elements that help to explain how an environmental campaign works. In the model presented in Figure 6.5 they are presented as the overriding essential elements. In this model *environmental responsibility* is connected to environmental awareness, ethics and behaviour. Environmental responsibility requires both an awareness of environmental problems and behaviour that complies with environmental ethics. Thus, environmental behaviour is only possible if environmental awareness and ethics exist.

Environmental damage arising from, for example, improper behaviour may also be due to human ignorance (Frey, 1985 : 39). Human ignorance is often caused through insufficient education, research, and information. Since environmental disasters may develop over a long period, a direct link with concrete human action may not be visible; therefore a lack of understanding and information is often the real reason why such disasters arise. If humans had sufficient information about the consequences of their actions, such disasters may not happen. This is illustrated by the second foundation element in the model, *environmental knowledge*. This model element consists of two parts; environmental education, research and available information on the one hand and environmental know-how on the other. The latter refers to knowledge on appropriate criteria and the means of technical, financial, managerial and organizational implementation of environmental action, such as how to carry out water testing, and how to construct purifying plants in order to meet defined standards.

The Blue Flag campaign offers pre-defined criteria for the environmentally appropriate management of beaches and local communities. In Figure 6.5, the environmental know-how of the Blue Flag campaign is placed between environmental ethics (what is right and what is wrong) and environmental behaviour, and is seen as a connecting element (how to do it properly). Environmental education, research and information are presented as important elements in the creation of environmental awareness, which is the main aim of the Blue Flag campaign. For Slovenia, Blue Flag's environmental information potential is especially important. Amongst other things, the Blue Flag campaign informs the public about environmental quality and, at the same time, the Slovenian FEEE-S is pushing for public availability of all environmental quality data in order to promote and speed up environmental problem-solving through public pressure.

The effectiveness of the Blue Flag campaign can be partially judged by how well it addresses the elements of this model. In that regard, Kernel (1997) examined the environmental education, awareness and behaviour outcomes of Blue Flag from the perspectives of national tourism organizations, national Blue Flage juries, FEE member organizations and national environmental organization in fourteen European countries. According to that survey 80 per cent of tourism organizations, 81 per cent of national FEE branch organizations and 60 per cent of environmental organizations believed that the campaign had raised environmental awareness. The results also showed that there was still a gap between awareness and environmental behaviour, with less than 30 per cent of respondents believing that the Blue Flag campaign actually changed the behaviour of visitors (Kernel, 1997 : 5).

Conclusion

Tourism can provide an incentive for 'cleaning up' the overall environment through control of water, littering, and for improving environmental aesthetics through landscaping programmes, urban planning and better building maintenance

(Inskeep, 1991 : 343). In the Mediterranean region there is much justifiable concern being expressed about marine pollution, and hence there is a significant role for a campaign like Blue Flag. The campaign has now reached a stage where it is sufficiently established in Europe for the possession of a Blue Flag to mean something to visitors, or at least to tourism businesses. The previously mentioned survey by Kernel (1997 : 5) revealed that 24 per cent of tourism organizations believed that visitors preferred Blue Flag beaches over others. Having a Blue Flag signifies a safe and clean beach with good water quality, while not having, or losing one, may raise questions about water quality in the public media (Frank, 2001; Henderson, 2001; Mansfield, 2001).

The number of Slovenian Blue Flag beaches is still relatively low : five Blue Flag sea beaches out of a potential thirty-two, representing only 15 per cent of the total. On the other hand, all three Slovenian marinas were awarded the Blue Flag logo in 2000 and 2001. the low number of applications from Slovenian beaches is due to the very complex criteria that have to be fulfilled by the beach operator, although more are preparing to apply in the near future. Nevertheless, the Blue Flag campaign in Slovenia can be regarded as a successful tool for addressing environmental problems and implementing internationally recognized standards.

Finally, it has to be emphasized that environmental impacts are not always controllable by the beach operator or tourism business. The Blue Flag is awarded on the basis of the water quality of the beach; yet the organization responsible may not be able to control sources of pollution whose origination, for example, might be located some distance away, being carried by wind and currents. Hence the need to link the management of resources in a given area through a broader coastal management plan, and to engage communities in the decision-making processes associated with such plans. In this regard, FEEE-S is now being challenged to change Blue Flag's image so that it comes to be seen as tool for progressing integrated sustainable development in coastal areas that is beneficial not only to the tourism industry, but also to local communities. according to Kernel (1997), such an aim is in line with how environmental organizations in European countries primarily consider the Blue Flag campaign. Forty-two per cent of those organizations, as opposed to less than 10 per cent of national tourism organizations expected Blue Flag to promote integrated coastal area management and control.

References

1. FEE (2001) : *Statutes*, Foundation for Environmental Education, European secretariat, Norwich.
2. FEEE (1990) : *The Blue Flag Campaign*, Foundation for Environmental Education in Europe, European office, Copenhagen.
3. FEEE (2001a) : *The Blue Flag Campaign 2001*, http:www.blueflag.org. (Retrieved 14.06.2001.)
4. FEEE (2001b) : *Unititled Document*, http :// www.blueflag.org/criteria/beachc.htm. (Retrieved 28. 05. 2001.)
5. FEEE-S (2001) : Internal databank. Foundation for Environmental Education in Europe-Slovenia, Portoroz.
6. Font, X. (2001) : Regulating the Green Message : The Phyers in Ecolabelling. In *Tourism Ecolabelling. Certification and Promotion of Sustainable Management*. Edited by Font, X. Buckley, R.C. Walling ford : CAB International, pp. 1-17.
7. Frank, B. (2001) : Talking the waters in the UK. *Sunday Times*, March 24, 2001, London http :/www.proquest.umi.com. (Retrieved 14.07.2001.)
8. Frey, B. S. (1985) : *Umweltokonomie*. V&R, Goettingen.
9. Hellenic Society for the Protection of Nature (2001) : *The Blue Flag, Guidance Notes to the Blue Flag Criteria for Beaches*, Hellenic Society for the Protection of Nature, Athens.
10. Henderson, M. (2001) : Clean beaches, *The Times*, June 6, 2001, London. http :/wwwproquest.umi.com (Retrieved 14.07.2001.)
11. Inskeep, E. (1991) : *Tourism Planning : an Integral and Sustainable Development Approach*. New York : Van Nostrand Reinhold.
12. Kernel, P. (1997) : *Survey of opinions among national interests about the Blue Flag Campaign*, FEEE, Copenhagen.

13. Lubbert, C. (1998) : Umweltkennzeichnungen for touristische Angebote : Einstellungen deutscher Urlauber—Ergebnisse eine Pilotstudie. Fachtagung '*Umweltkennzeichningen im Tourismus*' am 29 October, 1998 an der Ludwig-Maximilians-Universitat Munchen (LMU). Deutsches Winschaftswissenschaftliches Institute for Fremdenverkehr e. V. an der Universitat Munchen, Munchen, pp. 22-31.
14. Mansfield, P. (2001) : Postcard from Brighton. *Evening Standard,* June 27, 2001, London. http:/ www.proquest.umi.com. (Retrieved 14.07.2001.)
15. Middleton, V.T.C. (1997) : Sustainable Tourism : A Marketing Perspective, in M. J. Stabler : *Tourism Sustainability, Principles to Practice.* Wallingford : CAB International, pp. 129-42.
16. Mieczkowski, Z. (1995) : *Environmental Issues of Tourism and Recreation.* London : University Press of America.
17. Mihalic, T. (1992) : Definitions, kinds and possibilities of environmental tourism forms (in Slovene). Paper presented at the *Alpe Adria Tourism Forum,* March 1992, Ljubljana.
18. Mihalic T. (1996) : Ecological Labelling in Tourism, *In Sustainable Tourism in Islands and Small States. Issues and Policies.* Edited by Briguglio, L., Archer, B., Jafari, J. and Wall, G. Cassell, London, pp. 57-70.
19. Mihalic T. (2000) : Environmental management of a tourist destination. A factor of tourism competitiveness. *Tourism Management* 21, Special Issue, pp. 65-78.
20. Mihalic, T. (2001) : Environmental Behaviour Implications for Tourist Destinations and Ecolables. In *Tourism Ecolabelling, Certification and Promotion of Sustainable Management,* Edited by Font, X. and Buckley, R. C. Wallingford : CAB International, pp. 57-70.
21. OECD (1992) : *Tourism policy and international tourism in OECD member countries.* OECD (Organization for Economic Cooperation and Development), Paris.
22. Pizam, A. (1991) : The management of Quality Destination. *Proceedings of the Association Internationale d' Experts Scientifiques du Tourisme* (AIEST) : Vol. 33. Quality Tourism—Concept of Sustainable Tourism Development. Harmonizing Economical, Social and Ecological Interests, pp. 79-88. St. Gallen : Niedermann Druck.

7 Tourism Certification Programme in Europe's National Parks

The Context and Nature of PAN Parks

Tourism is one of the largest industries in Europe, and has the potential to become a key contributor to the preservation of rural European landscapes and social structures through the regeneration of economically depleted areas. Although coastal and city tourism are still the highest in terms of visitor numbers, it is rural and mountain tourism that is showing particularly strong growth in the European context, and this is mostly around protected areas. The IUCN (1994 ; in Blangy and Vautier, 2001) lists four reasons why the 1990s have offered increased opportunities for protected areas, all of which apply to Europe :

1. human populations are relatively stable and affluent;
2. there are declining pressures on land in many areas because of agricultural surpluses and reduced military activity.
3. there is a high level of public support for conservation; and
4. there is a climate of international cooperation.

Given these trends, the threat to protected areas in Europe has diminished, particularly from such activities as resource extraction and agriculture (WWF, 2000). Nonetheless, land use pressures remain evident due to limited land availability, with tourism and recreation being amongst the greatest contributors to such pressure in context of Europe's national parks (FNNPE, 1993). It is also the case that the increasing use of natural areas for these purposes has generated a stronger commitment by governments and the broader community to their preservation (Font and Tribe, 2000).

There are between 10,000 and 20,000 protected areas in Europe; although the number is high, many are generally smallholdings containing pockets of biodiversity and few are large enough to allow for the free roaming of large mammals. It is also evident that the level of protection, the presence of multiple use objectives, level of funding, and state intervention / permissiveness vary significantly between these areas. In response to these, and other issues, the European Commission developed Natura 2000 as their strategy for environmental conservation. As part of this strategy, two tourism-related projects have been identified as being particularly relevant to the implementation of this strategy (European Commission, 2000a, 2000b). The first one of these is the European Charter for Sustainable Tourism in Protected Areas, headed by the Parcs Naturels Regionaux de France under the auspices of the Europe Federation, and supported by the IUCN. The Charter developed by this project has been tested in ten European national parks, and these have been acknowledged as well-managed protected areas that have made continuous efforts towards making tourism and conservation compatible. The second, and the focus of this case study, is the PAN Parks network of protected areas. PAN Parks is the result of a partnership established in 1997 between the World Wide Fund for Nature-Netherlands and the Dutch Molecaten Group, a leisure and tourism-based corporation with assets of 45 million euros and an annual turnover of 13.5 million euros, which develops holiday villages in Europe.

The concept behind PAN Parks is one of creating 'a network of natural areas with an international reputation for outstanding access to wildlife and excellent tourist facilities, combined with effective habitat protection and the minimum environmental impact possible' (WWF, 1998 : 1). Given this goal PAN Parks has sought to develop :

- a recognizable network of well-managed, protected natural areas which welcome visitors and avoid potentially conflicting activities;
- a partnership between the authorities of protected areas, the local population, and commercial and nature conservation organizations;
- a way to promote well managed natural areas to create a balance between nature conservation, local development, tourism and recreation; and
- an organization to increase the number of well-supervised natural areas in Europe (WWF, undated : 3).

In essence the PAN Parks projects is trying to create a network of 'Yellowstone Parks in Europe. The intention being one of identifying protected areas holding wilderness characteristics and tourist attractiveness, not only of natural but also of pan-European importance, encouraging the sustainable environmental and tourism management of these areas, and promoting visitation to them. The concept of reproducing the success of American parks in tourism is an ambitious challenge for Europe. There are no more than 100 parks that would qualify on size alone. Most of these are located in Eastern Europe, where problems such as overstretched budgets, little tourism infrastructure, limited visitor management experience and where local use of parks for poaching and illegal harvesting exist. Yet the preservation of these areas in the medium term, and the link via corridors between the remaining pieces of wilderness in Europe in long term, could have an invaluable impact on the preservation of the regions' wildlife.

PAN Parks and the European Charter are working jointly to benefit from synergies between their projects. Cees Lager, CEO of the Molecaten Groups, sees the benefits in tourism development that are linked to nature conservation, and views the inclusion of non-financial returns on investment, such as nature conservation, as a key value in this project. At the same time, however, Lager notes that for the projects to be successful, acceptable financial returns must be forthcoming to those that invest in it. PAN Parks Accommodation BV is the limited liability company made up of investing partners and initially managed by Molecaten, that will seek investors to provide 'appropriate accommodation (to be called PAN Villages) at approved PAN Parks, to generate income for its shareholders and to provide financial support for the PAN Parks Foundations' (Pan Parks Foundation, undated : 7). Molecaten and other investors will 'help protect and develop many of Europe's most beautiful wilderness areas protect and develop many of Europe's most beautiful wilderness areas while enjoying a sound return on their investment' (Pan Parks Foundation, undated : 1). It is unclear at this early stage what percentage of profits will be distributed to shareholders, used for reinvestment purposes or allocated to the Foundation.

This case study discusses the process of engaging a core group of European parks in the development and implementation of habitat, visitor, tourism and business management strategies in their process of application for PAN Parks quality trademark, and ultimately to ensure a more sustainable use of the parks' resources. The first section reviews the applications to PAN Parks and the benefits from application as presented by the PAN Parks Foundation and perceived by the applicants. This is followed by a review of the key principles of the process of compliance assessment (Font, 2002; Font and Tribe, 2001) and how PAN Parks is following this process of setting up criteria, ensuring the criteria are assessable, verifying standards of applicants, certification of results and ensuring recognition and acceptance by the target audiences. Since PAN Parks is still in its early years, this case study focuses on the outcomes from the first stage and critically assesses the main challenges to be faced if the programme is to contribute to sustainable tourism.

The PAN Parks Candidates

For parks to qualify for inclusion in the PAN Park network they need to be large (usually over 25000 hectares), with evidence of outstanding environmental quality and management. The candidates listed in Table 7.1 were present at the first Candidate PAN Parks Conference, held in Holland in June 2001. PAN Parks aims to appoint another six out of a preliminary list of ten other parks as prospective candidates in the near future.

The parks that have so far been selected as official candidates for inclusion in the PAN Park network represent some of the richest natural resources of Europe. They are home to large mammals and predators such as wolf ; chamois, bears, lynx, moose and eagle. As example, there are 200 rare animal species in Bieszczady, 100 Marsican Brown Bears and sixty Appenine wolves in Abbruzzo, and 6300 chamois in Mercantour, Besides their animal wealth, these parks are also sites of high concentration of species. Triglav has combined 5500 species of flora and fauna within its boundaries. Abruzzo has one third of the higher order plants of Italy, and Oulanka has 500 species of vascular plants, which is unusual given its northern location. Mercantour is home to 2000 species of plants, including sixty species of orchids, 200 rare and 300 endemic species, due to landscapes ranging from Mediterranean (20 kilometres away from the sea) to Alpine (3000 metre high mountains with glaciers). Slovenasky raj has more than 2100 species of butterflies due to its high concentration of gorges and caves.

Many of the candidate parks have a wide range of facilities. Abruzzo has fifteen visitor centres and ten mountain refuges, Oulanka has thirty-six cooking and camp fires, thirty-two campsites and eights unlocked cabins for recreational use, and Triglav has thirty-two alpine houses and huts. Land use in these parks varies, and although they all have core conservation areas, poaching and illegal hunting are still common. Some parks, such as Triglav which generates 40 percent of its funds from tourism and recreation, are already benefiting from visitation; however, such parks tend to be the exception rather than the rule. In general most parks rely on governmental funds, with tourism benefits being captured

Table 7.1
Candidate Pan Parks

Name of area	*Country*	*Area (ha.)*	*Visitors per year*	*Strengths*	*Weaknesses*
(1)	(2)	(3)	(4)	(5)	(6)
Abbruzo National Park	Italy	43 950	2 000 000	1600 small-scale businesses in operation. Local people represented on board of directors.	No distinct management plan doucment.
Bieszczady National Park	Poland	29 200	250 000	Trilateral Man and Biosphere Reserve. 70 per cent of park is strictly protected.	Park is perceived as limiting to local development.
Fulufjallets Nature Reserve	Sweden	35 000	1 00 000	Local people are interested in PAN Parks.	Traditional use of resources.
Mercantour National Park	France	68 500	550 000	Partnership with Gites Panda. Twinned with Italian park.	Conflicts with shephereds on wolf issue. Local people have just started to realize importance of tourism.

(Contd.)

(Contd.)

(1)	(2)	(3)	(4)	(5)	(6)
Oulanka National Park	Finland	27 500	150 000	Park can raise income for itself. Local people are active in park management issues.	There is no co-operation with local companies. Park does not communication with local communities.
Slovensky raj National Park	Slovak Rep.	32 774	500 000	Comparative advantage in Slovakia, well-known park, Close working relationships with PAN Parks office.	Pressure on environment from high level of visitation. Land use problems due to contradictions in zoning.
Triglav National Park	Slovenia	83 807	720000	History of co-operation with local communities. No hunting on 25000 hectares.	Pressure on environment from high levels of visitation. Limited co-operation between groups associated with tourism in the park.

Source : Adapted from PAN Parks Courier, 2001.

by nearby communities. Oulanka typifies this situation, with its management noting that it gains no revenue from its 120 000 visitors, yet it is estimated that 30 per cent of the income from the neighbouring towns is attributable to tourists visiting the park.

Short-and Long-Term Benefits to the Parks

The current candidates for inclusion in PAN Parks are acting to pilot the processes and materials that have been developed for the project. Each candidate park must demonstrate that it is performing at a high level in at least one area covered by the scheme, and parks are encouraged to share information in order to reach acceptable benchmarks as they seek to move from 'candidate' status to become a verified member of it.

Parks can benefit from WWF support in training and resources to meet the scheme's criteria, and once they qualify certified parks can use the PAN Parks logo for marketing purposes. Table 7.2 shows a list of benefits categorized according to whether a park has been verified and certified, is a candidate park aiming for verification, or has made perspective enquiries but not yet entered the process as a candidate. The benefits of working towards the PAN Parks standards are not clear to every park, and in the last three years many parks have shown interest for a short period of time, after which they have decided not to go forward. Out of the current parks working towards certification (seven), the two in France and Italy, with longer experience in tourism management , have been most critical of the benefits that can be gained from the process, whereas parks with lower tourist numbers have shown more interest.

The benefits that PAN Parks lists in Table 7.2 generally coincide with park managers' expectations of the outcome from this process. In general, park mangers view PAN Parks as quality trademark, however, what each park seeks from the scheme is dependent on their specific circumstances (PAN Parks Courier, 2001). The anticipated benefits for each park include opportunities for increased, mainly international, tourism business (Fulufjallet, Mercantour, Triglav, Oulanka), networking and research opportunities (Abruzzo, Bieszczady, Mercantour, Slovensky raj, Triglav), and closer co-operation with local populations and stakeholders (Oulanka, Slovensky raj).

As regards tourism benefits, when Cees Lager, from the Molecaten group, introduced the first Candidate PAN Parks conference in 1999 he did so by highlighting the market demand for ecotourism that can be experienced in relative comfort. While the desire to service this market niche was central amongst his group's decision to support the PAN Park concept, there is no obligation on the part of participating parks to allow PAN Villages to be developed within their boundaries. At the commencement of 2002, only two candidate parks, Bieszczady and Fulufjallet, had decided to proceed with proposal to develop PAN Villages (PAN Parks Supervisory Board, 2000). Fulufjallet PAN Village, for example, is intending to include forty self-catering chalets with planning permission for a total of sixty-two, the construction of infrastructure will be completed by summer 2002 and the chalets by 2003, with the Village to be opened on 1 July, 2004 (PAN Parks Foundation, undated).

Table 7.2.

PAN Parks Benefits to Verified, Candidate and Prospective Candidate Parks.

Benefits	*Verified park*	*Candidate park*	*Prospective park*
Introduction of a PAN Park Village	(✓)		
PAN Parks Foundation support	✓		
Access to loans	✓		
Access to EU subsidies	✓		
Access to on-site conservation projects	✓	✓	
Training material and opportunities	✓	✓	
Inclusion in PAN Parks brochures	✓	✓	
Communication package	✓	✓	

(Contd.)

(Contd.)

Local partner website	✓	✓	
Benefits from PAN Parks research	✓	✓	✓
Access at the PAN Parks internet	✓	✓	✓
Promotion at the PAN Parks website	✓	✓	✓
PAN Parks Courier (magazine)	✓	✓	✓

Source : PAN Parks internal information not published.
(✓) PAN Park Village will be introduced on a longer-term basis.

Most candidate parks have stated that PAN Parks has given them a medium-term goal and a short-term pathway to put into practice a variety of actions that have been on the 'back burner' for some time. Community consultation and the development of visitor and tourism management strategies are the short-term benefits mentioned most often. Besides these general considerations, two examples can be given of the benefits of PAN Parks to prospective candidate parks to date. Firstly, PAN Parks is helping promote tourism to the Bialowieza National Park (Poland), a prospective candidate park (see http ://www.poland.panparks.org). Secondly, Fulufjallet Nature Reserve has submitted a proposal to the European Union to be reclassified as a National Park, which has been accepted and will become operational in 2002 in part due to the support of PAN Parks. To assess the possible long-term benefits of PAN Parks it is necessary to review the process that applicants will have to follow in their efforts to achieve certification.

Standards

A standard is a document approved by a recognized body that provides for common and repeated use of a prescribed set of rules, conditions, or requirements (Toth, 2000). Setting standards is one of the hardest elements of a project of this type, since varying geographical and other site specific conditions mean what is appropriate for one park may not be acceptable elsewhere. For example, slash and burn is a traditional practice in Finland that has been lost over the years, and in the Koli National Park (Finland) this practice has been reintroduced as a mean of rescuing traditions, yet forest fire is a major threat to national parks in the Mediterranean (Font and Tribe, 2000). Another major difficulty arises from differences in national legislation, practices and objectives. Ideally, standards should not be below any national legislative requirements, but if a standard reflects the highest level of current flow and practice this might be too demanding for some countries. For these reasons the standards PAN Parks has developed tend to be a mixture of environmental performance and environmental management (Font, 2002).

PAN Parks is developing its standards in the form of criteria, grouped under five principles (Anon, 2001). A manual of good practice for parks needing support to meet the requirements of these principles will be developed, which will include case studies from pilot sites (see the Discussion section later).

Principles and Criteria

PAN Parks has laid out five principles for assessment of each member park's performance and management (see Table 7.3). The first three principles are under the control of the park's management unit, whereas the fourth and fifth principles are more challenging, since they recognize the dependence between the park and its surroundings, and the need for the park to engage with a variety of stakeholders in determining limits and acceptable change from tourism.

The first principle relates to a park's natural heritage, and acts as a 'filter' to ensure that a park is worthy of inclusion in the Pan Parks project. The second principle concerns the degree of management effectiveness exhibited in the protections of the natural environment. The third principle relates to the park's visitor management strategy and plan, including the provision of education and interpretation to visitors. These first three principles could be seen as somewhat predictable given the objectives of the project, and it is therefore not surprising that they were the first agreed to. The two subsequent, principles are more innovative and therefore have received more attention here.

The fourth principle pertains to the sustainable tourism development strategy of the park and its zone of influence, ensuring that development around the park is in keeping with the values of the area, taking into account visitor needs as well as environmental, socio-economic and cultural constraints. This is a challenging principle since the park's management has limited influence over what takes place outside its boundaries. Nonetheless, park authorities need to see beyond their physical boundaries since the activities taking place in neighbouring towns and villages rely in many ways on the park, and also affect the use of the park's resources.

The fifth principle is linked to the quality of the park's business partners. It extends principle 4 by requiring the park to set up agreements with individual companies that commit themselves to being assessed against a set of criteria, which includes demonstrating how they can support the park's objectives and contribute to their implementation. This implies that parks will have to identify and communicate potential benefits to those businesses aiming to become partners. Organizations with which partnerships may be established extend beyond those involved in the tourism industry to encompass any business or association that can prove it has a vested interest in, or influence on, a park. It is also noteworthy that any international organization wishing to use a park will be encouraged to be certified by a relevant body (for example, Green Globe 21) or to be involved in recognizable programmes (such as the Tour Operators Initiative for Sustainable Tourism Development). Partner bodies will also be encouraged to be part of a forum involved in the sustainable tourism development strategy (principle 4). However, their involvement in decision-making will depend on their relationship to the area. For example, hotels, inbound tour operators and shops trading directly with tourists will have a greater say than outbound tour operators from overseas, since the former have made a long-term investment in the destination and rely on the long-term sustainable use of the park's resources, whereas the latter can easily move their business away from the area.

Table 7.3

Summary of Principles and Associated Criteria

Principles (1)	*Criteria* (2)
Principle 1 : Natural values. PAN Parks are large protected areas; representative of Europe's natural heritage and of international importance for wildlife and ecosystems.	• The area is adequately protected by means of an enforced act or decree. • The protected area is of Europe wide importance for the conservation of biological diversity and contains the best existing representatives of original natural ecosystems in the region. • The minimum area of the protected area is 25000 hectares.
Principle 2 : Habitat management. Design and management of the PAN Parks aims to maintain and , if necessary, restore the area's natural ecological processes and its biodiversity.	• Design of the protected area aims to maintain natural ecological values. • Regulations protecting the area are adequately enforced. • The protected area has an integrated management plan that is actively implemented. Regular monitoring and assessment of the plan are carried out and there is provision for updating and monitoring the plan in light of the results of this. • Management of the protected area makes use of zoning or some other system that ensures protection of the area's nature conservation values while allowing for human activities compatible with this. • If the protected area is zoned, there is

(Contd.)

(Contd.)

(1)	(2)
	an unfragmented core zone of at least 10 000 hectares where no extractive use is permitted and where the only management interventions are those aimed at restoring natural ecological processes. • If the protected area is not zoned, management of the whole area aims to maintain and, if necessary, restore key natural ecological processes. • The protected area's management system pays particular attention to threatened and endemic species. • In the case of a protected area adjacent to a national border, transborder co-operation in management is actively sought after.
Principle 3 : Visitor Management Visitor management safeguards the natural values of the PAN Parks and aims to provide visitors with a high – quality experience based on the appreciation of nature.	• The protected area has a visitor management plan that is actively implemented. Regular monitoring and assessment of the plan are carried out and there is provision for updating and modifying the plan in light of the results of this. • Visitor management safeguards the natural values of the protected area. • Under the visitor management plan visitors are offered a wide range of high-quality activities based on the appreciation of nature. • Visitor management creates understanding of and support for the conservation goals of the protected area. • The protected area has visitor centre, for which clear goals and a policy are set out in the visitor management plan. • The visitor management plan includes

(Contd.)

(Contd.)

(1)	(2)
	training programmes for staff and others involved in the provision of services to visitors.
Principle 4 : Sustainable Tourism Development Strategy. Protected Area Authority and its relevant partners in the PAN Parks region aim at achieving a synergy between nature conservation and sustainable tourism by developing a Sustainable Tourism Development Strategy (STDS), committing to it and jointly taking responsibility in its implementation.	• The protected area and its region have sufficient tourism potential and carrying capacity for sustainable tourism. • The present tourism activities do not arm the protected area in order to implement its nature conservation goals. • Protected Area Authority and local stakeholders have the opportunity to co-operate within the framework of an official forum that aims at developing Sustainable Tourism Development Strategy (hereafter STDS). • An Execute PAN Parks Organization (hereafter EPPMO) or an existing forum for co-operation, which could assume responsibility for implementing PAN Parks, has been established in which all relevant stakeholders have formally confirmed their support and commitment to the conservation goals of the protected area and PAN Parks Organization. The EPPMO (or similar) formulates, implements and monitors an STDS for the protected area and its surrounding region. • Tourism development and existing tourism activities, which are under the control of EPPMO, are based on sustainable use of the ecological resources of the region. • Tourism development and tourism

(Contd.)

(Contd.)

(1)	(2)
	activities are based on sustainable use of the socio-economic resources of the region, including minority and if necessary indigenous people issues. • Tourism development and tourism activities are based on sustainable use of the cultural resources of the region. • The STDS's communications and marketing strategy aims at informing all target groups.
Principle 5 : Business partners. PAN Parks' business partners as legal enterprises are committed to the goals of the protected area in their region and the PAN Parks Organization, and actively cooperates with other stakeholders to effectively implement the region's Sustainable Tourism Development Strategy as developed by the local EPPMO (see principle 4).	• PAN Parks business partners follow all national legislation related to their business. • Business partners support the protected area and its management goals. • PAN Parks business partners are committed to the PAN Parks Organization and its goals. • Business partners actively participate in the implementation of Sustainable Tourism Development Strategy as developed by EPPMO and verified by PAN Parks Organization.

The principles and associated criteria noted previously were field tested in 1999. Once a basic 'shell' was agreed, indicators were introduced to verify the criteria. These were tested in a second round of consultations that involved the self-assessment of seventeen national parks from fourteen countries. After this consultation phase was complete the principles and criteria were further evolved with the assistance of : the Société Générale de Surveillance (SGC) Hungary (principles 1 to 3) ; Europarc (principle four) ; and an independent consultant (principle 5). Flowing from this process was the present (September 2000) set of principles and criteria (Kun, 2001).

Assessment, Verification and Certification

The process associated with assessment, verification and standardization involves the following steps :

1. the park's management unit submits an assessment, which is made on the basis of the checklist (principles 1-3). Any area will be able to download the application form from the PAN Parks web page (www.panparks.org);
2. the assessment is evaluated by PAN Parks and a decision is made whether it seems to be worth verifying it;
3. the park, with expert support from PAN Parks, will devise a plan to meet the requirements of the criteria, and collect evidence for each one of the indicators, by a negotiated date;
4. the verifiers travel to the area to review evidence;
5. verifiers submit their recommendation to the PAN Parks Foundation; and
6. certification is awarded and/or recommendations for improvements of the park.

The assessment process (step 2) will be guided by the use of indicators that will serve to determine a park's performance against a specific principle and its associated criteria. In Table 7.4 an example of indicators has been given. If a park moves on to step 3 it is given the status of candidate and provided with training resources and other benefits. Candidature periods are negotiated individually with parks depending on their current position, demonstrating the openland and flexible approach taken by PAN Parks in encouraging applicants to set their own agendas. At the end of the candidature period the park will submit a report detailing their progress in meeting the five principles and their associated criteria. To assist parks in working their way through the candidature process. PAN Parks conducts workshops at which parks develop their initial draft strategies. The first of these was conducted in Holland in June 2001 and was attended by all the current (seven) candidate parks.

Table 7.4

Assessment Indicators Linked to Criteria (from Principle 3, Criterion 3.1)

Criterion	*Indicators*
The protected area has a visitor management plan that is actively implemented. Regular monitoring and assessment of the plan are carried out and there is provision for updating and modifying the plan in light of the results of this.	• Provide the visitor management plan (an English summary and copy (if available)). • Provide information of the plan's long- and short-term goals. • Provide information on the resources available for the implementation of the visitor management plan. • Describe how the effects of the visitor management plan's actions are being monitored. • Indicate how the plan can be revised accordingly.

Once a candidature period is over, and the park concerned has submitted a report, a verification process takes place. This involves a site visit and a review of desk evidence such as plans, minutes of meetings, procedures, surveys, assessments and so on. PAN Parks has opted for third party verification, involving the contracting of independent individuals (Kun, 2001). Other approaches to the verification process were considered, but they were found to have limitations. PAN Parks staff, for example, could have been used for this purpose, but it was felt that a conflict of interest might arise from having the same staff that provided support throughout the process being asked to do the assessment. Another option was to contract an external company to undertake all verifications; however, the small scale of PAN Parks does not make this feasible. PAN Parks plans to have eight parks verified by 2006.

During a workshop held in Zwolle, the Netherlands, on 11 April 2000, participants agreed that the PAN Parks Foundation must develop its own verification manual, which can be provided to a third party verifier in order to undertake the required field verification. With this goral in mind. Société Générale de Surveillance (SGC) Hungry was appointed to develop a verification manual including general guidelines and check lists. SGS is one of the world leaders in verification, testing and certification and has collaborated closely with Green Globe 21. Once developed, the manual will be tested and finalized through field trials in pilot areas. The manual will then be available to independent experts contracted as verifiers. The process for developing the manual and finalizing the principles and criteria system, including measurable and objective indicators, was due for completion in October 2001.

Exact fees for involvement in the programme, and the associated use of the PAN Parks logo, have yet to be set. Nonetheless, fees will be subsidized by 50 per cent for European Union countries and up to 75 per cent for EU Accession countries, including Eastern Europe, where most applicants are based. The fees will be used for third-party verification and for providing other services, such as consultants or training programmes. The cost of operating PAN Parks is much higher than the fees paid by members, and the operations of the secretarial function of the PAN Parks Foundation, membership services, and publications will require external funding. Such funding will be provided by the Molecaten group in the short to medium term; with its long-term capacity / willingness to do so likely to be linked to the success in establishing PAN Villages in, or adjacent to, participating parks. A complicating factor here is that once a park is certified and a village built (option under this scheme), if the park concerned later comes into question there is the potential for a conflict of interest to emerge between the accommodation and the certification arms. This is an issue that PAN Parks Foundation is aware of but has not yet determined how to resolve.

Recognition and Acceptance

Recognition and acceptance of the PAN Parks trademark will be driven by a communications campaign conducted directly by the PAN Parks organization, the parks themselves and the distributors of tourism products. This process will be costly, and as such it is one of the major drawbacks of certification systems of this kind. At present , PAN Parks are communicating with four groups : pilot PAN Parks and self-assessment participants, WWF-offices, (potential) investors and (potential) partners, all with different information needs (van Ladesteijn, 2000).

Assessing the Success of PAN Parks

PAN Parks started as a concept in 1997, and for the ensuing years has been in the development and piloting stage, mainly involving the organization of internal structures., development of system for compliance assessment, and establishment of links with potential candidates. It would appear that the experience to date of candidate parks has been positive for those in need of expertise in natural area and tourism management, which are mainly located in the more remote parts of Northern Europe, or in Eastern Europe. Those in wealthier areas, and with more experience in these areas, however, appear to be questioning the benefits of their involvement. Indeed, one potential fate of PAN Parks is for it to become a programme that engenders a more proactive approach to park management in the less developed parts of Europe.

Whether individual parks involved in the scheme become more sustainable than they otherwise would have been without input from PAN Parks is difficult to assess. It can be said, however, that principles 4 and 5 of the scheme that concern the engagement of local communities and organizations, along with businesses, in the development of national areas are in line with the more progressive attitudes evident amongst some parks managers (Blangy and Vautier, 2001). They also reflect the perceptions on conservation embodied in Natura 2000 (European Commission, 2000a, 2000b). Only once PAN Parks has progressed to the point where it has certified a number of parks, can the question of how successful or otherwise it has been in enhancing standards of natural area conservation, while at the same time facilitating tourism development of such areas, be answered. This question would make the subject of a worthwhile future study.

References

1. Anon (2001) : PAN Parks principles and criteria, principles 1-5, April 2001, draft for construction.
2. Blangy, S. and Vautier, S. (2001) : Europe, in Weaver, D. (ed.) *The Encyclopedia of Ecotourism,* Wallingford : CAB International, pp. 155-72.
3. European Commission (2000a) : *Sustainable tourism and Natura 2000, Guidelines, initiatives and good practices in Europe,* DG ENV, Brussels : European Commission.
4. European Commission (2000b) : Natura 2000, European Commission DG ENV Nature Newsletter, Issue 13, December 2000.
5. FNNPE (1993) : *Loving them to death? The Need for Sustainable Tourism in Europe's Nature and National Parks.* The Federation of Nature and National Parks of Europe : Grafenau, Germany.
6. Font, X. (2002) : Environmental certification in tourism and hospitality : progress, process and prospects, *Tourism Management* **23(3)** : 197-205.
7. Font, X. and Tribe, J. (2000) : Recreation, conservation and timber production : a sustainable relationship? In Font, X. and Tribe, J. (eds) *Forest tourism and recreation : case studies in environmental management,* Wallingford : CAB International, United Kingdom, pp. 1-22.
8. Font, X. and Tribe, J. (2001) : The process of developing an

ecolabel. In Font, X, and Buckley, R. (*eds.*) *Tourism ecolabelling : certification and promotion of sustainable management,* Wallingford : CAB International, pp. 87-104.

9. Kun, Z. (2001) : PAN Parks verification, draft 3.2, 11th September, 2000, WWF : Budapest, Hungary.
10. PAN Parks Courier (2001) : Summer 2001, Budapest : WWF Hungary.
11. PAN Parks Foundation (undated) *PAN Parks Accommodation BY,* Zwolle (Netherlands) : PAN Parks Foundation.
12. PAN Parks Supervisory Board (2000) : Resolutions meeting PAN Parks Supervisory Board (PPSB) on 29 September 2000.
13. Roerhorst, I. (2000) : PAN Parks business partners : Quickscan of environmental assessment systems for the tourism industry, Zeist Holland : WWF.

8 Perspectives on Sustainable Tourism in the South Pacific

Introduction

Any discussion of sustainable tourism, or tourism that respects any preferably enhances the environmental and sociocultural carrying capacity of a destination, must take into account the physical and cultural characteristics of the destinations that are being considered. Insularity is one such characteristic that can significantly influence the attainment of sustainable tourism outcomes. This chapter specifically considers the status of sustainable tourism in the South Pacific region as defined in Figure 8.1, a macro-region notable for its exaggerated insularity. The first of four major sections outlines the physical and human geographical characteristics of the study region, and this is followed by a generalized discussion of the regional tourism sector. The third section uses level of intensity as a basis for examining a variety to South Pacific destinations in order to assess the evidence for and against the existence of sustainable tourism practices. The fourth and final section considers the options for tourism in the study region in light of the preceding material. The chapter does not purport to be inclusive or all-encompassing in terms of the South Pacific destinations which are described or discussed. Furthermore, it does not attempt to draw any definitive conclusions about the presence of absence of sustainable tourism, but rather is intended to raise important issues for further investigation.

The Geographical Context

Any meaningful discussion of tourism in the South Pacific

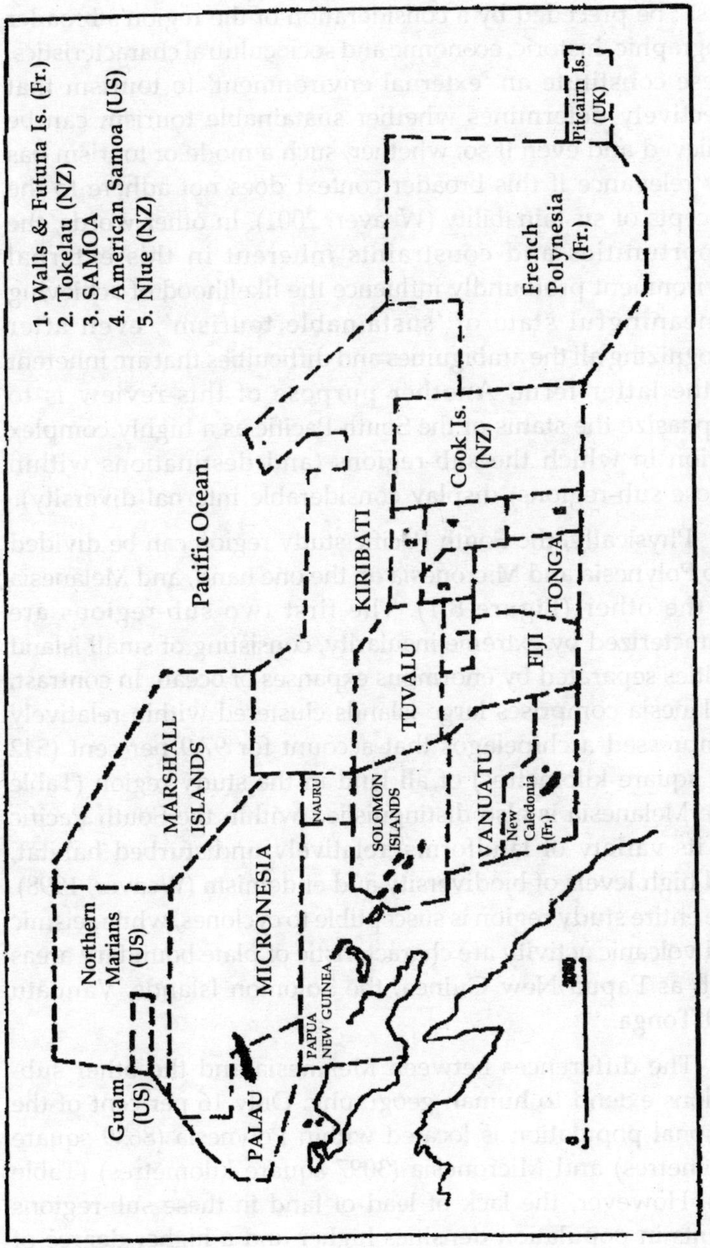

Fig. 8.1. The Pacific 2002.

must : be preceded by a consideration of the region's broader geographic, historic, economic and sociocultural characteristics. These constitute an 'external environment' to tourism that effectively determines whether sustainable tourism can be achieved and even if so, whether, such a mode of tourism has any relevance if this broader context does not adhere to the precepts of sustainability (Weaver, 2001). In other words, the opportunities and constraints inherent in this external environment profoundly influence the likelihood of achieving a meaningful state of 'sustainable tourism', even after recognizing all the ambiguities and difficulties that are inherent in the latter term. Another purpose of this review is to emphasize the status of the South Pacific as a highly complex region in which the sub-regions (and destinations within whose sub-regions) display considerable internal diversity).

Physically, the South Pacific study region can be divided into Polynesia and Micronesia on the one hand, and Melanesia on the other (Figure 8.1). The first two sub-regions are characterized by extreme insularity, consisting of small island entities separated by enormous expanses of ocean. In contrast, Melanesia comprises large islands clustered within relatively compressed archipelagos that account for 97.9 per cent (542 230 square kilometres) of all land in the study region (Table 8.1). Melanesia is also distinguished within the South Pacific for its variety of landforms, relatively undisturbed habitat, and high levels of biodiversity and endemism (Weaver, 1998). The entire study region is susceptible to cyclones, while seismic and volcanic activity are characteristic of plate boundary areas such as Papua New Guinea, the Solomon Islands, Vanuatu and Tonga.

The differences between Melanesia and the other sub-regions extend to human geography. Only 16 per cent of the regional population is located within Polynesia (8639 square kilometres) and Micronesia (3097 square kilometres) (Table 8.1). However, the lack of lead of land in these sub-regions results in population densities higher and a higher degree of

Table 8.1

Land Area and Population in the South Pacific

By state and region	*Land area (km²)*	*Population 1998 (000s)*	*Population/ km²*
Papua New Guinea	461 690	4599.8	10.0
Fiji	18270	802.6	43.9
Solomon Islands	28450	441.0	15.5
New Caledonia (Fr)	19060	194.2	10.2
Vanuatu	14760	185.2	12.5
Melanesia (Total)	**542230**	**6222.8**	**11.5**
Guam (US)	541	148.1	273.8
Fed. States Micronesia	702	129.7	184.8
Kiribati	717	84.0	117.2
Northern Marianas (US)	477	66.6	139.6
Marshall Is.	181	63.0	348.1
Palau	458	18.1	39.5
Nauru	21	10.5	500.0
Micronesia (Total)	**3097**	**520.0**	**167.9**
French Polynesia (Fr)	3941	237.8	60.3
Samoa	2860	224.7	78.6
Tonga	748	108.2	144.7
Wallis and Futuna Is (Fr)	274	15.0	54.7
Niue (NZ)	260	1.6	6.2
Cook Islands (NZ)	240	20.0	83.3
American Samoa (US)	199	62.1	312.1
Pitcaim Is. (UK)	47	< 1.0	1.0
Norfolk I. (Aus)	34	2.2	64.7
Tuvalu	26	10.4	400.0
Tokelau (NZ)	10	1.4	140.0
Polynesia (Total)	**8639**	**683.4**	**79.1**
South Pacific (Total)	**553966**	**7426.2**	**13.4**

human-induced environmental degradation both on land and sea. Ethnically, each of the sub-regions is associated with a separate indigenous racial group after which each region is named, allowing for a significant degree of intermixture and acculturation as a result of ongoing, historical contact, particularly in transitional border islands. Pre-European elements of these cultures remain robust, given that the South Pacific was one of the last regions to be formally incorporated into the global capitalist economy. This is especially true with regard to language and communal land tenure systems, while other attributes such as religion and economics, have been profoundly changed during the past 150 years of intensive European contact and subsequent acculturation. Fiji and New Caledonia are the only two entities where non-indigenous groups are roughly comparable in population to indigenous people. As a region, the South Pacific is characterized by high fertility rates and, despite high rates of out-migration steady population increase and resultant added pressure on natural resources (McKnight, 1995). Politically, the South Pacific shares with the Caribbean the distinction of having the highest concentration of dependent political units (*i.e.*, ten remaining dependencies), indicating that this region is also the last to be experiencing the formal de-colonization process. Melanesia has no remaining dependencies, but is characterized by a high level of political instability, as evidenced by recent upheavals in the Solomon Islands and Fiji.

In the South Pacific elements of physical geography, human geography and history have conspired to produce fragile environments and weak economic structures that are not indicative of, or conducive to sustainable economic development in the 'western' sense. Bertram and Watters (1985) characterize the South Pacific as a region where the MIRAB syndrome *(i.e., migration, remittances, aid and bureaucracy)* is prevalent, reflecting a reliance upon a narrow range of economic activities, and subsequently severe trade deficits and dramatic fluctuations in economic performance (Craig-Smith and Fagence, 1994). The MIRAB syndrome is most apparent on small outlying atolls, where insularity and isolation are exaggerated (Krause, 1995), but is also evident in Melanesia despite that sub-region's much greater endowment of natural resources. In terms of per capita GNP, many South Pacific states rank among the world's poorest, with Papua New Guinea, the Solomon Islands, Vanuatu, Kiribati, Samoa, the Marshall Islands and Micronesia all being below US$2600 following a adjustments for purchasing power parity (Weaver, 1998).

The Tourism Context

At a regional scale, the South Pacific is over-represented as an inbound tourist destination, with 0.13 per cent of the world's population, but 0.5 per cent of all international stayovers. This observation, however, is rendered all but meaningless by the highly skewed internal distribution of the sector, which is overwhelmingly dominated by inbound as opposed to domestic tourists. Just two small destinations, Guam and the Northern Marians (the island of Spain, specifically), account for almost 60 per cent of all stayovers, and this figure increases to over 80 per cent with the addition of Fiji and French Polynesia (Table 8.2). Tourist arrivals in the remaining eighteen destinations, and indeed, in the numerous peripheral islands of the last three named destinations, indicate a more incipient level of tourism development, and a much higher lever of return visits by former residents who tend to stay in local residences and spend less money. Interrelated factors that have contributed to this situation include isolation, the lack of infrastructure and accommodation, the scarcity of freehold land, and a lack of interest among potential investors, due in part to the presence of intervening opportunities in more accessible and established regional destinations such as Hawaii and Okinawa. In this context, Guam and Saipan can be seen as anomalies that have benefited from their proximity to Japan, the provision of infrastructure and other services as an outcome of World War II and their status as US dependencies.

Given the economic context, it is not surprising that South Pacific status and dependencies have been paying increased attention to tourism as a vehicle for helping to overcome the MIRAB syndrome and bringing into effect sustained economic development. This attention is not new. Tourism was already included as a component of development strategies in the late colonial and early post-independence period, when it was standard practice to uncritically endorse the sector as a panacea for underdeveloped countries in general. Jafari (1989),

Table 8.2
International Stayover Arrivals in the South Pacific

By state and region	1991 (000s)	1998 (000s) (A)	Percentage of region : 1998	Tourist/ resident ratio 1998 (B)	Intensity Category (AB)	Tourism as estimated percentage of GDP
(1)	(2)	(3)	(4)	(5)	(6)	(7)
Fiji	259	371.4	13.7	0.46	HL	17
New Caledonia	81	103.8	3.8	0.53	LL	3
PNG	37	67.5	2.5	0.01	LL	<1
Vanuatu	40	52.1	1.9	0.28	LL	15
Solomon Is.	11	13.2	0.5	0.03	LL	2
Melanesia (Total)	**428**	**608.0**	**22.4**	**0.10**		
Guam	737	1137.0	41.8	7.68	HH	na
Northern Marianas	422	490.2	18.0	7.36	HH	50
Palau	33	64.2	2.4	3.55	LH	10
Micronesia	8	11.0*	0.4	0.08	LL	na
Marshall Is.	7	6.4	0.2	0.10	LL	5
Kiribati	3	5.4	0.2	0.06	LL	1

(Contd.)

(Contd.)

(1)	(2)	(3)	(4)	(5)	(6)	(7)
Nauru	1	1.0	< 0.1	0.10	LL	n.a.
Micronesia (Total)	**1210**	**1715.2**	**63.1**	**3.30**		
French Polynesia	121	188.3	6.9	0.79	HH	23
Samoa	35	77.9	2.9	0.35	LL	13
Cook Islands	40	48.6	1.8	2.43	LH	23
Norfolk I.	na	29.0	1.1	3.18	LH	n.a.
Tonga	22	27.1	1.0	0.25	LL	6
American Samoa	18	21.3†	0.8	0.34	LL	5
Niue	1	17	0.1	1.06	LH	18
Tuvalu	1	11	< 0.1	0.11	LL	n.a.
Pitcairn Is.	n.a.	n.a.	n.a.	n.a.	LL	n.a.
Tokelau	n.a.	n.a.	n.a.	n.a.	LL	n.a.
Wallis and Futuna Is.	n.a.	n.a.	n.a.	n.a.	LL	n.a.
Polynesia (Total)	**238**	**395.0**	**14.5**	**0.58**		
South Pacific (Total)	**1876**	**2718.2**	**100.0**	**0.37**		

Sources : Europa World Year Book 1997 (GDP sales) ; WTO, 1997 ; 1998 data for Nauru from Fagence, 1999.

* 1997 data.

† 1996 data.

accordingly, refers to this as the era of the *advocacy platform.* By the 1970s, however, the negative impacts of poorly regulated tourism became more obvious prompting widespread criticism of the sector and the emergence of a *cautionary platform.* Along with the Caribbean, the South Pacific emerged as a focal point of this critique, with references to tourism as a 'new kind of sugar' and a 'pleasure plantation' (see, for example, Finney and Watson, 1975; Britton, 1980). The well-known and often-tested destination life cycle model of Butler, (1980), which foresees stagnation and decline as the likely outcomes of unregulated tourism development, may be seen as the culmination of the cautionary platform.

Actual attempts to put forward more benign models of tourism development are associated with the era of the *adaptancy platform* in the 1980s, which gave rise to supposedly more appropriate options such as alternative 'tourism', 'ecotourism' and, of course, 'sustainable tourism'. Explicit within this platform was the view that mass tourism was inherently bad and smallscale alternative tourism (*i.e.,* tourism that is deliberately structured to contrast with conventional mass tourism) inherently good for small underdeveloped Pacific and Caribbean islands in particular. Alternative tourism and ecotourism, therefore, were equated with sustainable tourism. This perspective is now being challenged by the *knowledge-based platform,* which espouses a less ideological and more scientific perspective toward tourism (though adoption of a scientific approach may itself be seen as an ideological decision). From this platform, mass tourism and alternative tourism can *both* be either sustainable or unsustainable, depending on the circumstances that pertain to any particular destination (Weaver, 2000).

Sustainable Tourism in the South Pacific

Since the early 1990s, virtually all South Pacific destinations have declared their interest in, and commitment to, sustainable tourism. Many planners and academics still adhere to the pro-alternative tourism biases of the adaptancy platform and argue that this is the only means for attaining sustainable tourism development in the region. Yet, by disassociating scale from sustainability, the knowledge-based platform holds that the attainment of sustainability does not necessarily depend on adherence to alternative tourism. Moreover, it has been argued that conventional mass tourism, in theory, confers sustainability-related advantages of scale that are not possible in alternative tourism (see, for example, Clarke, 1997). Intensity is used in this section as a criterion for placing South Pacific countries and dependencies into categories for discussion purposes, but given the above debate, no assumptions are made as to the advantages of high or low intensity relative to the attainment of sustainable outcomes. Rather, the evidence from the destinations themselves will be used to make such assessments. For classification and discussion purposes 'intensity' is constructed as a variable that arises from different combinations of absolute and relative criteria. The total number of inbound stayover arrivals represents the former while the latter is represented by the stayover / resident ratio. Of course, these are not perfect criteria since, amongst other reasons, returning former residents (who comprise a high proportion of stayover arrivals in destinations such as Tonga and Niue) are likely to stay in 'local' areas and blend into the local community, thereby not contributing to an obvious intensification effect. Cruiseship excursionists are omitted since this subsector occupies a relatively minor role in the region. Rankings of the listed destinations for both variables revealed gaps in the data that provide a logical basis for separating 'high' from 'low' intensity destinations. In both cases, the gap occurred between French Polynesia (188300 arrivals and a ratio of 0.79) and New Caledonia (103 800 and 0.53) (Table 8.2).

Classified accordingly, the destinations fall into four possible categories : low traffic / low ratio (LL), low traffic / high ratio (LH), high traffic / low ratio (HL), and high traffic / high ratio (HH) (Table 8.2). Although all destinations, and especially the archipelagic states, have significant internal variations in the intensity of tourism, there are several reasons for basing classification on the entire state or dependency. Firstly, it is usually difficult to obtain even the basic tourism data (except perhaps for accommodation) at the sub-national level. Secondly, it is not clear at what sub-national scale the classification should be made if this approach is adopted, since individual peripheral islands of a state may themselves display significant internal variations. Thirdly, whatever the internal differences, all regions and people within a single state or dependency are commonly affected in same ways by the national tourism industry, through the right to move internally in order to obtain employment, and through the dissemination of benefits resulting revenues. Though rejected as a basis for classification, internal variations nevertheless will still be recognized and taken into account, particularly in the section where options are discussed.

Low Traffic/Low Ratio (LL) Destinations

Low intensity destinations account for a clear majority of South Pacific states and dependencies, with several, such as the Pitcairn Islands and Tokelau, having virtually no tourist arrivals or facilities at all (Tokelau Apia Liaison Office, Samoa, personal communication, 1997). For those with at least some level of tourism development, the evidence does not always point towards sustainable practice or outcomes. The colonial heritage of most islands and the concomitant positioning of 'local' expatriates in positions of influence, for example, resulted in the marginalization of indigenous people during the 'involvement' phase of the tourism cycle throughout Melanesia (Douglas, 1997). This trend was, and still is, exacerbated by the lack of skilled locals in countries such as Tuvalu or Palau that have fewer people than a small English country town. A very similar situation pertained to other colonized small islands outside of the Pacific, such as the Caribbean islands of Antigua (Weaver, 1998). The situation has improved somewhat in the post-independence era, though business owned by ni-Vanuatu (native people of Vanuatu) still accounted for less than 10 per cent of total expenditure within Vanuatu's accommodation sector during the mid-1990s (Milne, 1997).

The alleged dispersal of the tourism sector during the early stages of the cycles is often deemed to be congruent with sustainable tourism in that the resultant benefits are more accessible to a wider sector of the local population. Moreover, carrying capacities are not unduly stressed by over-concentrations of activity within specific tourism districts. Again, the evidence from the LL destinations is contrary, as urban areas are substantially over-represented as locations for tourist accommodation. On Pohnpei (a Federated State of Micronesia), virtually all hotels are located in the capital city of Kolonia (Dahl, 1993), while almost two-thirds of registered accommodation in Papua New Guinea is found in the three largest urban centres (PNG Tourism Promotion Authority, personal communication, 1997). This pattern owes to a combination of factors, including prevalence of business-related tourism, the concentration of functions and services in urban areas, and the status of capital cities as international and internal gateways. Such concentrations, however, cannot automatically be considered unsustainable. Unlike beach environments, urban areas already accomodate a broad array of high-density activity within a highly modified and relatively cosmopolitan environment that usually has the infrastructural capacity to cope with this level of activity.

The Butler-type resort cycle implies that negative sociocultural outcomes are liable to occur as a function of increased tourism development. However, problems such as a pronounced demonstration effect, the commoditization of local culture and the entrenchment of the power and wealth of the local 'Big Men' are already apparent in incipient destinations such as the Solomon Islands (Lipscomb, 1998). The burning of Anuha Resort in 1988 by customary Solomon Islands landowners, though cited as an isolated event, is indicative of the resident antagonism that might be expected to result in the later, not earlier, stages of tourism development (Douglas, 1997). Similar negative sociocultural developments occurred in Tonga as early as the 1970s (Urbanowicz, 1989), while inter-clan rivalries in the Tufi region of Papua New Guinea occurred because of tourism in the early 'involvement' stages of tourism development (Ranck, 1987). These examples are not meant to suggest that attitudes towards tourism in all LL destinations are antagonistic or that all of the affected cultures and societies are being undermined. Rather, they indicate that such destinations are not immune to negative outcomes just because tourism is relatively undeveloped and smallscale, or 'alternative'. The sustainability of tourism at this incipient stage can also be negatively affected by external factors such as logging, which in the Solomon Islands is estimated to be undertaken at a level three times in excess of a sustainable harvest (Lipscomb, 1998). In Nauru, environmental problems focus around the mining-related devastation that has affected almost the entire interior of the island (Fagence, 1999). An additional dissuasive factor for tourism development in the Solomon Islands was the outbreak of civil war in 2000 and the concomitant descent into political and social anarchy. Whether environmental or sociopolitical, such hostile external environments could ensure that the destination does not progress beyond tourism incipience within the foreseeable future.

Substantial fluctuations in the level of tourist arrivals are often seen as conflicting with sustainability, yet characterize many LL destinations simply because a small drop in arrivals can translate into a large relative decrease when the overall visitor base numbers are low. In Tonga, the lowest visitation month (1600 in February, as a five-year mean from 1991 to 1995) is just 45 per cent of the peak month of December (3579) (TVB, 1996). For Vanuatu, the same calculation revealed a figure of 54 per cent for 1996 (2639 in February, 4813 in September) (Statistics Office, 1997). Such variations are partly climate-related, but also reflect the large impacts exercised by specific events, such as a monopolistic airline's decision to reduce flight frequency, on small volumes of traffic. As a result, LL destinations tend to experience high levels of vulnerability and uncertainty in their visitor flows, for reasons other than seasonality. Exacerbating this vulnerability is a common dependency on a small number of tourist markets. For example, the two principal markets in Tonga accounted for 53 per cent of all stayover arrivals in 1995, while the equivalent statistic for Vanuatu was 70 per cent in 1996 (with Australia also contributing 58 per cent).

Low Traffic/High Ratio (LH) Destinations

Low traffic/high ratio destinations receive small absolute

numbers of tourists in relation to the threshold established above, but still produce relatively large tourist/ resident ratios because of the small local population. The Cook Islands, Niue, Norfolk Island and Palau are four South Pacific destinations that fell into this category. In all four cases, the tourist/ resident ratio exceeds 1.0, and at least 10 per cent of GDP is represented by tourism. The Cook Islands is one of the most tourism-dependent LH destinations and resembles a more intensively developed destination as well from the perspective of foreign participation. External interests control just over half (50.6 per cent)of accommodation rooms, with the proportion increasing to 58 per cent on the main island of Rarotonga. One surprising development, however, is the decline of market concentration as the destination has become more developed. Contrary to the expectations of the destination life cycle, the dependency of the Cook Islands on its primary market (New Zealand) has actually declined from 55.7 per cent to 21.8 per cent between 1979 and 1995, largely as a result of growth in Asian origin regions (Burridge and Milne, 1996). The tourism sector of Niue, in contrast, is marked by extremes in market dependency and fluctuation. In 1995, New Zealand supplied 83.5 per cent of all arrivals. The number of visitors during the lowest month of that year represented only 20 per cent of the traffic arriving in the busiest month (80 versus 410 visitors) (UNDP, 1997).

High Traffic Low/Ratio (HL) Destination

Fiji is the only South Pacific destination where a large absolute number of stayover arrivals is offset by a low tourist / resident ratio, owing to the country's relatively large resident population. Such generalizations, however, mask the actual complexity of the Fijian tourism sector, which ranges from mass resort tourism along some coastal areas of Viti Levu to exclusive resort island tourism, urban tourism (in Suva) and village-based ecotourism. Segmented in this way, all categories are represented in Fiji, and it is fair to characterize this destination as a microcosm of South Pacific tourism in general. Like the Cook Islands, inbound markets are becoming more rather than less diverse, with the two primary markets accounting for 57.2 percent and 41.8 per cent of all stayovers in 1980 and 1993, respectively (Lockhart and Chandra, 1997). Another departure from the usual social impact assumptions is the finding by King *et al.* (1993) that Fijians in the vicinity of Nadi, with its concentration of beach-based resorts, tended to express favourable attitudes about the tourism industry.

The small, exclusive resorts, usually located on small offshore islands, are also complex with respect to their relationship with sustainability. The Turtle Island Resort offers a case in point. On the one hand, this resort caters to a very wealthy elite (= a very strong wealth differential between host and guest), is owned by an expatriate American millionaire, and requires its employees to remain isolated from their families for extended periods of time. However, the Resort has also engaged in a major programme of vegetation rehabilitation on the island, provides almost 100 jobs, and has a strategy to encourage Fijian participation at the managerial level. It also uses solar power to provide much of its energy requirements, and has established an eye clinic and other medical services for the residents of the adjacent islands (Evanson, 1997; Harrison, 1997). At least in this case, the positive effects would seem to outweigh the negative impacts, although no generalizations about exclusive isolated resorts should follow. A more serious issue for Fijian tourism as a whole is chronic political instability, the latest crisis being the 2000 coup attempt by George Speight that resulted in a dramatic decline in visitor arrivals (Hing and Dimmock, 2001). Notably, Turtle Island was specifically targeted for takeover by indigenous Fijian coup supporters over issues of land rights, though the extent to which associated activism was legitimate or politically opportunistic is unclear (King and Berno, 2001).

High Traffic/High Ratio (HH) Destinations

Only two South Pacific destinations, Guam and the Northern Marianas, have large absolute number of tourist visitors and high tourist/resident ratios arising from low resident populations. In several superficial respects, both destinations conform to the more mature phases of the resort cycle. Market concentrations in Guam, for example, is indicated by Japan's 75 per cent share of stayovers, which increases to 89 per cent with the addition of Korea (GVB, 1997). The comparable statistic for the Northern Marianas is 85 per cent (62 per cent from Japan and 23 per cent from Korea) (MVB, 1997). Foreign participation in the tourism sector, another indicator of maturity according to Butler (1980), is also very high in both destinations, with fifteen of thirty hotels (with 50 percent of all rooms) in Guam having Japanese general managers (GVB, 1997). The same situation pertains to seven of the ten largest hotels in the Northern Marianas (MVB, 1997).

Structurally, hotel size and room inventories are the largest within the study region. The average hotel size in Guam is 253 rooms, and the island provided 7601 rooms in 1997 (GVB, 1997). The Northern Marianas contained 3847 hotel rooms in 1997, virtually all located on Saipan (MVB, 1997). While these figures already raise concerns because of the small physical size of each destination, further increases are likely. As of 1995, the number of hotels rooms approved by the government of Guam was equivalent to the total amount in existence or under construction at that time. If announced or potential rooms are added, the inventory could increase to over 26 000 rooms . Among the approved hotels are two that each provide over 1000 rooms (Marbo Cave Resort, at 1200, and Nansay Resort, at 1100) (GVB, 1997). The hotel sector in Guam, as in most intensive beach resorts, is highly concentrated, with 83 per cent of all rooms (and about one-half of all approved hotels) located along a short stretch of coastline at Tumon 'village' (GVB, 1997). However, an equally vigorous process of golf course expansion (Table 8.3) enhances the influence of tourism as a consumer of land. In Saipan, 69 per cent of all hotel rooms are located on a five-mile expanse of beach in the southwest of the island (MVB, 1997). While no statistics are available indicating the contribution of tourism to Guam's GDP, this can be inferred from employment data. Of 48980 jobs in total as of March 1997, 11892 (24 per cent)were directly related to tourism, and another 8766 (18 per cent) were indirectly related to tourism, for 20657 in total (42 per cent) (GVB, 1997). The resultant figure is not inconsistent with the GDP statistic for tourism in the Northern Marianas.

Clearly, the current and potential intensity levels of

tourism in the two HH destinations are impressive and of obvious concern to those wishing to develop a sustainable tourism industry, especially when other factors such as ownership and market concentration are taken into account. However, just as some of the characteristics of LL destinations do not appear coherent with sustainability, certain traits of the HH destinations appear compatible. With respect to seasonality, the lowest visitation month in Guam, calculated as a mean value from 1992 to 1996, is 78 per cent of the peak visitation month (April = 79 800; March = 101900). The low/high month ratio for Saipan is a similar 84 per cent (GVB, 1997; MVB, 1997). Resident reactions to tourism on Guam, as well, do not indicate antagonism. Although solicited from only one segment of the market, an exit survey of US visitor in December 1996 revealed 'friendliness and courteousness of the people of Guam' as the local attribute given the highest rating on a Liker-type scale (6.1 of 7.0) (GVB, 1996). As for the physical carrying capacity of the island, high concentrations of tourism facilities and large hotel complexes may compensate in some degree for their obvious local stresses (high traffic, 'heat island' effect, induced housing development for hotel workers, etc.) in several ways. These include the provision of 'economics of scale' that allow for the effective management of waste, and the minimization of space required to house the tourist population (*i.e.,* upward instead of outward, and in one small area instead of distributed throughout the island). A strong tourism industry may also in theory possess lobbying capabilities that prevent competing resource stakeholders (*e.g.,* fishing and agriculture) from undertaking activities that undermine the attractiveness of tourism resources.

Tourism Options

The South Pacific tourism industry can be summarized as highly skewed, with most destinations being characterized by low visitor numbers and low tourist / resident ratios. Only two destinations exhibit the opposite tendency. Intensity, however, is clearly no a priori indicator of sustainability. Low visitation levels are inherently vulnerable to extreme fluctuation, and tourism, even in its incipient stages, is inevitably influenced in a negative way by the MIRAB syndrome and by longstanding patterns of dependency with 'mother' countries. Islands with low levels of tourism development, moreover, tend to possess rudimentary infrastructure that equates with low carrying capacity and subsequent threats to environmental sustainability despite small visitor intakes. That low intensity tourism does not automatically equate with sustainable tourism, therefore, should come as not surprise. The question of sustainability will always be mediated by the realities of the small island syndrome of underdeveloped and by a longstanding regional history of acculturation, sociopolitical instability, and environmental degradation.

Sustainable Mass Tourism

If this impeding impact of the small island syndrome is granted, then the pursuit of higher intensity tourism may be a rational option for some South Pacific destinations or portions thereof, since there is often no 'unspoiled paradise' to be undermined by the development of mass tourism. To the contrary, it is the more tourism intensive destinations that display higher prosperity levels on the basis of per capita GDP (allowing for anomalies such as the phosphate producing country of Nauru) (Europa World Year Book, 1997). This endorsement,, however, is not unconditional, and supposes that intensive tourism is not appropriate in all locations and that its implementation be carefully regulated so as to minimize any further disruptions to the destination's economy, culture or physical environment. Preferably, the onus should also be placed on the various stakeholders, and on large corporations in particular, to contribute to the gradual amelioration of these disrupted sectors and spaces. Such could be a pre-condition for anyone, local or expatriate, for obtaining permission to establish tourism-related facilities.

Deliberate 'Alternative Tourism' (DAT)

Although tourism scenarios are continuous in nature with respect to their intensity, it is still useful for conceptual purposes to contrast 'mass tourism' with 'alternative tourism' as ideal types situated at either end of the tourism spectrum (Weaver, 2000). Alternative tourism, as described above, was conceived in the early 1980s as a mode of tourism deliberately structured to contrast with the supposedly unsustainable characteristics conventional mass tourism. Accordingly, it was ideally characterized among other things by smallscale, local control, architecture that is congruent with the local culture and physical environment, and inter-actions with locals that are equitable and mutually supportive (Dernoi, 1981). A particular destination scenario can be said to gravitate, to a greater or lesser extent, toward one local type (*i.e.*, alternative tourism) or the other (*i.e.*, unsustainable mass tourism). At the less intensive end of the spectrum, most South Pacific destinations resemble 'alternative tourism' in at least some respects, though patterns of ownership, imports, market concentration and seasonality more typical of intensive destinations have already been identified. Clearly, the resemblance to alternative tourism in most of these destinations is superficial, as there is seldom any regulatory environment in place to ensure, as far as possible, that principles of local participation, environmental sustainability, etc., are followed. These places, essentially are merely in the early stage of the (modified small island) destination life cycle and accordingly can be described as circumstantial alternative tourism (CAT) destinations (Weaver, 1991,2000). This would seem to apply, for example, to Papua New Guinea, where 85 per cent of the 14000 short-term visitor arrivals in 1995 had visited nature-based attractions (PNG Tourism Promotion Authority, personal communication, 1997), but where little exists in the way of a formal ecotourism structure that adheres to core criteria of nature-focused attractions, learning outcomes, and sustainability (Blamey, 2001).

Several scenarios are possible for CAT destinations. In most instances, they will remain as such because there is no demand for any further tourism-related development, or such development is impractical due to inaccessibility or other factors. A second possibility sees these destinations following the S-curve trajectory that characterizes the Butler-type destination life cycle. A third scenario is the 'instant resort' phenomenon, wherein the area is earmarked for planned largescale resort development (*e.g.*, Cancun in Mexico). In both cases, a very rapid transition from LL status to LH or HH status is possible because of the small resident population. A fourth scenario entails the establishment of a regulatory environment that steers the destination toward the principles of alternative (and hence smallscale sustainable) tourism. Places that adopt this approach can be described as *deliberate* alternative tourism (DAT) destinations. Such a strategy is implicit in the planning of many South Pacific destinations. Applied at the sub-national level, such as in mountainous interiors or peripheral islands, it may be designated as a *regional* (DAT) strategy (or R-DAT). Applied to an entire country or dependency, the term *comprehensive* DAT (C-DAT) may be employed, as discussed in the following sub-section.

Comprehensive DAT (C-DAT) Destinations

C-DAT destinations are rare, although Dominica Bhutan would probably qualify if a global survey were to be conducted (Weaver, 1998). In the study region emergent C-DAT destinations include the Federated Micronesian State of Pohnpei, whose apparent pursuit of an environmentally sound, ecotourism-style policy (Office of Tourism & Parks, Pohnpei, personal communication, 1997), it should be noted, is motivated by the lack of beaches capable of supporting mass tourism. Nevertheless, pressure to pursue mass tourism is arising from concerns, over the impending termination of special post-independence financial aid from the US government, and from calculations revealing that an annual visitor intake of 50000 is necessary to compensate for the loss of those funding revenues (Dahl, 1993).

The Niue Strategic Development Plan identifies tourism as the sector with the greatest potential to facilitate sustainable development. A village-based strategy is being proposed as the centrepiece of a policy to 'develop a sustainable tourism sector whose activities are compatible with Niue's unique environment and culture, which are the country's principal tourist attractions' (UNDP, 1997). Tourism on Niue thus far is not seen as involving any substantial negative environmental or sociocultural impacts (De Haas and Cukier, 2000). Samoa is somewhat more evolved in the C-DAT direction, having already established such relevant mechanisms as the National Ecotourism Programme and the Samoan Ecotourism Network (Weaver, 1998; Zeppel, 1998).

Regional DAT (R-DAT) Destinations

Several larger South Pacific destinations are initiating strategies that explicitly recognize a role for both mass tourism and deliberate alternative tourism. For example, Vanuatu's Tourist Development Master Plan emphasizes a hierarchical spatial structure of 'Primary' tourist destinations (international / regional gateway and port, larger volume of visitation) and 'Longer Term' tourist destinations. The latter are characterized by local or regional airports, limited infrastructure, smallscale tourist facilities, retained local customs and village lifestyles, and controlled visitation to environmentally and culturally sensitive areas. The latter tend to involve the smaller peripheral islands (McVey, 1995; UNDP, 1995).

In Fiji, the R-DAT concept has long implicit in an 'islands policy' that discourages largescale tourism, in peripheral island locations, a concept that has also been practised in Bahamas with respect to the 'Family Islands' relative to Grand Bahama and Nassau, and in Trinidad relative to Tobago. While 'tourist resort islands' (such as Turtle Island Resort) are one option, most of these areas are designated as 'local subsistence islands' where 'only smallscale development will be permitted' (Lockhart and Chandra, 1997; 308-9). In contrast, large/scale tourism is being fostered in certain districts of the main island, including the Coral Coast and Nadi. Other districts of this island, particularly in the interior, are focusing upon alternative tourism and smallscale ecotourism in particular. One example among several is occurring at Abaca village in the Koronayitu forest of western Viti Levu. Its establishment in the early 1990s coincided with the formation of a national park in the areas. Abaca village initially constructed a traditional lodge to accommodate twelve visitors, and in 1993, the Abaca Ecotourism Co-operative Society Limited was registered to formalize the participation and ownership structure of the venture. Subsequently, another village was added to the scheme, and others have expressed an interest in joining. Each participating village is expected to dedicate a portions of their communal land to the national park, and I then entitled to hold shares in a company which promotes ecotourism in the area. In addition to the ecotourism revenues, tangible benefits to Abaca so far have included the formation of a medicinal plan arboretum, a tree seeding nursery, and the use of the tourism vehicle to transport children to school (Gilbert, 1997).

Part if the success of the Abaca venture is attributed to the village's proximity to the concentration of tourism activity at Nadi, and its subsequent linkages with the mass tourism sector of that area. According to Harrison and Brandt (1997), the cultivation of such opportunities as the 'add-on' to the mainstay resort product has long been a feature of the Fijian tourism sector. More recently, such relationships in Fiji and elsewhere are being formally recognized and promoted as a matter of mutual advantage to both types of tourism. Thus, the ideal outcome of the R-DAT strategy is the creation of synergies and symbioses between alternative and mass tourism, a possibility that is supported by Ayala (1996), Milne (1997) and Weaver (1998, 2001), amongst others.

Conclusion

Evidence from the diverse array of South Pacific tourist destinations suggests little or no correlation between scale of intensity and the presence of 'sustainable tourism'. Rather, the apparent presence or absence of sustainability, or indications of same, is dependent upon the unique circumstances that pertain to any given destination and the management responses that are made to these circumstances. Accordingly, there is no basis for supporting that tourism in intensively developed Saipan of Guam is any less sustainable than the incipient sector that characterizes Tuvalu or the Wallis and Futuna Islands, where government, infrastructure and society in general are ill-equipped to cope with even a small increase in arrivals. Complicating the issue of sustainability is the possibility that a destination may indicate this trait in some characteristics (*e.g.*, is environmentally sound) but not others (*e.g.*, is not locally controlled), thereby raising the question as to whether the destination is 'sustainable' in an overall sense.

Moreover, a characteristic that appears unsustainable in itself may have sustainable consequences. For example, the transformation of land of Guam to golf courses is associated with environmental problems and the loss of agricultural self-sufficiency. However, these golf courses may generate enough revenue to allow the importation of diverse foodstuffs and to facilitate remedial environmental measures. Increased importation of food, in turn, might increase dependency, though the alternative to dependency may be abject poverty. Similarly, the concentration of tourism within a small area of Saipan (a characteristic of destination life cycle maturity that is usually regarded as negative) reduces the need for sprawling tourism facilities in other parts of the island. Concurrently, it offers conditions conducive to cost-effective and environmentally beneficial site hardening, such as the installation of tertiary sewage treatment that depends upon high volumes of waste production.

An equally important issue is whether the concept of sustainability, and concomitant planning options as described above, can be seriously considered from a single-sector perspective. Various external environments over which tourism exercises little or no influence profoundly affect this sector in a direct or indirect way. The MIRAB syndrome is especially relevant to the South Pacific as is, unfortunately, the apparent increase in political instability and environmental degradation. Thus, for example, while deliberate alternative tourism appears to be emerging in the Solomon Islands, any judgments about its sustainability and longevity are rendered effectively meaningless by the fact that civil war and rapacious logging practices make most human activity in the Solomon Islands as a whole unsustainable. Adding to this uncertain environment, and especially relevant to South Pacific coastal areas and atoll-dominated countries such as Tuvalu an Kiribati, are the looming threats of rising sea levels and more numerous cyclones due to global warming. Whether sustainable mass tourism or deliberate alternative tourism is advocated for a particular South Pacific destination, the isolationist approach that typifies much planning and academic writing in the sector should therefore be rejected. The existing or potential impacts of these external environments must be taken into account when considering and implementing the options described above. Indeed, it can be argued that external environments are an omnipresent shadow theme that cannot be divorced from any considerations pertaining to sustainable tourism. In such a contex, it is unlikely that any mode of tourism development, no matter how sustainable in itself, will serve on its own as a panacea for the persistent problems of South Pacific destinations.

References

1. Ayala, H. (1996) : Resort Ecotourism : a paradigm for the 21st century, *Cornell Hotel and Restaurant Administration Quarterly*, **37 (5)** : 46-53.
2. Bertram, I. and Watters, R. (1985) : The MIRAB economy in South Pacific Microstates, *Pacific Viewpoint*, **27** : 497-520.
3. Blamey, R. (2001) : Principles of Ecotourism, In Weaver, D.B. (ed.), *Encyclopedia of Ecotourism*. Wallingford, UK : CAB International, pp. 5-22.
4. Britton, S.G. (1980) : A Conceptual Model of Tourism in a Peripheral Economy. In Pearce, D.G. (ed.), Tourism in the South Pacific : The contribution of research to development and planning. Proceeding of UNESCO Tourism Workshop, Rarotonga, June 10-13, pp. 1-12.
5. Burridge, K. and Milne, S. (1996) : Tourism, Development and the Travel Distribution System : The Case of the Cook Islands. Paper presented at Pacific Rim 2000, Rotorua, New Zealand, 4 November.
6. Butler, R. (1980) : The concept of a tourist area cycle of evolution : implications for management of resources. *Canadian Geographer*, **24** : 5-12.
7. Clarke, J. (1997) : A Framework of Approaches to Sustainable Tourism. *Journal of Sustainable Tourism*, **5** : 224-233.
8. Craig-Smith, S. and Fagence, M. (1994) : A critique of tourism planning in the Pacific, In Cooper, C. and Lockwood, A. (eds) *Progress in Tourism, Recreation and Hospitality Management*, Volume 6. Chichester, UK : Wiley, pp. 92-110.
9. Dahl, C. (1993) : Tourism Development on the Island of

Pohnpei (Federated States of Micronesia) : Sacredness, Control and Autonomy. *Ocean & Coastal Management,* **20** : 241-65.

10. De Haas, H. and Cukier, J. (2000) : Smallscale tourism and sustainability in Niue, *Pacific Tourism Review,* **4** : 1-6.
11. Dernoi, L.A. (1981) : Alternative Tourism : Towards a New Style in North-South Relations, *International Journal of Tourism Management*, **2** : 25-64.
12. Douglas, N. (1997) : Applying the Life Cycle Model to Melanesia, *Annats of Tourism Research,* **24** : 1-22.
13. Evanson, B. (1997) : The Unique Turtle Island Experience. Paper presented at the Eighth Pacific Science Inter-Congress, July 17.
14. Fagence, M. (1999) : Tourism as a Feasible Option for Sustainable Development in Small Island Developing States (SIDS) : Nauru as a Case Study, *Pacific Tourism Review,* **3** : 133-42.
15. Finney, B. and Watson, K. (1975) : *A New Kind of Sugar : Tourism in the Pacific,* Honolulu : East-West Centre.
16. Gilbert, J. (1997) : *Ecotourism means Business.* Wellington, New Zealand : GP Publications.
17. GVB (1995) : 1995 *Visitor Accommodations & Golf Course Plant Inventory.* Agana : Guam Visitors Bureau.
18. GVB. (1996) : *US Exit Survey December 1996 : Summary of Principal Findings.* Agana : Guam Visitors Bureau, Research Department.
19. GVB (1997) : Miscellaneous Tourism Statistics. Agana : Guam Visitors Bureau.
20. Harrison, D. (1997) : Globalization and Tourism : Some Themes From Fiji. In Oppermann, M. (ed.) *Pacific Rim Tourism.* Wallingford, UK : CAB International, pp, 167-83.
21. Harrison, D. and Brandt, J. (1997) : Ecotourism in Fiji : Making sense of the Muddle? Paper presented at the Eighth Pacific Science Inter-Congress, July 13-19.
22. Hing, N. and Dimmock, K. (2001) : A Fractured Paradise : Discussion of Issues Surrounding Fiji's 2000 Coup d'Etat

and Their Impacts on Tourism. Paper presented at the 2001 CAUTHE. National Research Conference, February 7-10.

23. Jafari, J. (1989) : An English language literature review. In Bystrzanowski, J. (ed.), *Tourism as a Factor of Change : a Sociocultrual Study. Vienna* : Centre for Research and Documentation in Social Sciences, pp. 17-60.

24. King, B. and Berno, T. (2001) : Trouble in Paradise Managing Tourism after the coups in Fiji, Paper presented at the 2001 CAUTHE National Research Conference, February 7-10.

25. King, B., Pizam, A. and Milman, A. (1993) : Social Impacts of Tourism : Host Perceptions, *Annals of Tourism Research,* **20** : 650-5.

26. Krausse, G. (1995) : Sustainable tourism for remote atolls in the Pacific. *International Journal of Sustainable Development and World Ecology,* **20** : 166-81.

27. Lipscomb, A. (1998) : Village-Based Tourism in the Solomon Islands : Impediments and Impacts. In Laws, E., Faulkner, B. and Moscardo, G. (eds) *Embracing and Managing Change in Tourism : A Case Book,* London : Routledge, pp. 185-201.

28. Lockhart, D. and Chandra, R. (1997) : Fiji : crossroads of the South Pacific. In Lockhart, D. and Drakakis-Smith, D. (eds) *Island Tourism : Trends and Prospects*, London : Pinter, pp. 302-1.

29. McKnight, T.L. (1995) : Oceania : *The Geography of Australia, New Zealand and the Pacific Islands*, Englewood Cliffs, NJ, USA : Prentice Hall.

30. McVey, M. (1995) : *Vanuatu : Tourism Sector Review,* Tourism Council of the South Pacific.

31. Milne, S. (1997) : Tourism, dependency and South Pacific Microstates : beyond the vicious cycle? In Lockhart, D. and Drakakis Smith, D. (eds) *Island Tourism : Trends and Prospects.* London : Pinter, pp. 281-301.

32. MVB. (1997) : *Hotels & Motels in the CNMI as of February 4, 1997.* Saipan : Marianas Visitors Bureau.

33. MVB. (1998) Miscellaneous Statistics. Saipan : Marianas Visitors Bureau.

34. Ranck, S. (1987) An Attempt at Autonomous Development : The Case of the Tufi Guest Houses, Papua New Guinea. In Britton, S. and Clarke, W. (eds) *Ambiguous Alternative : Tourism in Small Developing Countries*. Suva, Fiji : University of the South Pacific, pp. 154-66.
35. Statistics Office (1997) Vanuatu. Miscellaneous Tourism Statistics. Port Vila.
36. TVB (1996) : *Visitors Statistics 1995*. Nuku' alofa : Tonga Visitors Bureau, Research & Statistical Section.
37. UNDP (1995) : *Tourism Development Master Plan* (Vanuatu). United Nations Development Programme and World Tourism Organization.
38. Urbanowicz, C. (1989) : Tourism in Tonga Revisited : Continued Troubled Times? In : Smith, V. (ed.) *Hosts and Guests : The Anthropology of Tourism*. Second Edition, Philadelphia : University of Pennsylvania Press, pp. 105-17.
39. Urbanowicz, C. (1997) : *Tourism and Private Sector Development Programme, Niue : Final Report*. United Nations Development Programme and World Tourism Organization.
40. Weaver, D. (1988) : The Evolution of a 'Plantation' Tourism Landscape on the Caribbean Island of Antigua. *Tijdschrift voor Economishce en Sociale Geografie* **79** : 319-31.
41. Weaver, D. (1991) : Alternative to Mass Tourism in Dominica. *Annals of Tourism Research* **18** : 414-32.
42. Weaver, D. (1998) : *Ecotourism in the Less Developed World*. Wallingford, UK : CAB International.
43. Weaver, D, (2000) : A Broad Context Model of Destination Development Scenarios, *Tourism Management*, **21** : 217-24.
44. Weaver, D. (2001) *Ecotourism*, Brisbane : John Wiley & Sons.
45. WTO (1997) Yearbook of Tourism Statistics. Volume 1. 49th edn. Madrid : World Tourism Organization.
46. Zeppel, H. (1998) : Land and Culture : Sustainable Tourism and Indigenous People. In Hall, M.C. and Lew, A. (eds) *Sustainable Tourism : A Geographical Perspective*. Harlow, UK : Longman, pp. 60-74.

9 Mekong Tourism

Introduction

The Mekong River basin area with its peculiar history and great political, economic and social differences (the Mekong sub-region comprises Burma, Cambodia, Laos, Thailand, Vietnam and Yunnan in Southern China) is a region in which many of the issues and problems associated with tourism development can be observed. Until the 1980s, Thailand was the only country among the Mekong riparian states, which was fully integrated into the global capitalist system and had systematically developed a tourist industry to boost foreign exchange earnings and investment, as well as prestige in exchange for readily available cultural and natural resources. Over the last 20 years, tourist arrivals in Thailand have risen from one million to almost ten million annually.

Other Mekong countries remained more or less isolated form the rest of Southeast Asia after the Second World War because of post-colonial turmoil, the emergence of different political systems and American anti-communist warfare in Indochina. While Burma followed its own self-styled 'Burmese Path to Socialism', China—and later Laos, Cambodia and Vietnam-were part of the socialist block. Travel to, from and within these countries was restricted, and much of the poor tourism-related infrastructure dated back up colonial times.

With the collapse of the state socialist block in the late 1980s, all Mekong nations decided to reform their economies and boost tourism as an industry in the hope of quickly catching up with the Asian 'newly industrialized countries' (NICs). The growth of political and economic regionalism since the beginning of the 1990s has been vital for the emergence of several cooperation frameworks involving the Mekong Basin area, all of which prioritize the development of tourism and related infrastructure. Clearly, the recent tourism expansion into the Mekong sub-region has not happened incidentally or inevitably, but is the result of political will and substantial promotional efforts.

However, there is a clear tension in the Mekong Basin area between the requirement to meet the vast majority of the population who are poor and the prevailing policies of growth-driven economic development in the region. A central question is whether benefits from tourism can actually 'trickle down' and contribute to improve the living standard of disadvantaged social groups and indigenous peoples. Deprivation, uneven distribution of wealth, social inequalities and rapid depletion of natural resources, which set the stage for political, social, ethnic and ecological conflict, feature prominently in Mekong countries and make tourism a highly insecure industry.

Thailand has often been described as a negative tourism model because reckless development has resulted in the environmental degradation of many places, exacerbated economic inequalities and contributions to undesirable changes in society, such as the proliferation of the sex industry, AIDS, drug abuse, gambling, crime and cultural erosion. Government official and industry leaders framing the Mekong tourism development have acknowledged that the industry causes a plethora of problems and responded by incorporating the notions of 'sustainable tourism' into their policies and plans. They maintain that with improved planning and management, past mistakes can be avoided in new destinations.

Has a new era in tourism development begun that can reverse the negative trends so that Mekong's neighbouring countries will be spared from a tourism onslaught as experienced in Thailand? To answer this question, this chapter begins by examining regional tourism plans with a focus on the Greater Mekong Subregion (GMS) scheme initiated by the Asian Development Bank (ADB). The next section presents case studies that suggest that destructive tourism projects persist and are spreading throughout the Mekong basin area despite the constant rhetoric of sustainable tourism or ecotourism. Finally, the last section discusses the question of sustainability by taking into account some broader issues such as the impact of globalization and lessons learned from the Asian economic crisis. It will be argued that the often ill-defined and reductionist sustainable tourism policies need to be replaced by holistic and people-centred development initiatives, if the goal is to work towards a sustainable future.

Tourism and Regional Development

Over the last decade all Mekong countries, except China, have become members of the Association of Southeast Asian Nations (ASEAN). This grouping has forged transborder economic cooperation programme in the form of so-called 'growth triangles' with tourism development playing a prominent role. ASEAN even has its own Travel Association (ASEANTA) and declared 2002 as 'Visit ASEAN Year' under the theme 'ASEAN-Asia's Perfect 10 Paradise'. In 1996, ASEAN also set up its own working group on Mekong Basin Development Cooperation, with the major proposal under this initiative being the creation of a regional rail network for freight and passenger traffic, linking Singapore with Yunnan via Kuala Lumpur, Bangkok, Phnom Penh, Ho Chi Minh City and Hanoi.

The Mekong River Commission (MRC), under the auspices of the United Nations Development Programme (UNDP), has presented plans for the Mekong subregion, providing for 'economic growth together with environmental protection and cultural enrichment', which includes tourism and related infrastructure development (MRC, 1995).

Another initiative is the Quadrangle for Economic Cooperation (QEC) which emphasizes the improvement of land, water and air transport to promote tourism and trade. Formed in 1993 by a group of Thai business people and backed by influential Thai and Chinese politicians, the investors promoting QEC have been especially eager to win concessions and attract funds to build roads and to develop tourism projects in the border areas of Thailand, Laos, Burma and Yunnan. Their plans involve the establishment of hotels, resorts, casinos and shopping centres, as well as 'model cultural villages' catering to adventurous 'ecotourists'.

However, the most prominent framework and prime mover of Mekong tourism is the ADB's GMS scheme.

The GMS Tourism Programme

Since its formation in 1992, the GMS initiative has endorsed more than 100 development projects in the field of transport, energy, tourism, telecommunication, environment and human resource development. While seven priority projects are directly related to tourism, thirty-four projects pertain to road, railway, water and air transport, and more than fifty deal with hydro-electricity generation. The GMS tourism working group has successfully garnered support from governments, international development agencies, large industry associations, as well as corporations to promote the subregion as a single tourism market (ADB, 1996; PATA, 2001).

Apart from the ADB, representatives of the six Mekong countries' national tourism organizations (NTOs), international tourism associations such as the World Tourism Organization (WTO), the Pacific Asia Travel Association (PATA), ASEANTA, the UN Economic and Social Commission for Asia and the Pacific (ESCAP) and specialized UN agencies, have been involved in the GMS scheme. The Tourism Authority of Thailand (TAT), which has eagerly marketed Thailand as a 'gateway' to other Mekong countries, has also played a key role in the programme. Since 1996, TAT's office in Bangkok has accommodated the GMS tourism working group's secretariat known as the Agency for Coordinating Mekong Tourism Activities (AMTA).

Thailand also hosted the first Mekong Tourism Forum (MTF)—an annual event initiated by the GMS tourism working group—on the occasion of PATA's annual conference in Pattaya in April 1996. The MTF seeks possibilities to realize the 'Mekong Dream'—a concept designed by PATA to promote 'hassle-free' air and overland travel between Mekong countries since lack of accessibility, insufficient provisions for safety and difficult immigration regulations are seen by the industry as the main obstacles to regional tourism growth (Chandler, 1995). In addition, to raise market awareness of the subregion's tourism resources, a world-wide campaign was launched at the MTF 1996 event to promote thirty cultural and natural tourist sites as 'Jewels of the Mekong'.

While working towards the removal of all barriers to travel in the Mekong Basin area (including physical, economic, organizational and legal barriers) that have so far discouraged foreign visitors and investors, the GMS initiative has emphasized 'sustainable development' and 'ecotourism' as worthy goals.

The 'Concept Plan for tourism development in the Greater Mekong Subregion 1999-2018', outlines the GMS strategy for the next 20 years. The major goal is 'to consolidate a "Mekong" cultural tourism, ecotourism and adventure tourism network by linking destinations, circuits and roots' by the end of 2006. By 2018, it anticipates the GMS region will be 'one of the world's most important ecotourism and cultural tourism destinations' and 'a safe, accessible and "good value" (value for money) destination to experience the rich, natural, historical and cultural heritage of the peoples and places along and adjacent to the Mekong/Lancang River' (AMTA, 1998).

Whereas ecotourism has nurtured notions of smallscale and controlled development, this plan aims at luring millions of additional international visitors to the Mekong subregion. Moreover, the list of priority projects proposed in the study are in line with the ADB's GMS mega-infrastructure programme and reflect a heavy emphasis on improving transportation systems involving navigation, highway construction and air route expansion.

The study says 'In the long term, there will be emphasis on the creation of networks and gateways, transportation nodes and international standard facilities to accommodate all segments of the tourism market throughout the subregion' (AMTA, 1998). In other words, there will be a focus on ecotourism and other alternative tourism forms such as 'village tourism' as long as there are major bottlenecks in infrastructure, which restrict largescale tourism. Once all gates have been thrown open and the necessary facilities are in place, the plan is to tout for all shades of tourism, which ultimately means a shift to the development of main-stream mass tourism.

Meanwhile, it is widely acknowledged that the majority of the Bank's projects not only fail to meet standards but are responsible for severe impacts on local communities and the environment.

For instance, the ADB put forward a proposal in 1996 for conservation management in watershed areas which involves the gradual relocation of some 60 million mountain people in the subregion. This massive resettlement programme has been legitimated with the claim that the widespread practice of shifting cultivation is a major cause for environmental destruction. In addition, a countless number of people are likely to be displaced and lose their Traditional livelihoods by the Bank's more that fifty large dam projects.

According to ADB's belief, in the name of 'development' and 'poverty reduction', local communities should abandon their traditional self-reliant lifestyles and economic activities and turn to ecotourism as an alternative source of income in new locations. At the 9th Ministerial Meeting of the GMS Economic Cooperation Programme held in Manila in January 2000, Warren Evans, manager of the ADB's Environment Division, said 'We need to persuade hill communities that it's in their best interest to conserve rather than exploit natural resources by encouraging community participation in ventures such as ecotourism. They can discourage poachers and illegal loggers and operate sound tourist facilities'.

To introduce a comprehensive conservation programme that involves unprecedented mass evictions and inevitably degrades indigenous societies and cultures and then to offer tourism as compensation is certainly one of the deepest ironies manifest in the GMS scheme. Much more so as tourism studies reveal that only a tiny proportion of tourism income actually reaches villages. For instance, Mingma Norbu Sherpa, a Nepalese representing the Worldwide Fund for Nature (WWF) argued at the ADB's first 'pro-poor tourism seminar that in many cases, tourism's benefits do not make it to a country's outer reaches, even though those areas bear the impact of tourism. He cited Nepal's famous trekking areas as an example, where local people receive only 2 per cent of the tourism revenue.

Shivakumar, a development consultant based in Cambodia, concludes that the ADB and other donor agencies are primarily committed to creating a conducive environment for private corporations, rather than making a serious effort to lift weak and peripheral social groups out of poverty. In general, most projects developed by the donors, particularly the ADB and Japan, are capital-intensive while, at least in the short term, labour-intensive projects are needed in these nations to challenge poverty. They have not been able to propose a plan to combine simultaneously, in a balanced and mutually reinforcing manner, economic growth with welfare, empowerment, cultural renaissance, social transformation and sustainability. These observations lead one to conclude that reduction of poverty is not the priority of these projects. . .' (Shivakumar, 1997 : 11).

The following example will demonstrate how damaging tourism activities have proliferated throughout the Mekong subregion over the past decade and posed severe pressure on local people and the environment.

Real-Life Tourism Tales

(1) Mass 'Ecotourism'—Thai Style

The rapid growth of tourism in Thailand during the 1970s

and 1980s, particularly the upsurge of sex tourism, attracted severe criticism for its negative effects on Thai society.

The impact of mass tourism in Thailand on the local people, their culture, natural resources and built environment has been substantial. Two striking effects of over-zealous profit-oriented tourism development efforts have been : (1) the disproportionate shift of capital to mass tourism-related construction and real estate developments at the expense of other sectors such as agriculture and small industry which are locally oriented ; and (2) the promotion of over-consumption and excessive local resources with attendant new social and environmental pressures on local people and environments. (Pholpoke, 1998)

Coinciding with government and industry efforts to diversify Thailand's tourism products to shed its worsening image as a 'spoilt' destination, has been the growing interest in 'ecotourism'. Acknowledging that tourism in the past had caused severe damage, Seree Wangpaichitr, the former TAT Governor, said in an interview with the *Bangkok Post* in June 1998 : 'Ecotourism is the heart of long-term tourism development.' He further argued that the mass tourism promotion by the TAT is not incompatible with ecotourism : 'The strategy is to distribute the mass of tourism to a great number of places so that resources will not be over-exploited while distributing the economic benefits to the wider public'.

Unfortunately, Thailand has longstanding experience with the mismanagement of forests, beaches, marine areas and other natural assets, and many hotels, resorts and other facilities have encroached on officially 'protected areas'. Repeated attempts by the Tourism Authority of Thailand (TAT) and the Royal Forestry Department (RFD) to open up national parks to private tourism businesses have elicited great controversy. Since 1997, the RFD has worked on a proposal to grant leases to operators of illegal tourist facilities on resort islands—a highly disputed plan that is expected be approved by the government in the near future.

Many observers were amazed by the strong opposition of local residents and environmentalists towards the filming in 1999 of 20th Century Fox's movie 'The Beach', starring Leonardo DiCaprio, in Phi Phi Islands' National Park in Southern Thailand, which involved profound landscape changes at Maya Bay. But the protest actions and the related lawsuit filed by local government agencies and citizens against the film company and authorities, who gave permission to 're-design' to part of the park, need to be seen in the context of the fierce struggle for the protection and enforcement for Thailand's national park laws. Opponents repeatedly pointed out that 'The Beach' affair, which even led to an international boycott campaign against the Hollywood movie, was a precedence case, and the fight to save Maya Bay was not about just one island but about the fate of all parks in the country. The reason given by Thai officials for allowing the controversial film project to go ahead was to boost the country's tourism industry and income for local communities. But critics have warned that such incidents make a mockery of conservation efforts and the legal system, and set a bad example whereby commercialism can override any other issue in Thailand.

Indeed, the situation is worsening. Under the pretext of ecotourism promotion, the RFD has recently implemented massive tourism-related infrastructure projects–some involving logging operations—in parks countrywide, funded with loans from the World Bank and Japan. The frenzied construction of roads, parking lots, visitor centers, bungalows, camp sites and nature trails neatly coincided with the RFD's 'Visit National Park Year 2000' aimed at attracting more than 20 million domestic and international tourists to the parks during that year.

In Thailand, ecotourism development in nature reserves generally proceeds without the involvement of surrounding local communities in decision-making and without adequate discussion on who owns the land and natural resources, how land should be used, where and how tourist facilities should be built, visitor volume or regulations on tourist conduct; all of which has created and aggravated ecological problems and conflict between the government, private industry and communities. For instance, when the RFD proposed to increase the land area protected by national parks in northern Thailand a few years ago, some 10,000 people–primarily from ethnic minority groups—reflected the RFD's plans to evict, them from their lands and held street demonstrations in the city of Chiang Mai (Pleumarom, 1997/98).

The social injustice inherent in 'tourism-cum-conservation' projects is evident as they stop the access to land and natural resources of one social group—poor villagers who have often inhabited the area for generations–and open these areas for other groups–investors and paying ecotourists.

Whenever the Thai economy is in trouble, the government resorts to tourism as its saviour. With agriculture and industry staggering in the 1980s, it seized on services and declared 1987 'Visit Thailand Year'. Following the financial meltdown in 1997, the previous government of Chuan Leekpai responded with the 'Amazing Thailand' promotional campaign. Facing a new economic downturn, the present government, under Thaksin Shinawatra, vowed to boost foreign exchange earnings from tourism by 50 billion bath (US$1.1 billion) in 2001. The target required that the country attracted an additional 1.9 million foreign visitors. Under the new plan, many thousands of hitherto undeveloped villages were earmarked for 'community-based ecotourism' projects. In the interim, a well-formulated conservation policy to counter the impact of increased visitor volume and spatial expansion of tourism was conspicuously absent. This suggested that the country's natural resources will further be sacrificed for short-term economic gains.

(2) Golfers' Dream—a Farmer's Nightmare

Since the late 1980s, golf has been aggressively promoted as a lucrative tourism business. Starting out from Thailand, the gold course boom spread into other Mekong countries causing immense environmental and social conflicts.

In the late 1980s and early 1990s, some 200 courses were built in Thailand. The construction of golf complexes—often involving other largescale developments such as hotels, residential houses, shopping centres, entertainment facilities, power plants, access roads and even airports—came under heavy attack for environmental reasons. Many of the projects were accused of encroaching on parkland and driving off farmers from their land (Pleumarom, 1994).

Golf courses require large stretches of land and replace biodiversity-rich wilderness areas and fertile agricultural lands. Another major concern is the enormous waste of water resources for such projects. According to the Mahidol University in Bangkok, the turf of an 18-hole international standard golf course consumes up to 6500 cubic metres of water per day which is equal to the daily household demand of 6000 city residents or 60,000 villagers. While scarce water reserves are being diverted to keep the courses green, nearby communities are suffering due to the lack of drinking and irrigation water. In addition, the excessive application of chemical fertilizers and pesticides necessary to maintain the courses covered with foreign grass species threatens to pollute air, soil, and water, and create health risks for both wildlife and humans. Alarming reports were published in the Thai media about caddies and greenkeepers affected by acute chemical poisoning—*e.g.*, headache, nausea, respiratory illnesses and skin diseases.

In the southern Lao province Champasak, Thai investors had plans to build a mega-resort project, including golf courses, hotels, casinos, a power station and an international airport, in a pristine area at the famous Lee Pee waterfalls on the Mekong River. Although the developments promoted the resort as an 'ecotourism' venture, it was met with resistance by Lao and Thai environmentalists as well as local villagers because it would have involved deforestation, ecological disruption of the fragile Mekong river system, displacement of villagers, and probably undesirable social and cultural changes in nearby communities. Consequently, due to increasing public protests and financial difficulties the controversial project was halted.

Vietnam has also built a number golf courses to attract foreign tourists. Citizens protested when developers flattened a public forest in Thu Duc near Ho Chi Minh City for the construction of the Golf Vietnam Club. The Thai developers of the King's Island Golf Resort at the Dong Mo dam reservoir near Hanoi built a golf course at the edge of the lake below the reservoir's spill way level without considering rising water levels during the rainy season. During devastating floods in 1994, provincial officials allowed the release of large amounts of water from the reservoir to save the golf resort, which resulted in the destruction of the rice crops in neighbouring faring areas. Despite a 1995 governmental decree that prohibited converting more rice lands to other purposes, the South Korean conglomerate Daewoo received an investment license to build a gold course on the rice fields at Kim No village on the outskirts of Hanoi. Violence broke out at the construction site, when angry farmers, who had no been properly informed about the project, tried to stop an army unit from plowing up the land for golf course.

In Cambodia, several golf course projects surfaced around Phnom Penh, near the Angkor Wat temple complex, and in Sihanoukville as part of the huge Naga Island casino resort proposed by a Malaysian company. For the construction of the Singapore-financed Cambodian Country Club at the Bang To Yab Lake outside of Phnom Penh, the developer wanted to drain a large stretch of marshland and remove more than 450 families who lived beside the lake (mostly fruit and vegetable growers). But the villagers refused to leave and protested to the authorities who, in turn, treated them as illegal squatters and refused to compensate them.

In military-ruled Burma as well, golf courses have sprung up at tourist sites, including luxury golf-plus-casino resorts such as the Golden Paradise Resort near Tachilek in the Golden Triangle and Andaman Club on Thathay Kyun Island in the South. For the development of the Myanmar Golf Club in Rangoon, the army blockaded the site to scare off the people who had been living there for decades. When this failed, the government arrested one member of each family and sent them to jail. The remaining families were then moved against their will to a 'new town' far outside of the city.

(3) Cultural Heritage for Sale–the Case of Angkor Wat

In order to lure and entertain visitors, culture (as manifested in historical and religious sites, rituals, arts and crafts) has often been distorted beyond recognition in the process of being re-packaged as a tourist product. The famous twelfth century Angkor temple complex at Siem Reap—the most sacred site and national symbol of Cambodia-is a glaring example as to how culture heritage is no longer for local people to celebrate, but increasingly coommoditized to lure foreign visitors.

With the Cambodian government aiming for 1 million foreigners a year to visit Angkor Wat, grave concerns have been raised that the temple area and its surroundings could be destroyed within a few years. In 1995, UNESCO's World Heritage Committee even threatened to remove Angkor from the list of protected sites because Cambodian authorities had not met the necessary requirements such as adopting a cultural preservation law to deter the theft and smuggling of antiquities. Thousands of invaluable artifacts have been stolen from the temple complex since it has opened to tourists. The government has vowed to take precautionary measures to ensure that protection zones at the historical and religious sites are respected. But this may not be enough to save Angkor due to inefficient bureaucracy, corruption and the absence of a functioning legislature and sufficient capacities to scrutinize, monitor and control projects.

Conservationists in and outside Cambodia were particularly appalled at the proposal for a US$20 million Angkor Wat high-tech sound–and–light show saying it would turn the temples into a 'carnival-like attraction 'or a 'Disney-like inane entertainment place' In 1995, the Malaysian YTL company claimed it would promote 'the biggest and best cultural events of its kind in the world '. The plan was to stage up to four performances per night, inn which the temple as well as selected bas-relief carvings on, its inner wall s would be illuminated in lights and voices in different language be heard from loudspeakers. In Thailand where tourist shows at historical monuments have become common-place, such activities have provoked debates regarding the extent to which old, fragile buildings are damaged.

The YTL company had also wanted to develop a 1095-hactare sits near the northwestern temple into a tourism zone include several luxury hotels, golf courses, a commercial centre, a hospital and other facilities-a project which was expected to attract more than US$1 billion investment. In January 1996, even king Norodom Sihanouk voiced strong concern about the commercialization' of Angkor and pressed for a review of YTL's plans for the light-and-sound show and hotel and the tourism complex in the area. However, since Prime Minister Hun Sen.'s bloody coup against the co–Prime Minister Prince Norodom Ranariddh in July 1997, which resulted in a dramatic tourism slump in Cambodia, little has been hearted regarding YTL's Angkor show and accompanying developments.

In all-out effort to revive Cambodia, ruined tourism industry following the political turmoil, in 1999 the government adopted an 'open-skies ' policy to increase international flights Siem Reap, the gateway to the Angkor temples. Additionally, it organized an extravagant 'Angkor 2000' millennium show. Tourism officials ' hopes that the combination of direct flights from overseas and spectacular promotion events would make Angkor part of an international 'must-see' itinerary were being realized. In addition, the opening of new overland routes to Siem Reap from Thailand attracted more visitors and investors to the area and fuelled the construction of more tourism facilities around Angkor. As a results, renewed warnings of threats to the temples were been voiced in public, and there were growing worries that local people would be increasingly exposed to the effects of uncontrolled tourism.

(4) 'A Fascist Disneyland'—Tourism and Human Rights in Burma

In 1996 the Burmese military government, which has been

condemned by the international community because of its gross human rights violations, launched an ambitious tourism promotion campaign 'Visit Myanmar (Burma)Year'. The junta hoped to attract more than 250 000 foreign visitors to the country during 1996-97 to increase currency earnings and gain recognition in the international community after decades of isolation and a bloody military crackdown on the pro-democracy movement in 1998. while Burmese tourism authorities and the industry stepped up promotion to sell the country as the 'Golden Land', critics increasingly delivered descriptions of Burma as a 'prison' for its citizens and a 'fascist Disneyland' for visitors (Lawrence, 2001).

Insisting that, in a country where people are denied basic rights, tourism cannot benefit that country, Burmese opposition groups and international human rights organizations have called for a tourism boycott to Burma. Democracy leader and Peace Nobel Prize laureate Aung San Suu Kyi has repeatedly urged foreign investors and tourists to stay away from the country until democratic reforms have been achieved. The argument is that the income generated through tourism helps to sustain the oppressive regime and is spent on buying weapons and expanding military action against its citizens. Since every foreign visitor entering the country has to purchase foreign exchange certificates equivalent to US$200, and many tourist facilities are state-owned, a considerable proportion of tourist dollars goes directly into the junta's coffers. In addition, members of the military run their own tourism-related businesses or have formed joint ventures with private companies to increase their personal wealth and economic power (Lawrence, 2001).

The close links between the development of the tourist industry and human rights abuses have been well documented by official agencies such as the United Nations Human Rights Commission, the International Labour Organization (ILO) and Burmese and international civic groups.

Drawing on reports from Rangoon, Mandalay, Pagan, Taunggyi, Maymo and other places earmarked for tourism development, it is estimated that tens of thousands of families have been forcefully moved from their homes and land to pave the way for hotels, resorts and tourism-related infrastructure. Most of the displaced people do not receive any compensation and have to resettle in areas which lack proper sanitation, electricity and water supply. Equally deplorable is the fact that ordinary people are forced into providing their labour to upgrade tourist sites and to build roads, railways and airports, in order to meet the increased transportation requirements for travel and tourism.

Burma's ethnic minorities, who have already suffered for decades under forced assimilation policies by the state, are now being lured away from their villages to serve as 'exotic' attractions in hotels or so-called 'model villages'. In addition, thousands of Burmese women and girls, many of them from ethnic groups, have become victims of a burgeoning domestic sex trade and are being trafficked to Thailand to work as prostitutes.

That 'Visit Myanmar Year' turned out a failure can be partly attributed to the success of strong global movement against Burma's tourism policies. Since 1997 tourist numbers have plummeted as a result of the Asian economic crisis and increasing international sanctions against the county. During the fiscal year 1998-99, Burma attracted only 120 000 foreign visitors, less than half as many that year junta had expected when it announced its 1996 tourism campaign. Yet, Burmese officials remained optimistic and announced a new campaign aimed at increasing the number of tourists to Burma by ten times to 1 million in 2001.

Discussion : The Question of Sustainability

The above investigation on tourism policies and practices in the Mekong region reveals the vast gaps between 'sustainable tourism' as a theoretical ideal : what has been planned, and what has been actually achieved. The grim realities, as described in the various case studies, leave serious doubts as to whether tourism development can be propelled towards more sustainability in the long term.

This is not to say that initiatives that have successfully managed to avoid major damage by fostering community based and environmentally sound tourist activities do not exist. It also should not be denied that some tourism companies have taken positive voluntary measures to mitigate impacts such as pollution. However, such 'success stories' are limited to a few micro-projects, and they have certainly not posed a real challenge to the status quo or considerably contributed to the redirection of the tourism industry as a whole.

A hard look at the overall situation leads us to the conclusion that the policies pursued by governments, national tourism authorities and supernational bodies, such as the Asian Development Bank, for the development of Mekong tourism have been those most suitable for promoting the industry rather than for the protection of the environment and the benefit of local communities. Put simply, in the words of Wall, tourism promotion in Asia over the recent years 'has consumed massive amounts of capital and has failed to create a sustainable product. It appears that there has been an implicit belief that tourism development is about the construction of high quality hotels and that, once these are in place, all else will follow' (Wall, 1998).

Indeed, little has been done to develop effective mechanisms to monitor and control developments aimed at curbing environmental degradation, social and cultural erosion and economic marginalization of the poor. Management plans, if there any, are often ignored, and environmental, zoning and construction laws are not being properly enforced. Many critical tourism-related issues—such as corruption, social vices, encroachment of public lands and diversion of natural resources, displacement of local and indigenous communities, and political suppression and human rights abuses—are typically neglected by tourism policymakers and project managers. In the light of this, it is easy for critics to assert that 'sustainable tourism' in the Mekong region is little more than empty rhetoric and a public relations exercise to ward off public criticism.

What is it that makes it so difficult for tourism to deliver sustainable development, and why does there seem to be no prospect of significant positive change? Some explanations and aspects for further analysis will be provided in this last section.

Firstly, sustainable itself is not a fixed and agreed term, and thus is subject to interpretation. Associated with this are the various potential limitations of the concept that have been identified by various researchers. Wall (1997) notes that 'While [sustainable tourism] has drawn attention to the need to achieve a balance between business and environmental interests . . ., as a single-sector concept, it fails to acknowledge the intersectoral competition for resources, the resolution of which is crucial for sustainable development'. Addressing the issues of power and vested interest, Mowforth and Munt (1998) state that 'the principle of sustainable tourism are open to manipulation in the service of operators and others in the industry. That is not to say that the principles are not worthy of attention by all those in the industry; but it does suggest that the motives of those who apply them should also be scrutinized'. Finally, Wheeller (1997) contends, 'there are continual exhortations on the need to adopt a holistic approach to the subject of tourism development, planning and sustainability. . . A truly holistic approach would be one that embraces realism. Sustainable tourism unfortunately fails, at the practical level, even to acknowledge it.'

In fact, the planning for 'sustainable tourism' in the Mekong region has largely remained a theoretical exercise without sufficiently taking into account the milieu in which tourism is evolving. Therefore, Majone's argument is worth savouring : A practical problem is not solved by offering a theoretical solution that does not take into consideration the limitations upon which the context imposes. Thus, it is quite misleading to employ ideal standards in evaluating or comparing alternative policy instruments; the standards must relate to the particular context in which the instruments are used. And because the context in which public policy is made includes values, norms, perceptions, and ideologies, technical considerations are insufficient as a criteria of choice' (cited in Hall, 1994).

It is also important to note that the concept of 'sustainable tourism' is deeply rooted in Western environmentalism that often takes the form of 'enlightenment' and is dependent on achieving a certain level of prosperity and development. This, however, often appears to be at odds with the livelihood-based environmentalism in Southeast Asia and other parts of the Third World, where poor peasants and forest dwellers are struggling to defend and reclaim land an natural resources for economic and cultural survival (Hirsh and Warren, 1998). A better understanding of these contradictions may help to explain why so many ecotourism projects based on Western conservation ideals are resisted by local people and subsequently fail.

What is also often ignored is that globalization has induced its own particular political dynamics in the region, which are to the detriment of the commitment to achieve sustainable development. In this context, Parnwell's study on how Mekong tourism has become part of the global race-to-the-bottom is instructive (Parnwell, 1998). Highlighting examples of human rights violations in Burma, sex tourism and the HIV/AIDS crisis in Thailand, and the environmental impacts of golf tourism in the region, he argues 'the impact of tourism depends crucially upon the ownership of regulatory power' and explains how transnational agencies and corporations work through and with influential local actors and institutions—what he calls 'conduits of capitalism'. His conclusion is that regulation *for* the global tourism industry is taking precedence over the regulation *of* its development. As a result, local people and especially the poor and marginalized, are exposed to greater political, social, economic and ecological insecurity (ibid.).

Since in poor countries, especially, tourism's economic viability is seen as a prime criterion for sustainability, the old question of who actually benefits from tourism needs to be raised a new in the face to globalization and liberalization.

Third World tourism is mainly driven by foreign industry interests, and the economic gains for destination countries are often greatly overestimated.

A 1990 study on Thailand by the Bangkok-based National Institute and Development Administration, for example, came up with disillusioning results. At least 60 per cent of tourism revenue, amounting to US$4 billion in 1989, had been lost to 'leakage', being used for the import of goods and services and profits to foreign tourism corporations and other remittances (TDSC, 1991/92). A new study prepared by UNCIAD on the 'The Sustainability of International Tourism in Developing Countries' presents even more alarming findings (UNCTAD, 200). It emphasizes that the economic, social and environmental sustainability of Third World countries' tourism industries is increasingly threatened by levels of financial 'leakages' that can easily reach 75 per cent, and escalating 'predatory practices and anti-competitive behaviour' of travel and tourism corporations based mainly in Europe and the United States. The UNCTAD report further points out that the combined impact of these factors undermines the economic viability of local enterprises and the ability of countries to allocate necessary resources for environmental protection and sustainable development (ibid.). Under these conditions, the proclaimed goals of sustainable tourism to enhance local economic benefits and the preservation of natural and cultural resources are extremely difficult to achieve.

Important lessons regarding the fragility of the tourism industry can be learned form the Asian economic crisis that began in June 1997 with the financial meltdown in Thailand (Pleumarom, 1998; Wall, 1998). It showed how much tourism is part of the fickle global economy, as well as being an industry that undergoes boom-and-bust cycles with serious consequences for the stability of national and regional economies.

There is little doubt that the inflationary tourism policies in the Mekong subregion in the early 1990s greatly contributed to the 1997 'crash'. During the era of the so-called 'bubble economy', indiscriminate and unsustainable investments led to the rapid conversion of lands into opulent tourism resort complexes. With progressive economic liberalization, the tourism, real estate and construction industries boomed in all Mekong countries, backed by local banks and global speculative capital.

In the immediate aftermath of the economic slump, Asian tourism markets almost collapsed. In Thailand, the currency devalued and major corporations—many of whom had expanded into Mekong's neighbouring countries—were exposed for having mismanaged their way into massive indebtedness. Many tourism developers went bankrupt or were forced to downsize their projects. In particular, golf course and resort businesses, which had become a new symbol of globalized leisure enhancing the tourist lifestyle in Southeast Asian societies, experienced a dramatic downturn.

Many tourism-related infrastructure projects initiated by regional cooperation initiatives, including those of the ADB, were put on hold, as resources were needed to strengthen Asian countries' financial systems. In Thailand, for example, the International Monetary Fund (IMF), the World Bank and the ADB granted a US$17 billion loan, which included a rigid Structural Adjustment Programme (SAP).

At that time, I had suggested that in environmental terms at least, the Asian crisis could be a blessing in disguise (Pleumarom, 1998). As a result of decreasing numbers of travellers, for example, airlines closed unprofitable routes, sold off aircrafts and cancelled orders for new aircrafts, and governments cut budgets for airport expansion and construction, which raised the prospect of less pollution and less damaging developments. Also, the malaise of rampant land grabs, park encroachments and environmental degradation in relation to tourism projects no longer seemed as threatening as before because Asian developers were cash-strapped (ibid.).

As it has turned out, however, Mekong tourism promoters not only returned to 'business as usual' but governments in the region have made all-out efforts to compensate for the heavy debts, declining growth and decreasing foreign exchange reserves through even more rapacious resource extraction policies. A case in point is Thailand's present policy, aimed at turning every corner of the country into a tourist site and excessively boosting the number of tourists. Simultaneously, public and private investments in environmental programmes have significantly decreased because of the financial downtown.

Another question that should be asked is : Can tourism be sustainable in a region deeply affected by political instability, human rights problems and socio-economic crisis? In the context of the preparations for 'Visit ASEAN Year 2002', for example, tourism officials admitted that the event could be seriously hampered by political turmoil and social unrest in Southeast Asian nations but at the same time they tried to portray the problems as 'isolated incidents' to engender the notion of a 'carefree' holiday for consumers. As Richter notes :

Scarcity, deprivation, inequality, remnants of colonialism and the proxy wars of the superpowers set the stage for random violence, ethnic conflict, revolution, and even hostage-taking.....The very underdevelopment that exacerbates the resolution of political demands and frustrates economic aspirations is a potential asset in attracting tourism. Thus we have a paradox : nations, which are veritable hellholes for most of their citizens are sold as 'unspoilt paradises' to outsiders. (Richter 995)

The concept of 'sustainable tourism' implies a high degree of public participation in the process, and public participation implies that local communities will have a degree of control over the tourism development process (Hall, 1994). However, the healthy-sounding weeds of 'local participation' and 'community control' often appear incredible and even bizarre, when applied to such destination countries as Burma, with no democracy or freedom for its own indigenous population. And 'Can a few corporate giants substitute for popular participation?' asks Shivakumar (1997). As regards tourism planning and management, regional initiatives such as the ADB-led GMS tourism scheme rely too much on foreign consultants, who often have little knowledge of local situations, whereas 'the type of subregional projects so far proposed defy the spirit of local participation and sustainable development to which most donors and multilateral institutions commit themselves...(*ibid.*)

The Mekong countires—particulary Burma, China, Vietnam and Laos–provide few opportunities for public participation in government decision-making. The exception to this generalization is Thailand, which has a relatively well-established civil rights and environmental movement, and a free press. Given the lack of individual freedom to speak out on development issues in the region, thus task has by default fallen to a number of non-governmental organizations who, in turn, have sought to draw attention to the problems of tourism development, pressing for holistic and people-centred development policies that are not narrowly confined to tourism.

As outlined in the previous sections, major problems and conflicts have emerged because many rural and indigenous communities lost control of their land, natural and cultural resources and the political process as a result of 'top-down' tourism development. This being the case, one of the most urgent future tasks is to develop policies and tools to protect local people against uncontrolled and damaging tourism and to give them more power in development and conservation projects in general.

A number of grassroots-oriented organizations are already working in this direction and have put forward proposals aimed at a tackling fundamental problems in development and natural resource management. For instance, an alliance of civil society organizations and local community networks in Thailand have developed a 'People's Agenda' that calls for a comprehensive reform of government policies and urges policy-makers to take the following actions :

- assert sovereignty over natural resources and not to relinquish control to transnational corporations;

- develop alternative economic systems based on the self-sufficiency of local communities, their use of natural resources and local knowledge systems;
- base its policies on natural resource management on a holistic view of nature and the diversity of natural ecosystems, cultures and knowledge systems;
- ensure local people's participation in drafting policies on the management of natural resources;
- guarantee, as well as strengthen, the rights of local communities to manage natural resources; and
- support the efforts of local community networks towards sustainable management of natural resources and local economic development (Rajesh 2001).

Importantly, the previously outlined agenda calls for just and equitable land reform that favours small-scale farming communities, and demands 'Foreign or Thai land-owners must be prevented from accumulating and controlling large areas of cultivable lands for speculative or non-farming purposes' (ibid.). This proposal aims to resolve the escalating land conflicts flowing from speculative investments in hotels, golf resorts and other land-consuming tourism-related developments that involve the expropriation of village commons, agricultural lands and natural areas, and, thus, increasing hardships for smallscale farming communities.

At the present time, there is little evidence that 'bottom-up' development alternatives such as the 'People's Agenda', based on the principles of economic equity, social justice, cultural integrity and ecological sustainability, are being heeded in tourism development planning, even though such grassroots-oriented proposals could be the key to root out the causes the problems. What are needed is more informed debate and public pressure to steer the tourism 'power-that-be' towards a more holistic and people-centred approach and to persuade them to reorient their policies and practices accordingly. As Teo and Chang aptly note,...one should not underestimate the salience of local players in the global game. It is by them that the success or failure of tourism development is ultimately decided (Teo and Chang, 1998).

References

1. ADB (1994) : *Promoting Subregional Cooperation Among Cambodia, the People's Republic of China, Lao People's Democratic Republic, Myanmar : Thailand and Vietnam : Tourism,* Asian Development Bank (Interim Report).
2. ADB (1996) : *Greater Mekong Subregion : Sixth Conference on Subregional Cooperation,* Kunming, Yunnan, People's Republic of China, 28-30 August.
3. AMTA (1998) : *Concept Plains for Tourism Development in the Greater Mekong Sub-region, 1999-2018,* Agency for Coordinating Mekong Tourism, Bangkok.
4. Bello, W. (2000) : *ADB 2000 : Senior Officials and Internal Documents Paint Institution in Confusion,* Focus on the Global South, Bangkok.
5. Bello, W., Cunningham, S. and Li Kheng Poh (1998) : *A Siamese Tragedy : Development and Disintegration in Modern Thailand,* London/New York/Oakland, CA/Bangkok.
6. Burma Peace Foundation (1995) : 'Forced labour on tourist projects', *Forced Labour in Burma—A Collection of Documents, 1987-1995,* No. 4, New York.
7. Chandler, N. (1995) : 'River of dreams : the Mekong Alliance', *PATA Travel News,* March.
8. Cohen, E. (1996) : *Thai Tourism : Hill Tribes, Islands and Open-Ended Prostitution,* Bangkok.
9. *Economist, The* (1997/98) : 'Golfonimics : 'Asia in the Rough', 20 December-2 January.
10. G.A. G'M Updates (1993-1996) : A documentation series published by the Global Anti-Golf Movement.
11. Ghimire, K.B. (1991) : *Parks and People : Livelihood Issues in National Parks Management in Thailand and Madagaskar,* United Nations Research Institute for Social Development (UNRISD), DP 29, Geneva.
12. Hall, C.M. (1994) : *Tourism and Politics : Policy, Power and Place,* Chichester.

13. Hirsch, P. (1998) : *Seeing Forests for Trees : Environment and Environmentalism in Thailand,* Chiang Mai.

14. Hirsch, P. and Warren, C. (eds), (1998) : *The Politics of Environment in Southeast Asia : Resources and Resistance,* London/New York.

15. Human Rights Watch (1994) : *A Modern Form of Slavery : Trafficking of Burmese Women and Girls into Brothels in Thailand,* Asia Watch Women's Rights Project, New York.

16. Laird, J. (2000) : *Money Politics, Globalization and Crisis : The Case of Thailand,* Bangkok.

17. Lawrence, N. (2001) : 'Nice country-shame about the dictatorship', *The Irrawaddy,* January 2001.

18. Meyer, W. (1998) *Beyond the Mask : Transdisciplinary Approach of Selected Social Problems Related to the Evolution and Context of International Tourism in Thailand,* Saarburecken/Fort Lauderdale.

19. Michaud, J. (1993) : *The Social Anchoring of the Trekking Tourist Business in a Hmong Community of Northern Thailand,* Paper presented to the Fifth International Conference on Thai Studies, School of Oriental an African Studies, University of London, 5-10 July 1993.

20. Mowforth, M. and Munt, I. (1998) : *Tourism and Sustainability : New Tourism in the Third World,* London/New York.

21. MRC (1995) : *Preparation of the Mekong Basin Development Plan,* Bangkok Mekong River Commission Secretariat.

22. NCGUB (1995) : 'Position on Visit Myanmar Year-1996', National Coalition Government of the Union of Burma, Press Release by the exiled Burmese Government. Washington, 25 May.

23. Parnwell, M.J.G. (1998) : 'Tourism, globalization and critical security in Myanmar and Thailand', *Singapore Journal of Tropical Geography* **19 (2)**.

24. PATA (2001) : 'A river runs through it', Pacific Asia Travel Association, *Asian Hospitality,* 7 September.

25. Pholpoke, C. (1998) : 'The Chiang Mai cable-car project : local controversy over cultural and eco-tourism', Hirsch, P. and Warren, C. (*eds*), (1998), *The Politics of Environment in Southeast Asia : Resources and Resistance,* London/New York.

26. Phongpaichit, P. and Baker, C. (1998) : *Thailand's Boom and Bust*, Bangkok.

27. Pilger, J. (1996) : 'In a land of fear', *The Guardian-Weekend*, 4 May.

28. Pipitvanichtham, P. (1997) : 'Issues and challenges of ecotourism in the national parks of Thailand', Bornemeier, J., Victor M. and Durst, P.B. (eds), (1997), *Ecotourism for Conservation and Community Development*, Proceedings of an International Seminar held in Chiang Mai, Thailand, 28-31 January 1997, Bangkok.

29. Pleumarom, A. (1994) : 'Sport and environment : Thailand's golf boom reviewed', *TEI Quarterly Environment Journal* **2(4)**.

30. Pleumarom, A (1997/98) : 'Trekking tours : walking on the rights of local people', *Watershed* **3(2)**.

31. Pleumarom, A. (1998) : *Tourism, Globalization and the Politics of the Environmental Agenda*, Keynote to the 5th Congress of the World Leisure and Recreation Association (WLRA) on 'Leisure in a Globalized Society : Inclusion or Exclusion? Sao Paolo, Brazil, 26-30 October.

32. Pleumarom, A. (1999) : 'Mekong tourism brings disasters, *The Nation*, 2 February.

33. Poonyarat, C. (2001) : 'Megaplans for tourism bring worries, *International Press Service*, 3 September.

34. Rajesh, N. (2001) : 'A people's agenda for change', *Watershed* **6(3)**.

35. Richter, L. (1995) : Political instability and tourism in the Third World. Harrison, D. (ed.), *Tourism in Less Developed Countries*, Chichester/New York/Brisbane/Toronto/ Singapore.

36. Sesser, S. (2000) : 'Ecotourism Bulldozes ahead', *Asian Wall Street Journal*, 30 June.

37. Shivakumar, M.S. (1997) : *Sub-regional Economic Integration and the Poor : A Critique on the Development Initiatives in the Mekong River Basin*, Phnom Penh.

38. Smith, M. (1994) : *The Impact of Tourism and Burma's Cultural Heritage*, Article 19, The International Centre Against Censorship, London.

39. Srisang, K. (1991/92) : 'An alternative to tourism', *Thai*

Development Newsletter, No. 20.

40. Sutcliffe, S. (1994) : 'Burma : The Alternative Guide', Burma Action Group, London.
41. TDSC (1991/92) : Regarding tourism development in Thailand, Thai Development Support Committee, *Thai Development Newsletter,* No. 20.
42. TEI (1994) : 'Tourism, Ecology and Sustainable Development', Thailand Environment Institute. Special Issue of the *TEI Quarterly Environment Journal* **2(4)**.
43. Teo, P. and Chang, T.C. (1998) : 'Critical issues in a critical era : tourism in Southeast Asia', *Singapore Jounal of Tropical Geography* **19 (2)**.
44. Tim-Team (1994) : The Forced Tourism Boom in Burma', Tourism Investigation and Monitoring Team, Bangkok.
45. Tim-Team (2000) : *Tourism Projects in Thai National Parks funded by the World Bank/Overseas Economic Cooperation Fund (OECF) Social Investment Programme, httpn : // www.twnside.org.sg/title/iye7.htm.*
46. Tourism Authority of Thailand (TAT) (1995) : *Ecotourism in Thailand,* Papers presented at the ecotourism seminar organized by the TAT in cooperation with the Walden Mills Group in Bangkok, 7-8 December, 1995.
47. Towards Ecological Recovery and Regional Alliance (TERRA) (2000) : 'ADB : Development as if Corporations Matter', *Watershed* **5 (3)**.
48. UNCTAD (2001) : *The Sustainability of International Tourism in Developing Countries,* Paper presented to the OECD Seminar on Tourism Policy and Economic Growth, Berlin, 6-7 March 2001, http ://www.oecd.org/dsti/sti/transport/tourism news/UNCTAD.pdf.
49. Wall, G. (1997) : 'Is ecotourism sustainable?', *Environmental Management* **21 (4)**.
50. Wall, G. (1998) : Reflections on the state of Asian tourism', *Singapore Journal of Tropical Geography* **19(2)**.
51. Wangpattana, A. (2000) : 'Deconstructing the ADB', *Watershed* **5(3)**.
52. Wheeller, B. (1997) : *Here We Go, Here We Go, Here We Go Eco,* Centre for Urban and Regional Studies, University of Birmingham.

10 Examples from the UK Coast

Introduction

The growth of tourism in the UK reflects the expansion of the industry worldwide. At the turn of the turn of the twentieth century the UK Government (DCMS, 1999) has calculated that British tourism :

- employs 1.75 million people in 125 000 businesses;
- has accounted for one in six of all new jobs created in the last ten years;
- is worth $53 billion a year; and
- brought 25.5 million overseas visitors to Britain in 1997.

This well-developed tourism economy is heavily dependents on the environment, heritage, culture and the diversity of local landscapes and local communities.

At the Earth Summit in 1992, the UK Government made a commitment to Agenda 21, the global environmental and development 'blueprint'. Whilst there is little explicit reference to tourism within Agenda 21, much is relevant; and local government is perceived to have an important role to play in its delivery. Local authorities were urged to develop and adopt a Local Agenda 21—a sustainable development strategy at the local level—by 1996. Local Agenda 21 guidance favours establishing partnerships with other sectors including businesses, voluntary organizations and community groups.

A national UK strategy for sustainability (DETR, 1999) advocated inclusive social progress, effective environmental protection, prudent use of natural resources, and high and stable levels of economic development and employment. At the same time, consultation on how the UK might work towards sustainable tourism (as defined by Tourism Concern/ WWF, 1992) stressed the positive potential contribution of a sustainable approach, and sought views on key issues associated with meeting the economic and social requirements of people within a framework of resource conservation (DCMS, 1998a). Issues examined included transport, community benefits and management of visitor flows. In terms of planning imperatives, the consultation stated that sustainable tourism should be accessible, particularly to public transport and those cycling or on foot, and it should be based wherever possible on an existing well-located infrastructure.

Key outcomes of this exercise have been the publication of a new UK Tourism Strategy (DCMS, 1999) and Sustainable Tourism Roundtable Guidance for local authorities (IDA, 1999). The former announced the formation of a new national body for tourism with sustainability at the heart of its mission. The latter translated sustainable tourism into six guidelines on the basis that tourism should :

- integrate activity, long term planning and partnership development;
- maintain and develop diversity;
- support local economies;
- use resources sustainably;
- involve local communities, stakeholders and the public; and
- research, share learning and experience.

Monitoring the delivery of sustainable tourism is, however, proving far more elusive than establishing guidelines. Miller (2001), in attempting to develop indicators for sustainable tourism, identified considerable expert disagreement over what constitutes sustainability and its conceptual boundaries.

This chapter focuses on coastal tourism. A series of case studies are presented as being reflective of the range of issues associated with the sustainable development of coastal tourism in the UK. The main contention of the chapter is that sustainable coastal tourism must focus on inherent strengths. For the rural coastline these relate to the physical environment, for the urban coastline a unique heritage. Neither should be compromised by tourist activity.

Coastal Tourism

The EU Demonstration Programme on Integrated Coastal Zone Management (ICZM) defined the coastal zone as 'a strip of land and sea of varying width depending on the nature of the environment and management needs. It seldom corresponds to existing administrative or planning units. The natural coastal systems and the areas in which human activities involve the use of coastal resources may therefore extend well beyond the limit of territorial waters and many kilometres inalnd' (EC, 1997 : 6). This is particularly applicable to coastal tourism given that tourists are usually confined to a relatively narrow area, but the infrastructure needed to support their activities including, for example, water and food supplies, transport access and accommodation for service staff, encompasses a much wider region.

ICZM has been defined as 'the process which brings all those involved in the development, management and use of the coast within a framework which facilitates the integration of their interests and responsibilities to achieve common objectives' (DoE, 1996 : 1). The framework should highlight and account for the interrelationship between individual issues and the management of the coast as a whole, since decision-making within one locality or one sectoral area is likely to impact upon others. In practice ICZM is still in its infancy and the intensification of use in the marine and coastal environments has become a significant issue only relatively recently. Johnson and Seabrooke (1996) suggested that new approaches and institutional support are needed to manage the marine and coastal environment effectively, efficiently, and above all in a manner which does not permit these environments to become degraded.

To date, relatively little work on marine tourism as a subject area in its own right has been undertaken (Orams, 1999). However, it is well documented that tourism has the potential to have a major impact on coastal areas. French (1997) stated that it is the intensity of tourism in a small unit area that differentiates it from other forms of development. Particularly acute negative environmental impacts are :

- over-exploitation of natural resources to satisfy tourist demand;
- loss of natural habitat and biodiversity as a result of resort development; and
- increased pollution, arising particularly from sewage effluent treatment and disposal problems.

Authors such as Cooper *et al.* (1998) have also highlighted positive and negative sociocultrual impacts, such as changes in local culture, congestion and crime, which affect both hosts and guests. These too are very evident on the coast, often changing the cultural heritage of traditional fishing communities, for example.

The 20, 000 kilometre UK coastline has a long history of tourism. The physical variety of the UK coast has often determined the type of tourist activity. Tidally dominated coasts are popular for water-based recreation; wave and wind dominated coasts for beach activities; and built up urban coasts have historically engineered sea front environments to 'accommodate' tourist facilities (including piers, beaches protected by sea defenses, and mass tourism attractions). Increasingly, however, the UK coastline is being valued for environmental conservation, including many area of international environmental sensitivity. To date for example, 100 coastal and marine Special Protection Areas have been classified under the EC Birds Directive (Directive 79/409/EEC

(OJ L103, 25.4.79) on the conservation of wild birds) and thirty-five marine Special Areas of Conservation have been identified under the EC Habitats Directive (Directive 92/43/EEC (OJ L206, 22.7.92) on the conservation of natural habitats and wild fauna and flora).

Strategic approaches are required to integrate environmental considerations within coastal tourism policies and plans. Detailed tourism planning is needed to identify issues liable to have an adverse effect on sustainability. This should focus on both physical and socio-economic aspects. Minimizing the negative physical aspects of tourism can be achieved through the development of environmental risk assessments, determination of carrying capacities and identification of sustainability indicators. The latter include measurements of destination quality such as ecological impacts, energy efficiency and pollution control. Maximizing the local economic and social benefits of tourism requires support for the local economies including sustainable tourism related employment. It should also pay attention to local community involvement, cultural impacts and health issues. Dumashie (1997) suggested that coastal tourism planning should involve the correct definition and balancing of location specific assets and liabilities. Examples, which she cited, are given below :

Assets	**Liabilities**
Good scuba diving	Sand storms
Brisk sailing	Jellyfish infestations
Good fishing	Strong currents
Attractive moorings	Endemic diseases
Cruising trips	Sea fog
Exotic hinterland	
Historic towns	

Management tools and techniques are also important, including environmental assessment of tourism projects, management plans for destinations, environmental auditing and life-cycle assessment of destinations, visitor surveys, environmental monitoring, and promoting the role of best practice, training and education.

Many sustainable tourism principles are not new. They reflect, for example, values enshrined in the UK town and Country Planning system. Nevertheless, British coastal tourism decision-makers, and the communities involved, need to re-examine their tourism policies and practices. The following examples provide a 'snapshot' of work in hand.

Examples of Sustainable Coastal Tourism Thinking

Urban Coastal Regeneration—Redcar and Cleveland Borough Council : Many British seaside resorts, established in Victorian times, are suffering from a decaying infrastructure and outdated accommodation provision. They have been slow to adapt to structural change in holiday trends. Additional reasons for resort decline include improved personal mobility, insensitive architectural designs of the 1960s, lack of investment and environmental degradation. The principal trend is for more British people to take their main annual holiday abroad, using domestic seaside resorts for shorter breaks. Over a period of twenty years market share has declined significantly. Trips taken to the seaside, nights spent at the seaside and money used at the seaside, as recorded by the UK National Tourist Boards, have all continued to decline in the period 1991-1997.

Recognizing the problem, reviews of resort issues by the English Tourist Board and Association of District councils highlighted the need for a strategic approach, creation of an identifiable marketing image, partnership approaches and improved standards of visitors care.

Redcar and Cleveland Borough Council has been part of an EU-funded pilot study to demonstrate and evaluate the way forward in terms of developing successful resort regeneration action plans. This study comprised two European Network Projects that specifically examined the problems of resorts and the potential for achieving effective revitalization with minimal funding. Lane (1999) summarized the findings of both projects and, in particular, concluded that resorts are a key function and element of the coastal zone. He also concluded that the suggested regeneration action plan methodology parallels the framework suggested for the preparation of Local agenda 21 Action Plans. Essential elements within a five-year regeneration action plan rolling programme are considered to be :

- establishing a vision, the political will and overall commitment to regenerate;
- research to create a better understanding of visitor needs and tourism infrastructure;
- generation of ideas including those of community groups and organizations and thus identifying the key issues such as zoning of development;
- formulation of policies, specific targetable actions and monitoring programmes; and
- provision of funding including attracting private sector investment.

The advantages of addressing this issue include reducing the potential for transformation and degradation of more natural sections of the coast. A central conclusion of the EU project was that 'existing resort areas provide a tremendous tourist resource and can handle, with minimum impact, substantial numbers of visitors' (Lane, 1999 : 4).

The UK Government is currently encouraging resorts to collect relevant baseline data (DCMS, 1998b) and has tasked development agencies with raising the profile of resort regions to maximize chances of EU and other funding applications. The recently published strategy calls for 'imaginative, market led and sustainable regeneration programmes' and favours niche marketing, creating opportunities for all sectors of society, as one solution to reversing this economic decline (DCMS, 1999).

As a result, many UK resorts are now working to establish a new identity and focus, investing in upgraded well-designed modern facilities, and striving to manage visitor flows in order to minimize seasonality. Action orientated plans, based on visitor survey information and involving resort communities, have been adopted. Environmental issues are acknowledged as paramount to resort action planning and the creation of a high quality, vibrant and effectively managed beach area continues to be seen as a key feature.

This example illustrate at least some elements of sustainability. It represents a holistic and integrated coastal tourism management policy, within which attempts are being made to balance the environmental needs of the destination with the investment returns required by the private sector. However, a sustainable vision will not be enough. Public funding is needed to build new attractions, renovate accommodation and improve public transport links. To be sustainable, redevelopment of this kind has to respect the scale, nature and character of each coastal resort, as well as reflecting the importance of the hinterland environment behind the beach. It must also tackle social inequity and deprivation.

Pump Priming—The Wales Tourist Board

Wales has a coastline of 1200 kilometers, which includes the only UK coastal national park and a unique coastal heritage. The Wales Tourist Board's (WTB) role is to provide pump-printing finance, ideas and advice for tourism operators. WTB has embraced sustainable tourism in four key aims. These are to :

1. develop and market tourism in suitable ways which bring social and economic benefit to Wales;
2. offer high standards of product, quality and service;
3. support and promote Welsh culture and the Welsh language; and
4. protect and improve the environment, the natural beauty of the country and its buildings.

In this context sustainable tourism has been interpreted as being about developing and marketing local products and produce, minimizing the environmental impacts of local visitor services and encouraging partnerships. Greenow (1999) highlighted the following examples of progressive steps, which illustrate how this is being achieved in Wales.

South Pembrokeshire Partnership for Action with Rural Communities (SPARC)

This rural development initiative has involved the local community in all aspects of tourism development. Thirty-seven villages have been involved working in the region of outstanding natural beauty around the Pembrokeshire Coast National Park. SPARC has facilitated tourism planning based on initial assessments of communities. The result is a tourism programme that reflects shared community vision and therefore fosters local support. Green and heritage holiday packages using local cycle routes, public transport and luggage transfer services have been developed. This links with the efforts of 'greenways' an attempt to integrate an improved environmental transport network, which includes footpaths, cycle routes and an enhanced public transport service. Wales currently has two new National Cycle Routes, which take advantage of traffic-calmed roads and off-road byways. The Landsker Borderlands Trail, for example, is one of several trails successfully promoted to the Dutch, German and UK markets, for which some 60 per cent of incoming travel is by train. Alternative holidays, based on environmental and cultural interpretation, are generating significant income for the local economy. This last point, reducing the leakage of tourism generated spending, is an important element of sustainable tourism. The aim is also to achieve a balance between the needs of the visitor, the destination and the host community.

'Greening Your Business' Manual

The WTB have produced detailed guidelines for tourism operators, published in Welsh and English in the form of a manual. During 1998 manuals were sold commercially and issued to businesses securing WTB grants. As well as explaining the rationale for environmental action, the manual offers practical ideas for more environmentally friendly working practices whilst maintaining an attractive environment for tourists. Attention is given to :

- energy and water conservation (*e.g.*, low energy light bulbs, insulation, thermostat settings, preference to showers over baths);
- purchasing (*e.g.*, local supplies, organic food, minimum packaging); waste and recycling (*e.g.*,materials management, composting, sewage disposal);
- visitor environment (e.g., access to gardens, home grown food, Welsh culture); and
- public transport opportunities.

In this instance encouraging the careful and efficient use of renewable and non-renewable resources and avoiding waste engenders sustainability.

Green Sea Partnership

The Green Sea Partnership is a public and private sector partnership, which includes WTB and the major public utility Dwr Cymru/Welsh Water, to co-ordinate and improve beach facilities and resources. Evidence of improvement in beach and coastal water quality has been the increase, from two in 1995 to thirteen in 1998, in the number of beaches gaining European Blue Flag awards. A Rural Beach Awards category has also been establishing for small, quiet beaches without recreation infrastructure. The Partnership aims to survey 120 of these smaller beaches annually. Public and private sector partnerships of this type can encourage sustainable tourism, not least by raising awareness of business benefits associated with good environmental practice and through the adoption of 'environmental management tools'. An informed public is more likely to visit and respect beaches demonstrating high environmental standards.

Managing Visitor Flows—the National Trust

The National Trust for Places of Historic Interest or Outstanding Natural Beauty is the UK's largest voluntary conservation organizations, with a membership of 2.2 million and an annual income of over $83 million. Whilst the National Trust is a charity, and thus perhaps not strictly a tourist operator, the organization channels income from visitors into maintaining and enhancing landscapes and local culture. It is also an example of a voluntary organization whose core activity relates to sustainable development.

In 1965 the National Trust launched Enterprise Neptune, a campaign to save the coast both for and from the public, which aimed to :

- acquire unspoilt coastline for permanent preservation and public access;
- alert people to the increasing pressures and threats to the coast; and
- raise funds for the purchase of unspoilt coastline.

Over 35 years this initiative, now renamed the Neptune Coastline Campaign, has been spectacularly successful, raising over $33 million enabling the acquisition and management of 960 (or 1 in 6) kilometres of the coastline of England, Wales and Northern Ireland (Scotland has its own National Trust). This has included a wide diversity of coastal sites with different problems. Among them are a number of extremely popular sites where visitor management strategies and techniques have been implemented to promote sustainable tourism, at the same time respecting and integrating biodiversity conservation objectives. The National Trust encourages people to enjoy their coastal properties whilst at the same time promoting good stewardship. An educational programme entitled the 'Coastal Guardianship Scheme' involves local people with their coastal properties. Three of these coastal 'honey pot' sites are described below.

The Farne Islands

The Farne Islands off the north-east coast of England are home to large colonies of nesting seabirds. Yearly visitor numbers rose from around 3000 in the 1970s to over 50 000 in the mid-1980s, enthused by media wildlife coverage. The National Trust determined to limit visitor numbers and negotiated permits with local boat owners. The result is that now only eight boats have permits. They transport a maximum of 3000 visitors per day to one location for a one-hour visit; walkways are roped and boardwalks prescribed where needed; and nesting birds take little notice of the 'ecotourists'. Over time this approach has worked well, achieving improvements in both habitat conservation and the quality of the visitor experience. Visitors can observe seabirds at close quarters, they understand that their visit is not damaging the environment, and local boat owners benefit. In this case sustainable tourism is clearly about 'demand regulation', but it is also an example of tourist activity responding the intrinsic value of the coastal environment and not prejudicing its long-term future.

Kynance Cove

The National Trust acquired Kynance Cove in Cornwall in 1935. The beauty spot attracts in excess of 100000 visitors annually. In 1986 land adjacent to Kynance Cove was acquired. Prior to this the headland had been in private ownership and visitor facilities comprised a number of 'ad hoc' buildings, a large car park and eroding cliff top footpaths. The National Trust has demolished unsightly structures, incorporated a new car park within the landscape, restored and re-routed footpath access. Visitor income now funds environmental conservation.

Studland Bay

Studland Bay, at the western extremity of Poole Harbour in Dorset, is possibly the UK's most popular rural coastal destination, attracting up to 1,250,000 visitors each year. The National Trust owns a six-kilometre stretch of beach together with an immediate hinterland of dunes, marshland and lowland heathland of high nature conservation importance. Facilities, including a visitor centre, car parks and raised boardwalks, have been developed to accommodate large numbers at peak times. The visitor management strategy concentrates visitors in an area with high carrying capacity and protects fragile areas.

Heritage Interpretation—Dorset County Council

Much of the country of Dorset's coastline is designated as Heritage Coast and much, including Studland Bay, is owned and managed by the National Trust. The Jurassic Coast Project is a three-year feasibility study that aims to address the fact that 80 per cent of the region's tourism income is derived form 20 per cent of visitors. The coastline, which is highly regarded for its landscapes, rural beaches and pretty villages, attracts large numbers of day visitors but these visits are restricted to a relatively short summer season.

A solution to improving the local standard of living, whilst simultaneously protecting the environment, is based on the region's outstanding geological heritage. The coastline reveals a complete Jurassic sequence from east to west (150 million years of geological history) and incorporates the largest coastal mudflow in Europe. Rapidly eroding cliffs are the source of world famous landforms such as Old Harry Roacks, Durdle Door and Lulworth Cove; spectacular fossils, including recent new dinosaur finds; and evidence of a fossil forest and dinosaur footprints. With the support of European Union funding, Dorset Country Council is attempting to use this unique earth science legacy to generate 'out of season' tourist interest, extend visitor stay time and maximize economic benefit to the region. The initiative epitomizes sustainable tourism principles and reflects the dynamic nature of coastal conservation. In the past the conservation ethos has been preservationist. The Jurassic Coast Project will enhance opportunities for visitors to enjoy landscapes, ecology and local character and culture by maximizing the potential of information and communication technology to explain the dynamic nature of coastal processes. Niche tourism will feed on, rather than diminish, local distinctiveness and diversity. In this instance geology provides the linking theme and is the basis for a World Heritage Site bid for this stretch of coastline.

For Dorset country Council an investment in heritage

interpretation provides the key to a more sustainable approach. Working, papers have highlighted new educational initiatives, an interpretation strategy and a marketing approach. This supports the viewpoint that tourism can be a positive activity with the potential to benefit resident communities, visitors and the destination. It also complements the work of Purbeck Heritage, a partnership of councils, landowners and conservation bodies, together with Purbeck District Council's management plan to promote more sustainable forms of tourism in the region. Tourism planners in Dorset hope that special interest breaks, employing local experts, will benefit accommodation providers at times when tourist numbers are low. Geo-tourism potential (see Hose, 1996 and 1998) can be realized in the 'shoulder' months when coastal scenery is more dramatic and when fossils uncovered by winter storms are more likely to be found. Dorset Tourism Data Project statistics indicate that visitors drive around the coat to a series of short stay places of interest. The Jurassic Coast Project aims to provide these visitors and educational groups with sufficient interest in one place.

A site-specific focus for a more sustainable approach is Portland and the Isle of Purbeck. This 'island', linked to the coastline by a causeway, has been dominated by the quarrying industry and by its role as a strategic military base. Quarrying for Portland stone continues but the Royal Navy is relocating its operation. A Quarry Park, incorporating both working and abandoned quarries, is proposed as a tourist and educational alternative. A combination of unique geographic position, wildlife interest, spectacular views, cultural interest associated with buildings, structures and artefacts (including a sculpture park) made from Portland stone provide a 'one stop shop'. The focus on cultural heritage will create opportunities for local people to share their knowledge and enthusiasm with visitors. Increasing the participation of local people and communities in this way is indicative of an emphasis on social responsibility, another key element of sustainability.

Conclusions

Sustainable tourism acknowledges the fundamental link

between long-term planning, conserving the environment, economic gain and profit ability from tourism operations, and social equality. Appropriate tourism policy and planning on a holistic and integrated basis is required by all stakeholders. Success is based upon :

- maintaining and improving levels of natural capital stock through accurate and objective assessment of resources;
- controls to observe carrying capacities;
- an adequate investment in resource efficient ancillary services;
- opportunities for all parties to contribute, particularly local involvement;
- raising public understanding and promoting intergenerational equity;
- effective environmental policies, tourism management plans, and equitable economic and employment benefits; and
- long-term monitoring, assessment and feedback.

In a review for Tourism Concern, Leslie and Muir (1996) argued that take up of Local Agenda 21 within local authority tourism strategies in the UK was poorly funded and left significant room for improvement. Like so much of the hype generated by the sustainable development concept, much remains on paper rather than in practice. Since then the UK Government has at least attempted to raise the profile of sustainable tourism but politicians are still searching for easily measureable ways to ensure that tourism practice does not contravene sustainable development principles.

The UK coastline is an example of a natural resource that has been used and abused for many years. The case studies selected suggest that increased voluntary efforts to deliver sustainable tourism are currently being made. In these cases the management of tourist activities has the potential to reshape the industry. A number of urban coastal resorts, such as Redcar and Cleveland, are planning positive regeneration projects. In hitherto unspoilt rural areas a sustainable approach is being developed on a partnership basis, by government agencies, voluntary organizations and local groups.

However, the case studies chosen also illustrate the absence of a coherent and comprehensive approach to the sustainable management of the UK coastal zone. Local government is leading much of the drive towards sustainable tourism at the coast and sustainability is not yet a mainstream concern for most private sector providers. Consequently, sustainable development ideals and actions have little prominence in the most popular coastal destinations such as Blackpool, Skegness or Newquay.

It could also be argued that the majority of UK tourists themselves give little thought to sustainability. Mass tourism along parts of the southern Spanish coast represents the antithesis of sustainability. However, some 1.5 million UK tourists holiday each year in the Spanish resort of Benidorm on the Costa Blanca, and on the Catalan coast, which includes the Costa Brava. Some environmentalists consider that pollution and over-development, much associated with tourism in these areas, have pushed their coastal ecology to a 'critical point'.

All the examples cited are attempting to combine protection or enhancement of the coastal environment, economic wellbeing of coastal communities, a healthy distinctive local culture, and maximum visitor satisfaction. Nevertheless, it also clear that better networks are needed to both apply the results of research and to promote and share good practice. Sustainability must be fully recognized as part of coastal tourism policy and decision-making, and its success or otherwise needs to be measured, judged and broadcast. Ultimately, in order to realize quantifiable gains, a proactive approach from the tourist industry will be required, along with a more responsible approach by tourists to their interactions with the natural and built environment.

Acknowledgements

The author would like to thank Mike Greenow, Wales Tourist

Board; Richard Often, National Trust; Peter Lane, Redcar and Cleveland Borough Council; and Richard Edmonds, Dorset Country Council for providing detailed information on selected case studies.

References

1. Cooper, C., Fletcher, J., Wanhill, S., Gilbert, D. and Shepherd, R. (1998), *Tourism : Principles and Practice*, Second edition, Longman, Harlow.
2. DCMS (1998a) : *Tourism—Towards Sustainability*. Consultation document, Department for Culture, Media & Sport, London.
3. DCMS (1998b) : Measuring *the Local Impact of Tourism* (A guidance pack for Local Authorities). Department for Culture, Media & Sport, London.
4. DCMS (1999) : *Tomorrow's Tourism—A growth industry for the new Millennium*. Department for Culture, Media & Sport, London.
5. DETR (1999) : *A better quality of life, A strategy for sustainable development for the United Kingdom*. Cm 4345. Department of the Environment, Transport and the Regions, London.
6. DoE (1996) : *Coastal Zone Management—Towards Best Practice*. Department of Environment, London.
7. Dumashie, D. (1997) : The benefits and risks of coastal tourism, *Exclusive Economic Zone Catalogue,* See Edition, pp. 84-9. Combined Service Publications, UK.
8. EC (1997) : *Better management on coastal resources—A European Programme for Integrated Coastal Zone Management,* (Official publication of the European Communities, Luxemberg.
9. French, P.W. (1997) : *Coastal and Estuarine Management* Routledge, London.
10. Greenow, M. (1999) : Practical Balance, The Leisure Manager August 1999, pp. 25-27, *Journal of the Institute of Leisure and Amenity Management*, UK.
11. Hall, C.M and Page, S.J. (1999) : *The Geography of Tourism and Recreation*, Routledge, London.
12. Hose, T.A. (1996) : Geotourism, or can tourists become casual rockhounds? In Bennet, M.R., Doyle, P., Larwood, J.G. and

Prosser, C. (eds), *Geology On Your Doorstep*, Geological Society, London, pp. 207-28.

13. Hose, T.A. (1998) : Selling Coastal Geology to Visitors, In Hooke, J. (ed.), *Coastal Defence and Earth Science Conservation*, Geological Society, London, pp. 178-95.

14. IDA (1999), *Local Agenda 21 Roundtable Guidance : Sustainable Tourism*, Sustainable Development Unit, Improvement and Development Agency, London.

15. Johnson, D.E. and Seabrooke, W. (1996) : Sustainable enjoyment : the need for leisure management at the coast. In Goodhead, T.J. and Johnson, D.E. (eds), *Coastal Recreation Management*. E&FN Spon, London pp. 23-42.

16. Lane, P. (1999) : *Tourism and Resort Action Plans—Identifying a Methodology*, Fact sheet 99/7, Institute of Leisure and Amenity Management, Reading.

17. Leslie, D. and Muir, F. (1996) : *Local Agenda 21, Local Authorities and Tourism-a UK Perspective*. A report prepared for Tourism Concern by Glasgow Caledonian University.

18. Miller, G. (2001) : The development of indicators for sustainable tourism : results of a Delphi survey of tourism researchers, *Tourism Management* **22** : 351-62.

19. Orams, M. (1999) : *Marine tourism : Development, Impacts and Management*. Routledge, London.

20. Tourism Concern/WWF (1992) : *Beyond the Green Horizon*. Tourism Concern, London.

11 Towards Sustainability Monitoring

Introduction

In response to monitor a decade of unrestrained growth, British Columbia's tourism industry is under intense scrutiny as regards its impact on the community and environment. As a consequence several of the province's industry and community leaders have begun developing strategies that are designed to focus tourism development in more sustainable directions. A critical component of such strategies involves developing and implementing monitoring processes that provide credible measures of how well tourism is doing in achieving sustainability goals. In this regard, one of the province's most significant tourism destination communities has taken the lead in the development and use of a comprehensive monitoring programme. Over the past six years, the Resort Municipality of Whistler has been systematically monitoring its progress towards its identified growth management goals. This case study examines this monitoring programme with a view to determining its performance against recommended sustainability assessment processes.

The Role of Indicators

To assess progress towards more sustainable forms of tourism, there is a need for relevant monitoring systems. Ideally, these systems should focus on assessing the extent to which existing best practices in tourism are aligned with, and help to achieve, core sustainability goals. In this regard sustainability monitoring should be focused on examining progress towards reaching a combination of ecological, social and economic imperatives (Arrow and Bolin, 1995; El Serafy, 1991; Goodland and Daly, 1996; International Council for Local Environmental Initiatives and International Development Research Centre, 1996; Maclaren, 1996; Robinson and Van Bers, 1996; and Bossel, 1999).

Indicators can be used to measure progress towards sustainability goals, and when tracked over time, can also help identify trends in the condition of a phenomenon that has significance beyond that of the measurement itself (Dilks, 1995). For example, an indicator of transportation modes into a resort area could help to measure progress towards the achievement of non-renewable resource consumption and air-pollution goals. Ideally indicators used for assessing progress in the sustainability area should :

- be selected on the basis of input received from a broad base of stakeholders ;
- be designed to meet the varying informational needs of these different audiences ;
- include objective measurements (*e.g.*, biophysical measurements such as water quality parameters);
- include subjective measurements (*e.g.*, stakeholder perceptions and attituteds); and
- signal where necessary the need for comprehensive studies of more complex relationship (Maclaren, 1996a).

Developing Indicators

Researchers and practitioners have identified several processes for developing sustainability indicators (Campbell and Maclaren, 1995; Fraser Basin Management Programme *et al.*, 1995; Dilks, 1995; Maclaren, 1996a, 1996b; Manning, 1999). Many of these processes have commonalties that appear to be applicable in the context to tourism communities. These include visioning, scooping, determining indicators selection criteria, selecting indicators, analyzing and reporting findings, and soliciting feedback.

Visioning

A variety of methods have been suggested for collecting the information needed to create a truly community based Vision of an area's sustainability goals. These methods include using a combination of town all meetings; workshop brainstorming sessions; livingroom focus groups questionnaire surveys; key informant or expert consultations; open house meetings and displays; and public meeting panel discussions to identify the set of goals to be achieved through tourism development activities (Stettner, 1993; Gill, 1996; Jamal and Getz, 1997).

Scoping

This second step involves establishing the scope of the monitoring programme. By creating an understanding of the role and benefits that a credible monitoring programme can create for existing tourism organizations and other community stakeholder groups, practical decisions need to be made with regard to :

- scope (politically, spatially, temporally); what development issues should be addressed; and
- how to determine what relevant data might be collected and by which methods within a monitoring programme.

By collaborating with tourism operators, local businesses, community and environmental groups (as well as neighbouring communities), and regional and provincial governments, a priority set of issues can be identified for monitoring. A balance must be found between providing an all-encompassing set of indicators and the fiscal realities of collecting, assimilating and interpreting the information (Dilks, 1995). This scoping exercise should address not only the range of issues and indicators to be measured, but also the spatial scale and range of audience to whom the findings of the monitoring programme's activities should be targeted. For instance, depending on the situation, the target audience might range from primarily community decision-makers, to business operators, to provincial government policymakers. All of these stakeholders may play distinct but important roles in influencing the way in which development unfolds in tourism areas. In each of these cases, it may be necessary to establish different levels of indicator reporting sophistication (*e.g.*, range and number of indicators) in order to ensure relevance to each group (Brugman, 1997).

Choosing an Indicator Framework

Indicator frameworks provide systematic means of structuring the identification and selection of relevance subjects/issues be monitored. A variety of different frameworks have been developed for application in varying sustainability monitoring contexts. Generally they fall into five broad categories.

Domain-Based Frameworks

Domain-based frameworks can address a variety of tourism performance issues. These include not only economic performance indicators commonly associated with tourism industry activity, but also critical social and ecological concerns, which often provide the underlying foundation for much of tourism's potential sustainability. Depending on the circumstances, specific domain-based indicators can be selected or accentuated in order to emphasize critical linkages between environment, economy and society (Daly and Cobb, 1994; Maclaren, 1996a; Robinson and Van Bers, 1996). However, domain-based frameworks do no necessarily link indicators directly with specific management goals, thereby, reducing their overall utility for monitoring progress towards sustainability.

Goal-Based Frameworks

Goal-based frameworks focus on identifying indicators that can respond directly to sustainability goals (Manning and Clifford, 1995; Maclaren, 1996a). In a tourism community context, these goals may include such concerns as : achieving specified resident satisfaction levels; maintaining targeted visitor traffic levels; providing a specified supply of affordable employee housing; and protecting a specified amount of sensitive habitat for conservation purposes. Such frameworks are particularly useful in systematically reducing the number of indicators required for monitoring purposes. This makes monitoring and assessment processes more manageable in many cases. The overriding weakness with goal-based frameworks is that the separateness of each indicator reduces opportunities for identifying important inter-relationships between various factors affecting tourism's sustainability. For example, goals such as resident housing and environmental conservation can be pursued in isolation and may ultimately conflict with one another, but would not necessarily be considered within a goal-based indicator framework.

Sectoral Frameworks

Sectoral indicator frameworks respond to the needs and structures of existing institutional organizations. Typically, they focus on issues linked to the functions and focus of specific management groups. From a tourism community perspective, sectoral frameworks might describe indicators of existing land use, housing, transportation, recreation, and social infrastructure service conditions. Over time, the indicators measured in such frameworks can be useful in assessing the impact of specific management responses to particular development issues. However, this type of compartmentalized approach to monitoring tends to reduce the range of ecological, economic and social influences on specific issues.

Issue-Based Frameworks

Issue-based frameworks address specific 'hot' topics such as traffic congestion, resident housing, and wildlife conservation. While valuable in short-term management contexts, these issue-based frameworks often lack the systematic rationale needed to provide a comprehensive perspective on issues having longer-term sustainability implications.

Causal Frameworks

Causal frameworks provide indicators that are useful in systematically measuring existing conditions, stresses, and responses related to sustainability issues (Hardi, 1995; Maclaren, 1996b). The strength of these frameworks lies in their ability to determine potential causal relationships between economic, social and environmental factors. Causal frameworks provide indicators that normally address issues concerning what is actually happening (*i.e.*, state or condition indicators), why is it happening (*i.e.*, pressure or stress indicators); and how management is addressing the pressure (*i.e.*, response indicators).

Within causal framework, performance cab be evaluated by comparing indicator trends with set management goals. For example, in the case of a mountain stream within a tourism community, an indicator or its condition (state) might be the water flow during low tourism visitation periods compared to its flow during peak visitor traffic periods. Per capita water consumption rates (pressure) might be used as an indicator of what current stresses are placed on the stream by visitors. Finally, a set of water conservation practices (response) might be used to assess the extent to which various water restriction targets are feasible under varying management regimes. While a very systematic approach to monitoring, past applications of causal frameworks have typically failed to address the within-domain interactions of essential components and structures within ecosystems (Rennings and Wiggering, 1997).

An Integrated Pressure—State—Response Indicator Option

Combining the strengths of the previously described indicator frameworks can provide more comprehensive alternatives for sustainability monitoring (Hammand and Adriaanse, 1995; Hardi, 1995). For instance, a domain-based approach combined with a pressure—state—response (PSR) system can offer a valuable integrated approach to systematically assessing tourism's progress towards a variety of interrelated goals (Manning, 1993; Manning and Clifford, 1995). Most importantly, this approach facilitates the integration of policy initiatives across sustainability imperative domains. In essence, this means that the relationship between various management response indicators within one domain cab be examined in the context of a state and pressure measure in another domain. For example, an economic response indicator of increased resort promotion can be compared with environmental pressure indicators such as habitat area lost.

Identifying Potential Indicators

Numerous indicators are available to tourism and community planners. These include lists of 'core indicators' derived from general community and regional planning contexts (Dilks, 1995), as well as those designed specifically for tourism (Manning and Clifford, 1995). Many of these lists can be obtained on the World Wide Web. For example, the Sustainable Communities Network (http ://www.sustainable.org) and Hart Environmental Data (http ://www.subjectmatters.com/indicators) offer extensive indicator lists. Additional potential indicators can also be developed which respond to unique local sustainability goals. Community visioning may provide guidance concerning what these potential indicators might be.

Selecting Indicators

Selecting a final set of key indicators from the long list of measurement options can occur in a number of different ways. For example, practical considerations such as data affordability and availability issues, as well as the perceived relevance to potential users, many help determine the overall appropriateness of specific indicators. Each indicator must be judged according to its appropriateness on a predetermined scale (Gosselin and Belanger, 1993; Long and Perdue, 1994; Dilks, 1995). Since conflicts may arise amongst decision-makers concerning the relative importance of each selection criteria, there may be a need to weight the relative importance of each factor. Once a set of preferred indicators has been identified, a review determining the completeness and balance of the final set can be carried out to ensure that all the major dimensions of sustainability are represented. The final set should be modified as required. The PSR matrix, in particular, is a useful framework for making this final assessment of completeness.

Analyzing and Reporting Progress Towards Sustainability

After indicator measures have been collected, the findings should be analysed. Ideally this entails not only reporting individual indicator values, but also establishing historical trends in specific indicator values, and identifying progress towards specific sustainability goals. Furthermore, where feasible, cause and effect relationships between pressure, state, and response indicators should be attempted. This analysis phase may prove difficult as different opinions may exist about the meaning of indicator trends relative to sustainability goals. For example, the number of building permits issued in a tourism community may indicate economic prosperity to some, while it may indicate an unacceptably high rate of natural land conversion to those more interested in environmental preservation.

The reporting of the findings emanating from the collection process should be tailored to the target audience. For instance, a brief summary report with key indicators should be appropriate for the general public who may not be concerned with a lot of complex information. In contrast, a more detailed report can be prepared for technical staff. This information can also be made available to interested stakeholder groups upon request. Ideally, these reports should include :

- explanations of the significance of each indicator itself and an explanation of the types of value judgments incorporated into its selection;
- assessments of past trends and anticipated future trends in indicator values relative to established target levels;
- graphical representation of indicator trends; and
- where feasible, a discussion of linkages between indicators.

Soliciting Feedback

Soliciting feedback to indicator reports should also be actively pursued. This can be encouraged in a variety of ways. For example, it might be useful to seek feedback via television, radio and print media, as well as public meetings, public surveys and focus groups. All of these techniques can help to refine indicator selection, measurement, and interpretation processes. In any reporting process, an acceptable level of relevant indicator information must be displayed in order to maintain stakeholder interest and at the same time the effort expended must not unduly tax personnel and financial resources of paid and volunteer data collectors in the community (McCool *et al.*, 2001). Responses to requests for indicator refinement by the lead agency must also be evident or the process runs, the risk of stakeholder alienation.

The Whistler Case Study

Tourism development in general, and mountain community tourism in particular, are often characterized by a combination of conflicting demands placed on what are frequently limited and fragile natural resources (Stettner, 1993). Growth management is an approach to planning that seeks to capture the benefits of growth while mitigating its negative consequences. Typically, this involves implementing a range of management strategies including : protecting community sense of place; managing tourism related impacts; identifying community commercial and social priorities; securing stakeholder commitment to specific programme initiatives; and managing tourism demand towards specific community objectives (Gill and Williams, 1994). Such growth management strategies rely heavily on data in the form of indicators to chart progress towards more desirable and sustainable future conditions.

Since 1994, the Resort Municipality of Whistler has undertaken several initiatives to develop and implement a monitoring system that has several sustainability components. Originally enacted in 1976 to encourage compact development and discourage sprawl, Whistler's growth management strategy has expanded to become an integral part of the community's Comprehensive Development Plan and a focus for the municipality's monitoring programme. The growth management strategy addresses issues encountered in many mountain tourism communities (*e.g.*, alpine environmental protection, land use sprawl control, affordable housing provision, community and tourism infrastructure development). In this respect, Whistler's growth management strategy is both innovative and exemplary. However, what distinguishes Whistler's growth management initiatives programme from those of other tourism destinations is its monitoring programme. Initiated in 1994, the monitoring programme is intended to communicate information to the community on how the destination has been changing. This monitoring information is also used to encourage community discussion concerning the selection of appropriate strategies for managing future development and growth.

Many of the elements in Whistler's monitoring programme are consistent with the recommended steps for sustainability reporting described previously. The monitoring initiative addresses the influence of various growth pressures on : resident quality of life; natural environment quality; and affordable housing.

Whistler's Visioning Process

Whistler's Comprehensive Development Plan outlines several general goals that relate to an evolving 'vision' for the resort municipality. The vision is about the values, scope and priorities that should drive management activities in the resort municipality. The formal goals are to :

- enhance the Whistler experience, for those who live in Whistler and for those who visit and use the resort, by balancing the environmental, economic and social needs of the community and the resort;
- continue to move towards environmental sustainability, by fostering and participating in a wide range of environmental partnerships and management initiatives associated with maintaining the high quality of the area's natural and built environments;
- build a stronger resort community, recognizing that this is an important aspect of enhancing the resort; and
- achieve financial sustainability by implementing a range of public and private sector partnerships

designed to support the community economy, as well as introducing a range of innovative and cost-effective methods of delivering municipal services (RMOW, 1993; RMOW, 2002).

The community's monitoring programme has been designed to measure change in the community as a result of growth. However, it should be noted that there has been no explicit consideration of the principles of 'sustainability' (except perhaps in an intuitive context related to 'sense of place' criteria) in establishing the appropriateness of the types and level of growth taking place in the community.

Scoping the Whistler Monitoring Programme

The target audience for the Whistler monitoring programme has been loosely defined as 'community stakeholders'. These stakeholders consist primarily of permanent residents and second homeowners. Stakeholder participation has, on the whole, occurred via annual 'town hall' meetings, community attitude surveys carried out in 1991 and 1995, livingroom focus groups in 1995, and a variety of community visioning processes since 1997 (*e.g.*, community workshops, stakeholder group meetings, workbook surveys). The geographic scope of the monitoring programme was decided by the municipal planning department. It roughly matches the institutional boundaries of the municipality. Little explicit consideration has been given to temporal aspects of the data or indicator trends. Also, no limits have been placed on the amount of data, or number of indicators, reported. Reconsideration is currently being given to the scope of issues addressed by the monitoring programme.

The Use of a Sectoral/Issue-Based Indicator Framework

The data an indicators reported in Whistler's monitoring report have been presented in sectorally based categories related to : development; social characteristics; environment; community facilities and infrastructure, economic benefits; transportation; and resident and visitor satisfaction. This framework was selected by municipal planners in response to the institutional structures that existed at the time of the first monitoring programme. In 1965, the indicator framework was modified to incorporate both sectoral and issue-based indicators. While using the same basic framework, some of its content since then has been modified by the community's municipal planners in response to issues raised by stakeholders in the annual town hall meetings. For example, monitoring information dealing with the state of undeveloped valley lands, natural habitat conditions in protected areas, as well as air and water quality have been added in response to resident requests.

Indicator Selection Criteria

No explicitly defined criteria were used in selecting the indicators employed in the monitoring programme. However, municipal planning department representatives did use indicators that were : readily available (*i.e.*, existing data or easily measured); displayed historical or trend information; were comparable with existing data and information; and responded to stakeholder issues expressed at town hall meetings.

Indicators Selected

The Whistler monitoring programme reports information concerning all the indicators it selects. While no overriding 'key indicators' are highlighted, the most recent monitoring report (RMOW. 2000) includes over eighty indicators organized within a predominantly sectoral framework. Perhaps half of these indicators address some aspect of the concept of sustainability's environmental and economic imperatives.

Monitoring Programme Reporting

The resort municipality publishes its annual community and resort monitoring report for public distribution and reading. Typically, the report includes measurements associated with all of the selected indicator identified. In addition, an annual bulletin with summary indicators information is published. This document is intended to inform a wide audience and stimulate informed stakeholder debate about growth management issues.

Each year these reports, and an additional display of information, are viewed and discussed at an annual open house and town hall meeting. At the 1996 meeting, for example, formal discussion was encouraged around issues related to the most beneficial types of future land development, key growth management concerns, environmental programme issues, and future monitoring programme refinements. Similarly, in 1997, the focus of the town hall meeting was on seeking input to the municipality's vision statement that was in the initial phases of development at that time (Whistler, 2002). It was expected that this vision statement would eventually drive the focus of future monitoring efforts. Subsequent public meetings (1998-2001) have focused on specific sustainability issues, such as housing, transportation and watershed management.

The perspectives presented at these town hall meetings are considered by the municipal officials and staff when creating new policies and selecting new indicators for subsequent years. For example, transportation and affordable housing issues identified at previous town hall meetings have become municipal programme and monitoring priorities in subsequent years.

Notwithstanding these initiatives, gaining an appropriate level and representation of attendance at these reporting sessions is a continuing challenge. Efforts are under way to solicit feedback from younger people, as well as social and environmental stakeholder groups in the community, in order to create a more inclusive perspective concerning the impact of growth on Whistler.

Assessment of Indicator Performance

To date, Whistler has not placed a strong emphasis on linking each of its reported indicators to specific community sustainability goals. As a result it is difficult to assess whether or not the indicators have been effective in measuring progress towards these goals. Consequently, the municipality has not conducted a formal assessment of the effectiveness of the data or its indicators. However, there is some informal recognition that there is a need to create a more systematic linkage between the goals and the reported indicators. This recognition has emerged as the monitoring programme has matured, and as the demand for the inclusion of additional performance indicators has expanded.

Conclusions

In many ways, the Whistler Community and Resort Monitoring Programme represents an exemplary initiative. However, its full potential is not being achieved because the focus of the programme has been primarily to monitor various dimensions of growth impact as opposed to measuring progress towards the development of a more sustainable tourism community. As a consequence, there has been no clearly articulated vision, goals or process for the development of sustainability indicators (Table 11.1)

However, the Whistler monitoring programme is still valuable for a number of reasons. First, it was implemented with the clear objective of maximizing the involvement of a broad group of community stakeholders concerned about a wide range to tourism growth issues. In this context, stakeholders were invited to participate in community decision-making associated with such issues as community size, housing options, and environmental management. Second, the monitoring programme has also assembled a considerable amount of valuable information that is important for enlightened discussion by community stakeholders concerned about these and other growth related matters.

Despite the programme's best intent there is a growing sense that much of the monitoring information collected is not generating the type of discussion on pressing and emerging issues that it was intended to create. Possible explanations for this perceived apathy might include the lack of any well-accepted indicators of progress towards the resort community vision or goals, as well as the lack of a resort community vision

Table 11.1

Comparison of Sustainability Reporting and Whistler Growth Management Programme Monitoring Processes

Model Sustainability	*Reporting Process Criteria*	*Whistler Growth management Monitoring process*
(1)	*(2)*	*(3)*
1. Identification of Community Sustainability Goals	Use a multi-method visioning process (*e.g.*, town hall meetings, workshops. focus groups, open houses, surveys) to establish broad-based stakeholder defined sustainability goals.	Used goals established in Comprehensive Development Plan as proxy for community vision; input for CDP goals derived from limited number of open houses, information meetings and public hearings. No distinct focus on sustainability goals were identified.
2. Scoping	Determine target audience Consider spatial and temporal bounds Include Institutional partners Establish relevant number of indicators.	Community stakeholders were target audience. Spatial boundaries were lands within municipal jurisdiction Number of indicators and institutional partners were not established prior to implementation.
3. Choose indicator Framework	Select combinational framework which maximizes ability of indicators to assess progress	Used a combination of setoral/issue-based frameworks Framework evolved in response to

(Contd.)

(Contd.)

(1)	(2)	(3)
	towards sustainability (*e.g.*, PSR matrix/domain).	departmental organization and issues raised by stakeholders.
4. Define Selection Criteria	Select indicator criteria based on community values and sustainability goals determined through stakeholder involvement.	Formal selection criteria not explicitly defined; informal criteria were related to data availability, affordability and relationship to growth management.
5. Identify Potential Indicators	Use existing listings of indicators as base; use stakeholder input to refine listings to potentially viable sustainability indicators.	Used existing local and regional data which appeared to match best with stakeholder issues.
6. Select Final Indicators	Apply indicator framework and selection criteria to 'long list' and select a final set of indicators.	No formal process was used to select indicator list. No formal attempt was made to refine indicator listings based on sustainability or growth management goals.
7. Analyse	Compare indicator values and trends	No analysis with the exception of 'bed

(Contd.)

(Contd.)

(1)	(2)	(3)
Indicator Results	to specific indicator target levels based on community sustainability goals.	unit ceiling' and a few other indicators such as air quality was undertaken. Few established targets were used to assess indicator values against goals.
8. Report Indicator Results	Report a relevant number of indicators to the target audience and solicit feedback.	Annual monitoring reports and discussions at town hall meeting were used to present findings and solicit feedback.
9. Assess Indicator Performance	Assess indicator measurement relevance to identifying progress toward established sustainability goals.	No specific goals for most indicators were established; therefore, no assessment of indicator performance was conducted.

Source : Adapted from Cambell and Maclaren, 1995; Maclaren, 1996 a, 1996 b.

that reflects the principle and objectives of sustainability. Only in recent times has a comprehensive programme been implemented to develop a vision of Whistler that clearly identifies a set of consensus-based community priorities and directions (Whistler, 2002). The community's local government believes that this visioning process and its subsequent vision statement will help to refocus, refine and improve the community's monitoring programme. In addition, the municipality has been developing a comprehensive Whistler Environmental Strategy (1999 to the present) along with a complementary community wide sustainability awareness and engagement process called 'Whistler. It's our Nature'. Early observations indicate that these initiatives will stimulate the creation of a more focused monitoring process in the community.

Beyond the need for more explicit sustainability goal-indicator linkages, there are also lessons to be learned with respect to the development process for assessing tourism monitoring programmes. In particular, emphasis should be placed on :

- involving a broad and inclusive group of stakeholders in the scoping exercise, as well as the selecticn of relevant indicators tailored to the target audience;
- developing partnerships with other local and regional institutions affected by tourism so as to increase cost efficiency and comprehensiveness in the collection of relevant data;
- using less compartmentalized indictors frameworks (*e.g.*, pressure-state-response) which facilitate the reporting of tourism's growth on various dimensions of ecosystem integrity and natural resource consumption;
- using comprehensive indicator lists developed elsewhere to help guide the selection of relevant indicators which cover critical sustainability issues; and
- reporting the monitored indicator data to community stakeholders via a variety of communication mediums

(*e.g.*, monitoring reports, summary bulletins, newspaper articles) prior to and after public meeting presentations and workshops.

Whistler's monitoring programme was designed to disseminate relevant information to community stakeholders and stimulate enlightened discussion on future growth management decisions. However, it has only been partially successful in achieving this goal. Whistler and other resort communities considering the implementation of such programmes can enhance the appropriateness and relevance of their activities by taking a more sustainable community oriented approach to their monitoring programme. When taken together, Whistler's recent efforts, specifically : the generation of a vision statement for the area; the creation of a comprehensive environmental strategy; and the development of a sustainability awareness communication programme, point to the area being in a much better position in the near future to implement a truly focused and effective monitoring programme.

References

1. Arrow, K. and Bolin, B. (1995) : Economic growth, carrying capacity, and the environment, *Ecological Economics*, **15** : 91-5.
2. Bossel, H. (1999) : *Indicators for Sustainable Development : Theory, Methods, Applications*. Winnipeg, Manitoba, Canada : International Institute for Sustainable Development.
3. Brugman, J. (1997) : Is there a method in our measurement? The use of indicators in local sustainable development planning, *Local* Environment, **2(1)** : 59-72.
4. Campbell, M. and Maclaren, V. (1995) : *Municipal State of the Environment Reporting in Canada : Current Status and Future Needs*. Ottawa : Environment Canada.
5. Daly, H.E. and Cobb, J.B. Jr. (1994) : *For the Common Good : Redirecting the Economy Toward Community, Environment, and a Sustainable Future*, Boston : Beacon Press.
6. Dilks, D. (1995) : *Workshop Proceedings*. Measuring Urban

Sustainability : Canadian Indicators Workshop. Ottawa : Environment Canada.

7. El Serafy, S. (1991) : The environment as capital. In R. Costanza (ed.), Ecological Economics (pp. 168-75). New York : Columbia University Press.
8. Fraser Basin Management Programme, Georgia Basin Initiative/Minister of Municipal Affairs (1995) : *Navigating for Sustainability. A Guide for Local Government Decision Makers*. Vancouver : BC Ministry of Municipal Affairs.
9. Gill, A. and Williams, P. (1994) : Managing growth in mountain tourism communities, *Tourism Management*, **15 (3)** : 212-20.
10. Gill, A. M. (1996) : Rooms with a view : informal settings for public dialogue, *Society and Natural Resources*, **9** : 633-43.
11. Goodland, R. and Daly, J. (1996) : Environmental sustainability : universal and non-negotiable, *Ecological Applications*, **6(4)** : 1002-17.
12. Gosselin, P. and Belanger, D. (1993) : Indicators for a sustainable society, *Canadian Journal of Public Health*, **84 (3)** : 197-200.
13. Hammond, A. and Adriaanse, A. (1995) : *Environmental Indicators : A Systematic Approach to Measuring and Reporting on Policy Performance in the Context of Sustainable Development*. Washington, DC : World Resources Institute.
14. Hardi, P. (1995) : *Models and Methods of Measuring Sustainable Development Performance*. Winnipeg, Canada : International Institute for Sustainable Development.
15. International Council for Local Environmental Initiatives and International Development Research Centre (1996) : *The Local Agenda 21 Planning Guide*. Toronto, Canada : International Council for Local Environmental Initiatives.
16. Jamal, T.B. and Getz, D. (1997) : 'Visioning' for sustainable tourism development : community-based collaborations. In P.E. Murphy (ed), *Quality Management in Urban Tourism*, (pp. 199-220). New York : John Wiley & Sons.
17. Long, P.T. and Perdue, R. (1994) : Rural resident tourism perceptions and attitudes by community level of tourism. *Journal of Travel Research*, **11(3)** : 3-9.

18. Maclaren, V.W. (1996a) : *Developing Indicators of Urban Sustainability : A Focus on the Canadian Experience,* Toronto : Intergovernmental Committee on Urban and Regional Research (ICURR).

19. Maclaren, V. (1996b) : Urban sustainability reporting. *Journal of the American Planning Association,* **62(2)** : 184-202.

20. Manning, E. (1993) : Managing sustainable tourism : indicators for better decisions. In S. Hawkes and P.W. Williams (eds), The Greening of Tourism : *From Principles to Practice.* Vancouver, BC., Centre for Tourism Policy and Research.

21. Manning, E. (1999) : Indicators of tourism sustainability. *Tourism Management,* **20** : 179-81.

12 Environmental Impacts of Leisure and Tourism

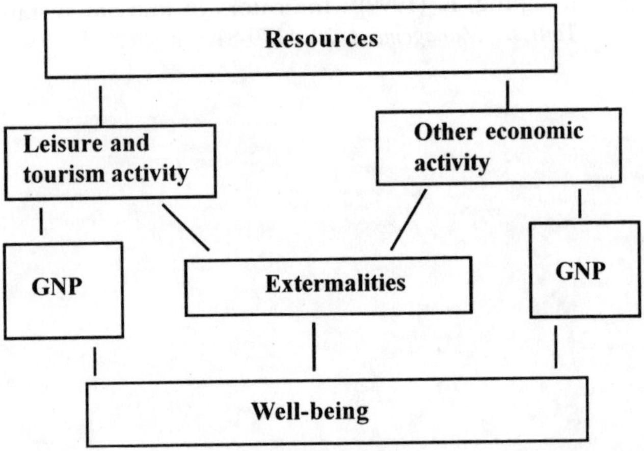

Objectives

Previous chapters examined the contribution of leisure and tourism to countries' national economies. Traditionally, economic analysis has measured impacts in terms of readily measurable variables such as employment, balance of payments and GNP. The objective of this chapter however is to examine the issues raised by environmental economics.

Environmental economics involves a wider view of the impact of economic development and growth, taking into account well-being rather than just measuring how much richer people become in monetary terms. Issues such as global warming, acid rain and resource depletion have been highlighted as threats to economic growth and even to the future of our species, and critiques and techniques developed by environmental economists can be readily used in the leisure and tourism sector.

First, questions can be raised about the validity of focusing measures of success solely on the uncritical use of GNP data. Second, environmental accounting techniques seek to include a wide rage of considerations when considering the cost and benefits of particular projects. These include effects on the natural and built environment, as well as raw material and waste product issues.

When subjected to environmental scrutiny, the leisure and tourism sector can display examples of previously unaccounted overall benefits as well as costs. Additionally, as well as being the perpetrator of negative environmental effects, the sector is sometimes the victim of environmental pollution caused elsewhere.

After studying this chapter students will be able to :

- distinguish between growth in GNP and growth in well-being
- distinguish between renewable and non-renewable resources (sources) and analyse the use of such resources
- understand the significance of waste disposal capacity (sinks) to the economy
- analyse the effects of the existence of open-access resources on resource use
- identify the existence of externalities and their contribution to well-being

Economic Growth and Well-Being

Previous chapter considered the contribution of the leisure and tourism sector to economic growth. Economic growth was measured by examining changes in real GNP per capita. Environmental economists point out that such figures may give a misleading impression about improvements in economic well-being for the following reasons :

- The environmental costs of producing goods and services which appear in GNP are not always accounted for

Exhibit 12.1. demonstrates some of these concepts in relation to the development of an airport.

Exhibit 12.1. Development and Well-being

The building and the running of an airport will add to GNP in terms of expenditure on building materials, fixtures and fittings, roads and access, staffing and consumables. However local residents will suffer form increased noise and atmospheric pollution as well as traffic congestion—none of these costs will appear in GNP data.

Whilst some local residents may benefit in terms of job opportunities, gainers and losers are often different people. The main gainers from the development are the shareholders of the airport company, airlines and tour operators, employees, and travellers themselves. Local residents are likely to form only a small fraction of these categories and so the benefits of such growth will be unevenly shared. GNP per capita figures only show average effects of growth.

Because of the extra noise, some residents will buy double glazing, more petrol will be used because of traffic congestion, and roofing contractors will gain more work because of vortex effects of aircraft (the tendency of aircraft engine thrust to cause intense patches of air currents which remove roof tiles). This is defensive expenditure. It is expenditure made to try to combat some of the ill-effects of the development. It does not leave anyone better off than before the development, but it contributes of GNP data, exaggerating the apparent benefits of the development.

Finally the development will involve loss of the natural environment. This represents the loss of an amenity to some people in terms of views or tranquility or open space, but again this fails to register in GNP data.

- The distribution of the benefits of economic growth is not always even.
- GNP figures may include 'defensive' expenditure.
- The destruction of the natural environment is not shown.

The discussion in exhibit 12.1 shows the need for caution in equating growth in GNP with growth in well-being. Indeed, some economists have argued that when a wider view of economics growth is taken, the costs may exceed the benefits. Such analysis has caused the questioning of policies which lead to fastest economic growth without regard to the wider consequences and some environmental economists have called for a halt or limit to economic growth.

The New Economics Foundation has produced andIndex of Sustainable Economic Welfare (ISEW) as an alternative measure of economic progress to that of GDP. It argues that while in 1997 GDP in the UK was over one and a half times higher than that in 1972, 'during the same period violent crime has quadrupled, the incidence of asthma has tripled, the number of workless households has tripled, car traffic has almost doubled and concentrations of climate changing gases in the atmosphere have grown to perilous levels'. The ISEW adjusts GDP accounts to take account of a wider understanding of welfare. Its five main adjustments are :

1. Defensive expenditure (spending to offset social environmental costs) are deducted.
2. An allowance is made for long-term environmental damage.
3. Net investment is included.
4. Changes in the distribution of income are valorized to reflect the higher marginal utility derived by extra income earned by poorer people.
5. A value for household labour is included.

Comparisons between changes in GDP and the ISEW over

time are striking. Whilst per capita GDP grew at an annual average of 2 per cent between 1950 and 1966 the ISEW only grew by an annual average of 0.6 per cent. But in recent years the indices have actually moved in different directions. Between 1990 and 1996 whilst per capita GDP has risen by an annual average of 1.1 per cent, per capita ISEW has actually fallen by an annual average of 1.3 per cent.

Externalities

The notion of externalities has already been briefly discussed. Externalities are those costs or benefits arising from production or consumption of goods and services which are not reflected in market prices. Because of this there is little incentive for firms to curb external costs, since they do not have to pay for them. Externalities can be divided into the following categories :

- Production on production. This is where one firm's external costs interfere with the operation of another firm, *e.g.* noise from discos and clubs which creates a noise nuisance to hotel residents.
- Production on consumption. This is where industrial externalities affect individuals' consumption of a good or service, *e.g.* aircraft noise affects people trying to listen to music; increase in crime levels in resorts; visual pollution of hotels, caravans and car parks affects enjoyment of landscape.
- Consumption on production. This occurs when for example external costs of consuming a good or service interfere with a firm's production process, *e.g.* traffic jams caused by a leisure park cause transport delays to local firms.
- Consumption on consumption. This is where the external effects of an individual's consumption of a good or service affect the well-being of another consumer, *e.g.* holiday-makers destroying coral reef, congestion around a football stadium causing inconvenience to other people.

Figure 12.1. Shows how firms tend to over-produce goods and services which are subject to externalities.

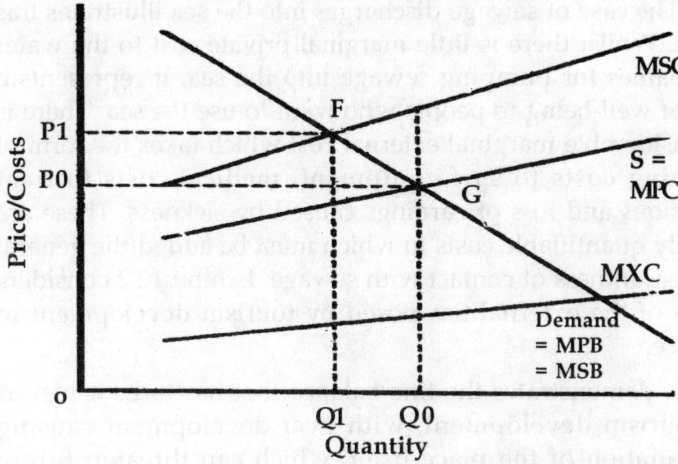

Fig. 12.1. External costs, private costs and optimum output. See text for details.

Demand curve D shows the marginal private benefit of consuming the good and, assuming there are no external benefits, it also represents the marginal social benefit. It shows how much consumers are willing to pay for extra units of output. Supply curve S shows the marginal private costs of production, *i.e.* costs per extra unit of output.

Producers will wish to expand their output to 0Q0 since the price they receive from extra units of production will exceed the costs of extra units of production up to that point. Beyond that point the extra costs of producing each good will exceed the price received for it. Thus 0Q0 represents the optimal market level of production.

Curve MXC represents marginal external costs, perhaps because of noise or other pollution effects. Adding MXC to MPC generates the marginal social cost curve MSC. Notice that now we include external costs, *i.e.*, previously unpriced environmental resources, the level of output 0Q0 is no longer optimal, since marginal social costs exceed marginal social benefits by the amount *FG*. A reduction in output to 0Q1 where

MSC = MSB would need to take place to provide the optimal social level of production.

The case of sewage discharges into the sea illustrates this point. Whilst there is little marginal private cost to the water companies for pumping sewage into the sea, it represents a loss of well-being to people who want to use the sea. There is a considerable marginal external cost which takes the form of cleaning costs to surf equipment, medical costs to treat infections and loss of earnings caused by sickness. These are readily quantifiable costs to which must be added the general unpleasantness of contact with sewage. Exhibit 12.2 considers some of the externalities posed by tourism development in Greece.

It demonstrates the fine balance that has to be achieved in tourism development, with over-development causing degradation of the place itself, which can threaten future demand and prosperity.

Another consequence that may stem from such development is that price inflation and property prices may rise, making it increasingly difficult for those not participating in the development, and thus benefiting from rising wages and profits, to remain in the area. This effect is termed economic dualism and occurs where a traditional and a growing sector of the economy exist side by side. The growing sector may increasingly threaten the traditional sector and participants in the traditional sector may only be able to access limited parts of the growing sector.

It is also possible to identify less obvious, distant, external costs of tourism and leisure developments. For large-scale resort developments, for example, consideration can be given to the sources of raw materials for building and the subsequent effect of quarrying for stone or forest depletion for timber.

Use of Resources

Environmental economics distinguishes between two types of resources. Non-renewable resources are those which have a fixed supply. Once they have been used up there will none

Exhibit 12.2. Tourism Curse Visited on this Blessed Aegean Isle

The Greek island of Amorgos is rugged, barren and beautiful.

But things are changing fast since locals can now make more money through tourism in 2 months than they could otherwise make in a year.

The tourism boom is taking its environmental toll. There are growing problems with water, sewage and rubbish, although officials are reluctant to acknowledge them.

'If we're careful we'll be all right. Out only real problem is plastic water bottles,' says Mr Vekris, a local mayor. You know the quality of our lives has really improved with tourism'.

And indeed it has. It has meant washing machines and colour televisions for local inhabitants, but these are luxuries that will ultimately be at the expense of Amorgos.

Source : Guardian, 6 September 1994 (adapted).

left for future generations. Renewable resources are those which are capable of being replenished.

Non-Renewable Resources

Landscapes, views, open spaces and tranquility represent non-renewable resources in the leisure and tourism sector. They are used up by general economic development as well as by leisure and tourism development itself. An important consideration concerning the use of non-renewable resources is the rate of depletion and hence the level of resources bequeathed to future generations.

The urgency of this problem can be illustrated as follows : Economic development uses up such resources. It also generates increases in incomes and leisure time and thus the demand for such resources. Thus we have the prospect of dwindling natural resources having to provide for increasing demands and thus degeneration occurring at a quickening pace.

Renewable Resources

An important renewable resource for large-scale tourism development in some parts of the world is water. Large-scale development requires considerable resources of fresh water. It is here that the technique of impact assessment is important. Forecasts need to be made of water use against water renewal, although in some circumstances the latter may be supplemented by water diversion schemes. If water is obtained from underground aquifers, these will eventually run dry or be subjected to salt or other pollution if the rate of extraction exceeds the rate of replenishment.

This problem is compounded by the free access problem, where it is not in anyone's interests to preserve water if everyone is drawing if from the same source.

Exhibit 12.3. Calls for Brake on Mountain Biking— Nicholas Schoon

The government is pondering whether restrictions on mountain bikes may be necessary because their growing popularity is damaging some of the nation's best scenery.

This week a report to be published by the Council for the Protection of Rural England will highlight mountain biking as one of the ways in which unrestricted countryside leisure and tourism are increasingly harming the environment. The cyclists often use footpaths, although the law says they should be restricted to bridle ways and byways. The broad, highgrip types they use are stripping out vegetation and leaving deep, muddy furrows.

Walkers and ramblers complain that they are irritated and frightened by mountain bikes that pass them at speed. Some regard the bicycles as an inappropriate, unnatural leisure pursuit in cherished landscapes such as the 11 national parks of England and Wales.

Source : Independent, 9 May 1994 (adapted).

Resources such as footpaths and public parks also have a renewable resource element to them. If the rate of wear of footpaths for examples exceeds the rate of regeneration of protective vegetation, degradation will occur, as illustrated in Exhibit 12.3.

One of the reasons for such overuse and degradation is that the use of footpaths and public parks is free to the user. In markets where prices prevail, price is an important factor in rationing the demand for scarce resources. Consumers economize on use so as to conserve their limited money income. Where price is zero, there is no incentive to economize. The use of unmetered water illustrates this point. For example, many people leave the tap on when they are cleaning their teeth, using a couple of pints of water where only half a cupful is needed since there is no incentive to economize to use. Figure 12.2 shows the economics behind this.

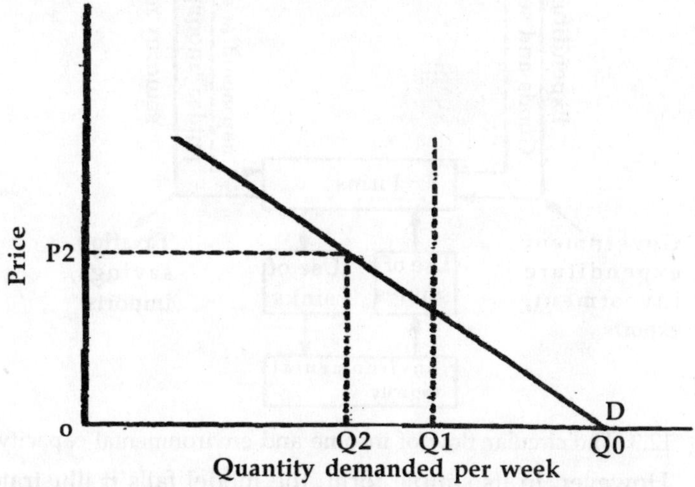

Fig. 12.2. Effects of zero price on demand. See text for details.

Curve D represents the demand curve for the use of a footpath. As price falls, demand rises. At price P2 demand would be Q2. If zero price is charged, demand rises to 0Q0. For some paths this may result in usage which exceeds the limits where the resource can regenerate itself. If 0Q1 represents the point of use beyond which regeneration cannot take place, then Q1 Q0 represents use which causes degeneration of the resource at zero price.

The Macroeconomy and Waste

Figure 12.3 recalls the simple circular flow of income model used earlier to underpin introductory macroeconomic analysis.

Factors of production are purchased by firms from households and combined to produce goods and services which are then sold to households. Household expenditure is financed from the income derived from selling factors of production to firms. Additionally there are leakages from the system in the form of taxes, savings and imports, as well as injections into the system of government spending, investment and exports.

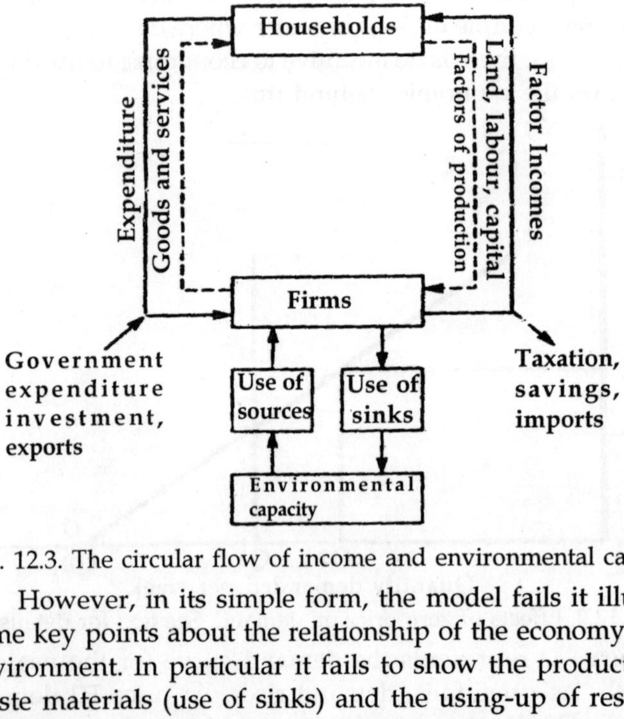

Fig. 12.3. The circular flow of income and environmental capacity.

However, in its simple form, the model fails it illustrate some key points about the relationship of the economy to the environment. In particular it fails to show the production of waste materials (use of sinks) and the using-up of resources (use of sources). In fact the production of waste materials is partially covered by the model and partially not. Exhibit 12.4 illustrates this point.

The article is about Newquay in Cornwall, UK, whose population of 100 000 is swollen by up to a million summer visitors. A key product of the tourism industry is sewage. This waste is collected and practically treated by South West Water, and this activity is picked up by traditional economics in the simple circular flow diagram as the use of factors of production to perform a service. However the raw sewage that is discharged directly into the sea represents the use of a waste sink and the simple circular flow model does not reflect this.

The circular flow model can show an increase in economic growth caused by tourism—increased expenditure, generating increased incomes which in turn allow increased expenditure—without highlighting a significant threat to such growth in terms of pollution effects. The use of the waste sink is free to South West Water and thus there is little incentive for it to amend its behaviour. There is, though, clearly a limit to the capacity of the sea to assimilate this waste. Where this assimilative capacity is exceeded, degradation of the sea occurs.

Environmental economics seeks to make the link between economic production—in this case tourism—on the hand, and the production of and the ability of the ecosystem to absorb waste on the other. It further seeks to amend economic models

Exhibit 12.4. Surfing in the Sewers

'I've just come back from a surf. The water quality wasn't too bad today because the wind was blowing offshore and the tide was going out. When the wind blows on to the shore and when the tide is high you still get the occasional pad or condom floating by.'

The surfers are from happy. And it's not hard to see why. A quick walk on to the headland and you notice the air begins to smell rich, sweet and vile. A brown slick drifts out to sea off the point. Tucked away beneath the cliffs is its source—the same old sewage outflow pipe, pumping out output all day long.

Source : Guardian, 5 August 1994 (adapted).

to incorporate this relationship so that such economic development can take place without causing feedback which would threaten economic development, or cause an unacceptable level of pollution.

Thus figure 12.3 adds an environmental dimension to the simple circular flow model to highlight that production uses sources and sinks and that the environment has a limited capacity to meet these demands.

Open Access and Overuse

There is a particular problem posed by open access to resources. The sea is an example of an open-access resource. It does not have a clear owner and therefore it is difficult to exert property rights over it—for example, preventing waste dumping. Because of this there is little incentive to reduce outflows into the sea.

The problem becomes more difficult with seas such as the Mediterranean. The Mediterranean coastline is shared by a number of countries. If one country should decide to reduce outflows of sewage into the sea, it will still suffer the ill-effects of the outflows from other countries who might even think that there is now more capacity for their sewage.

Exhibit 12.5 goes beneath the sea to record the destruction of an open-access resource.

Environmental Effects of Other Sectors on the Leisure and Tourism Sector

The general environmental concerns of global warming, ozone depletion, acid rain and atmospheric pollution each have impacts on the leisure and tourism sector.

The early 1990s for example witnessed successive years of poor snow conditions in European ski resorts. Global warming would clearly have an impact on the height of snow cover, thus putting low-level resorts out of business and shortening the length of the ski season. For example, a weather forecasting model at the UK Hadley Centre for Climate Prediction and Research predicts a 3°C increase in UK average

Exhibit 12.5. Reefs Under Threat

It took thousands of years to create the majestic coral reefs that lie under the earth's oceans. These vast limestone structures have been laid over the centuries by reef-building corals. They are home to a huge diversity of plants and over 200 species of fish.

The Great Barrier Reef, off the coast of Australia extends for some 2000 kilometres and is a magnet for scuba divers. The Belize Barrier Reef stretches for some 250 kilometres off the coast of Belize in central America.

But the reefs are under threat from industry, from agriculture and from tourism. Industrial fishing techniques using dynamite can blow up the fragile polyps that create the reefs. Rain forest clearance smothers the Belize Reef as thickly polluted run-off flows out of the rivers into the oceans.

Meanwhile, the tourism trade is set to kill one of its golden gooses. Whilst some boat operators practise good conservation methods and coach and cajole their clients to respect the coral, the growing size of the tourist tide threatens reef preservation. Boatloads of inexperienced snorkellers and divers regularly inflict unintentional damage, by touching sensitive polyps or smashing coral branches with a kick of a flipper.

But not all the damage is accidental. Some boat operators let their anchors drop on the reefs—the damage is evident by the clouds of debris thrown up. And some tourists seem unable to resist taking home just one small momento ('that won't make any difference'). For those who don't make the dive themselves there are plenty of willing hands—and souvenir shops in reef resorts are often full of rare shells and coral curios.

Source : The author, from press cuttings, January 1995.

temperatures between 1998 and 2100. This is based on estimated outputs and effects of greenhouse gases. The results are bad news for the Scottish ski industry since more of the precipitation that falls in Scotland will be in the form of rain rather than snow. Exhibit 12.6 demonstrates alarming possible effects of global warming.

Carbon dioxide emissions, the main source of which is fossil-fuel burning, are the main contributor to global warming.

Exhibit 12.6. 'Paradise' Islands Unite Against Sea-Level Threat : Alarm Over Global Warming—Geoffrey Lean

Fakaofu Atoll, the main island of the watery territory of Tokelau, has just one of the world's 400 million automobiles and it is making a lonely contribution to the island's impending extinction.

Tokelau, a group of islands administered by New Zealand—just 12 square kilometres of land in more than 250,000 square kilometres of Pacific Ocean—is expected, literally, to be wiped off the map by pollution. So are six other scattered strings of atolls, including similar dependencies and independent nations, among them the 1196-island state of the Maldives in the Indian Ocean.

As carbon dioxide emitted by fuel burned in the world's cars, homes and industries heats up the climate, many scientists believe that the seas will rise and eventually drown such low-lying islands.

Though small may be beautiful, however, it is also vulnerable. These islands' water supplies are usually limited and are increasingly being depleted by the tourism on which at least half their economies depend. Tourism increases pollution—only one-tenth of the sewage produced by the 20 million people who visit the Caribbean each year receives any kind of treatment. Increasingly dirty seas and oil spills imperil economies.

But the greatest threat of all comes from global warming. The highest point on the main island of Kiribas, in the Pacific Ocean, is 2 foot above sea level; and scientists' best estimate is that the seas will rise higher than this over the next century.

Source : independent of Sunday, 13 March 1994 (adapted).

Some commentators have predicted an increase in the average surface temperature of the earth of between 2 and 5° C over the next hundred years if carbon dioxide emissions double over the same period.

However not only are the physics and the chemistry of this calculation fraught with uncertainty, but so are the economics. It is difficult to predict the rate of economic growth and the subsequent demand for fossil-fuel burning for energy provision. Also there is a time lag between the emission of greenhouse gases and the effect on global warming.

Exhibit 12.7. Lights, Camera, Destruction

Twentieth-Century Fox, searching for a location to film Amex Garland's bestselling novel, The Beach, chose Maya Bay on Phi Phi Ley island, situated off southern Thailand. The film stars Leonardo Dicaprio and Tilda Swinton. However, Maya Bay's natural state of scrub bushes did not quite fit the imagination of the producer of the film, Andrew Macdonald. He wanted coconut trees and long clear views over sand and sea and ginned permission from the Thai forestry department to give the beach a makeover. The government added its blessing to the project saying that the film would benefit the economy by promoting Thailand.

However, John Vidal reported in *The Observer* that 'More than half of the level section of the beach has now been dug up and the sand dunes broken up. Hundreds of holes have been dug, destroying the roots of plants that hold the dunes together.' The actions of the film unit have attracted the attentions of local environmental groups. They staged a demonstration on the beach wearing Dicaprio masks and protested that the damage caused by digging up plants was damaging the ecosystem and would lead to beach erosion.

Ozone depletion may also affect the leisure and tourism sector. The ozone layer is a layer of gas around the earth which protects it form ultra-violet radiation from the sun. Recent thinning of the ozone layer has been attributed to use of CFCs—chlorofluorocarbons—which have been used in the manufacture of spray cans and refrigerators. The main harmful effects of ozone depletion are to increase the danger of skin cancer after exposure to the sun. Clearly this may affect the demand for holidays based around sunbathing.

Acid rain is the term given to acidic deposits caused mainly by the emission of sulphur dioxide into the atmosphere by industry. Its main effects in the leisure and tourism sector include :

- corrosion of buildings (particularly the stonework found on cathedrals)
- damage to trees (making forest areas less attractive to tourism)
- pollution of rivers and lakes

The external effects of specific industrial developments can also have an impact on the leisure and tourism sector.

Exhibit 12.7 illustrates the effects of the film industry on the tourism sector.

Positive Environmental Effects of Leisure and Tourism

Although much of the environmental debate focuses on the detrimental effects of economic development, there are also benefits which can be noted. The inflow of foreign tourists to London for example sustains a breadth of theatres that could not be supported buy the indigenous population. The existence of tourism in remote rural areas can make the difference between local shops remaining profitable, and therefore open, or not. Similarly the income and interest derived from tourists help to preserve heritage sites, contributing to restoration and upkeep. National parks and forest provide not only facilities for tourism but also habitats for flora and fauna.

Review of Key Terms

- Environmental economics = analysis of human well-being as well as the flow of money in the economy.
- Defensive GNP expenditure = expenditure that takes place to defend or protect one party from the external

Exhibit 12.8. Deforestation : The Tourism Alternative

In 1990 about 11 000 square kilometres of Amazonian rainforest were cleared and by 1995, that figure had jumped to more than 29 000 square kilometres. The latter represents an area equivalent to over 6 million football fields. The forest is being subjected to a series of developments which involve its wholesale destruction. These include industrial-scale agriculture schemes, cattle ranching and tropical timber cutting. To support these schemes there have been forest highway projects, energy distribution schemes and resettlement programmes.

The environmental consequences of this destruction are threefold. First, the Amazon rainforest is home to Amerindian settlements. Second, it contains almost 50 per cent of the world's terrestrial species and is a crucial site for maintaining biodiversity. The Amazon rainforest also plays an important role in the global carbon and water cycles. Trees are essential in reducing carbon dioxide levels in the atmosphere and bout one-fifth of the earth's fresh water flows down the rive Amazon. Meanwhile, carbon emissions from slash-and-burn clearance programmes add to global warming.

Niger Sizer, a senior associate with the World Resources Institute and lose Goldemberg who has an environment portfolio in the Brazilian government, suggest alternative uses of the forest to prevent its destruction, emphasizing the role leisure and tourism can play : 'Brazil is receiving hundreds of millions of dollars in international assistance administered by the World Bank to reduce deforestation. More careful use of these G-7 funds could go a long way towards combating the crisis... Investments could be made in alternative development, such as community forestry, non-timber products, education and tourism instead of subsidizing rainforest destruction'.

Source : The Author, 1999.

Exhibit 12.8 illustrates the potential for tourism to counter global deforestation.

effects of the activities of another (*e.g.* double glazing as a defence from noise pollution).

- Externalities = those costs or benefits arising from production or consumption of goods and services which are not reflected in market prices.
- ISEW = Index of Sustainable Economic Welfare.
- Non-renewable resources = those which have a fixed supply.
- Renewable resources = those which are capable of being replenished.
- Waste sink = part of the environment where waste products are deposited.
- Assimilative capacity = ability of sink to absorb waste.

Data Questions

Task 12.1 Cashing in on a hole in the sky : David Nicholson-Lord argues that green economics should replace Adam Smith

The adage that every cloud has a silver lining is even truer now that the sun is shining. This month saw the start of an alliance between Boots and the Cancer Research Campaign to promote 'sensible sun behaviour'. The benefits for the Cancer Research Campaign are obvious : extra money for research. But what's in it for Boots?

Here's a clue. There are five 'play safe in the sun' guidelines and at least three involve buying something : sunhats, sunglasses, suncream. Who sells sunglasses? Why, Boots does—in fact it is offering customers discounts if they trade in their old ones. Boots also sells suncream. The lucrative sun—protection market is worth £110m and Boots has about 47 per cent of it.

The hidden factor in all this is the gap in the ozone layer opening up 20 miles above our heads and letting in carcinogenic radiation. Skin cancer raters in the UK are double those of 20 years ago, and although lazing on foreign beaches is still largely to blame, the ozone factor is catching up fast. In the USA alone, accelerating ozone loss could cause an extra 200 000 skin—cancer deaths over the next 50 years. Profit margins on suncreams are about 50 per cent and the market is growing at around 4 per cent a year. Suncreams with a high protection factor make up 70 per cent of it. From a purefy business perspective, holes in the ozone layer are exceptionally good news.

There is another, more serious angle to this. When the Treasury does its sums, that portion of the £110m sun-protection market arising from worries about ultraviolet radiation will be added to GNP and will count as economic growth. Thanks to the hole in the ozone layer and the skin cancer epidemic, we will all be that little bit richer. As a way of measuring progress, this is clearly a nonsense, since the quality of our lives will undoubtedly be poorer.

Fortunately, some economists are developing a better way of assessing growth. Later this year the New Economics foundation, a group of 'green' economists, will produce the UK's first index of sustainable welfare, a form of alternative GNP measuring progress since the fifties, not only in income but in areas such as health, education, diet and environmental quality. These developments signify that the environmental movement is evolving a coherent critique of conventional economic theory which includes a response to the accelerating pace of planetary degradation—global warming in particular.

The global free market emerges as one of the villains. To a generation nourished on the idea that unlimited free trade is a food thing, this may be hard to accept. It rests on the assumptions that, first, cash relationships are invading and destroying areas of community life in which they have no place; and second, far from being a benevolent 'invisible hand'—Adam Smith's phrase—the market is blind to the environmental and social destruction it causes. Hence the global cash economy is a game that only the rich and powerful can win.

Which brings us back to Boots and the GNP. In the postwar era, GNP has been transmuted form being a purely statistical tool into a national political goal. Unscrambling it promises to be an exercise both cathartic and revelatory. An index of sustainable economic welfare developed in the USA, for example, shows that while the sum total of economic activity, measuring both 'good' and 'bad' expenditure, has continued to increase, improvements in welfare levelled off in the late sixties and since 1979 have declined.

In other words, we have lots more suncream, sunglasses and sunhats—but we can't really enjoy the sunshine any more.

Source : The Independent : 31 May 1993 (adapted).

Questions :

1 'Thanks to the hole in the ozone layer... we will all be that little bit richer.'

(*a*) Explain what is meant by this.

(*b*) Explain why 'this is clearly a nonsense'.

2 'The environmental movement is evolving a coherent critique of conventional economic theory' Explain the meaning of this statement.

3 Explain what economic 'goods' and 'bads' derive from leisure and tourist economic activities.

4 Should green economics replace Adam Smith?

5 Distinguish between GDP and ISEW using this article.

Task 12.2 Tourist Overcrowding Spoils Enjoyment of Historic Venue : Chester Approaches Saturation Point—David Nicholson-Lord

So many tourists are crowding into Chester, one of Britain's oldest and most beautiful ciues, that they are spoiling if for each other, according to the first 'environmental capacity' study by a local authority.

The study, to be published next month, highlights the dilemma faced by many historic towns where visitor numbers are nearing saturation point. It examines pedestrian densities in the city using a test of psychological 'comfort' developed by an American academic.

According to the English Historic Town Forum, centers such as Cambridge, York and Canterbury are struggling to cope with pollution, congestion and growing tensions between residents and visitors. Some towns are now trying to discourage visitors. The Chester study examined walking speeds, traffic flows and pedestrian numbers and found widespread evidence of tension caused by the 'competing demands for the limited street space in the heart of the city'. In much of the historic centre, pedestrian comfort was 'below acceptable levels' it said. 'In the most critical locations, [the] tension is strained beyond capacity.' The crowding was 'detracting from any pleasure of being in this historically rich environment'.

Chester, a city of 119 000, has an estimated 2–3 million visitors a year, most of whom crowd into a narrow centre inside the Roman walls. A spokesman for the city said pedestrian pressures were sometimes 'uncomfortable', adding : 'We are looking at what development Chester can sustain without further erosion of the fabric and the historic centre.' Pedestrianisation and new bus routes are being considered.

In a new guide for historic towns, the forum, and the English Tourist Board, urge then to adopt 'visitor management plans'. Stephen Mills, head of development at the board, said, many places felt they had too many visitors 'but you can't stop people coming—therefore you need to manage them in order to survive'.

In Cambridge, however, the council has refused to promote the town. One theme suggested—but not adopted—was the 'Great Cambridge stay away day, with the slogan : 'Cambridge is full—we don't want you.'

York, according to the forum, has reached a ceiling on visitors.

Bourton-on-the-Water, the most visited village in the Cotswolds, also 'suffers intensely form congestion and other problems'. In Bath, residents had turned hosepipes on open-top tourist buses.

Source : The Independent, 31 May 1994.

Questions :

1 What are externalities?

2 Classify the leisure and tourism-related externalities into :

(a) production on production

(b) production on consumption

(c) consumption on consumption

(d) consumption on production

3 What are the economic causes of 'crowding [that is] detracting from any pleasure of being in this historically rich environment [of Chester]'

Task 12.3 Fasten your Seatbelts and Prepare for Unsustainable Take-Off

The Heathrow Association for the Control of Aircraft Noise (HACAN) has recently published data from a number of sources about the effects that airports have on their local environment. These include :

- Sedative use increases by 8 per cent in areas affected by aircraft noise.
- Fourteen per cent more anti-asthma drugs are consumed by people living within 10 kilometres of an airport.
- Transport 2000 calculates that every return air ticket generates an average of four car journeys.
- Dr, Meyer Hillman, a transport specialist, has shown that every passenger on a return flight to Florida is responsible for a discharge of 1.8 tonnes of carbon dioxide.
- The Intergovernmental Panel on Climate Change is expected to show that aircraft emissions are responsible

for about 10 per cent of the world's carbon dioxide production.

- Mortality rates, are near Los Angeles Airport are 5 per cent higher than in quieter places.
- The reading ability of 12-14 year-olds who attend schools under flight paths is reduced by 23 per cent.
- Children exposed to aircraft noise are more likely to develop anxiety disorders.
- Airport expansion means more noise and less countryside.
- CO2 emissions are forecast to increase by 500 per cent by 2100.
- High-altitude carbon emissions from aircrafts are less likely to be reabsorbed by forests or oceans than other emissions, and are therefore more serious threats to the greenhouse effect.
- Sulphur dioxide emissions from aircraft on the polar routes contribute to ozone depletion.

Source : HACAN.

Questions

1. What externalities are associated with air travel?

2. Assess the impact of air travel on renewable and non-renewable resources

3. Are the quiet skies an example of open access over-use?

4. What evidence is there to suggest that the market equilibrium of air traffic exceeds the optimum social equilibrium?

5. How should GDP figures be adjusted to take account of the externalities of air travel?

13 Sustainability and 'Green' Leisure and Tourism

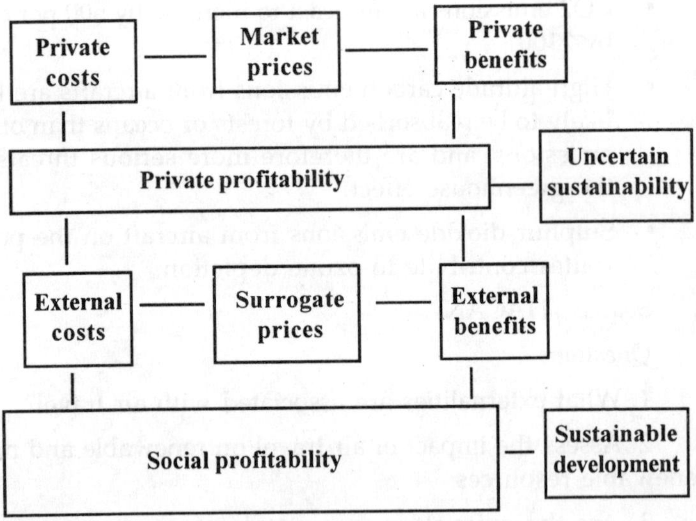

Objectives

Chapter 12 examined the environmental impacts of the leisure and tourism sector. It considered ways in which the market failed to signal long-term problems of resource depletion, waste production and disposal, and other unpriced externalities. It highlighted the distinction between what was most profitable for firms and what was most profitable for society as a whole. It chronicled a wealth of evidence of undesirable results if the market was left to dictate future developments without any regard for wider environmental considerations.

This chapter examines strategies for utilizing environmental economic analysis to enable development of the leisure and tourism sector to take place with due regard to possible side-effects. The aim of such analysis is to prevent the side-effects of development causing socially unacceptable damage to the environment or indeed to stifle the very developments themselves.

By studying this chapter students will be able to :

- understand the limitations of the price mechanism in allocating resources in respect of environmental considerations
- explain the meaning of sustainable development
- utilize the concept of cost-benefit analysis to determine the value of a project to society as a whole
- evaluate a variety of methods to impute value to unpriced externalities
- evaluate different policy instruments for encouraging sustainability and environmental consideration
- understand the range of influences on environmental policy

The Price Mechanism and the Environment

The market economy does in fact have an in-built tendency to conserve resources. In the model where competing firms seek to maximize their profits, since profit is defined as total revenue minus total costs, there is a constant pressure to economize on resources and hence minimize costs. Exhibit 19.1 is a transcript of a report on the Radio 4 Today Programme which shows this principle in action.

However the current market price of resources is not always an accurate measure of its true cost. This is particularly the case for unpriced open-access resources such as the sea. Chapter 12 explored the fact that, whilst the costs of sewage pumping into the sea were minimal for water companies, considerable pollution costs are incurred by other users of the sea. Similarly the loss of landscape and views caused by tourism destination development is not apparent in the profit and loss accounts of the organizations involved. Equally the price mechanism does not give due regard to the future.

Exhibit 13.1. Costs of Green Business a Lie

Sue MacGregor :	Now, a book published this week appears to knock on its head the old adage that it costs business the earth to protect the environment : the authors of the book say the opposite is often the case. Roger Harabin reports on a news story that seems almost too good to be true.
First woman :	This is your room, sir.
Roger Harabin :	Hotels gobble power, and power pollutes.
First woman :	You've got the television over here; over here we've got a mini-bar, fully stocked...
Roger Harabin :	But one hotel group has switched on to a little-used form of power generation that's cleaner than others. At the Russell Hotel in central London the secret is in the basement. Here under the plush reception rooms is the hotel's very own generating station. In a normal power station the heat from making electricity goes to waste, but the Forte group has installed a system called combined heat and power which pipes the hot water to warm the bedrooms. The manager, Ben Sington, says the savings are enormous.
Ben Sington :	When they told me that they were going to give me a machine in this useless piece of space, and give me £6000 worth of savings a year I couldn't believe it, and it's true, it has given me that.

Source : The Today Programme, Radio 4, 12 September 1994 (adapted).

Overexploitation of non-renewable resources such as coastline, countryside, rivers and mountains may leave future generations materially worse off than the current population. These considerations mean that the market often leads to overproduction and overdevelopment of projects where there are considerable unpriced externalities.

Meaning of Sustainable Development

There is considerable debate about the precise definition of sustainable development. It should also be noted that several levels of sustainability may be considered. At the widest level, sustainability of world economic development embraces those planet-threatening issues of global warming, resource depletion and ozone loss. Sustainability can also be considered at a national economy level, at a regional level, at a tourism destination level and at an individual leisure or tourism project level.

The 1987 *Brundtland Report* for the World Commission on Environment and Development defined sustainability as 'development that meets the needs of the present without compromising the ability of future generations to meet their own needs'. It therefore laid considerable emphasis on what is termed 'intergenerational equity'.

Key elements in this approach to sustainable development are first, the rate of use of renewable and non-renewable resources and maintenance of natural capital. Implicit here is that renewable resources should not be used beyond their regenerative capacities. Additionally, where non-renewable resources are used up, future generations should be compensated by the provision of substitute capital in some form so that, at the minimum, a constant stock of capital is maintained across generations.

The second key element in the *Brundtland Report* is consideration of the effects of development on waste sinks.

Sustainability has also been defined as growth which is not threatened by feedback, for example, pollution resource depletion or social unrest. This can be related to tourism destination development. In this case sustainability would be that level of development which did not exceed the carrying capacity of the destination and thus cause serious or irreversible changes to the destination. It is development that can sustain itself in the long run.

It is also possible to consider environmental costs and benefits when considering specific projects. This approach considers the total social and private costs against the total private and social benefits of project with a view to summarizing its total social value, taking into consideration environmental impacts as well as market profitability.

The key principles of sustainability can be summarized as :

- consideration of externalities
- consideration of depletion of non-renewable resources
- tailoring use of renewable resources to their regenerative capacity
- tailoring of economic activity to the carrying capacity of the environment

Since the operation of the free market in its present form does not guarantee the inclusion of the above principles in resource allocation, it follows that the implementation of sustainable development will involve modifications of free market activity. These implementation issues are considered in the remainder of this chapter.

Cost-Benefit Analysis

Individuals are constantly, if unconsciously, performing private cost-benefit analyses when making purchasing decisions. They compare the costs to themselves of purchasing an item (its price) with the benefits of purchase (the satisfaction they receive). Similarly, firms compare the costs of producing an extra good or service with the benefits (revenue) received from doing so. Cost-benefit analysis makes similar comparisons except that it includes the wider costs and benefits to society as well as those accruing privately to firms and individuals.

For a project or development to be socially acceptable the sum of the benefits to society (including external and private benefits) must exceed the sum of the cost to society (including external and private costs). This may be written as

$$\Sigma B > \Sigma C$$

where Σ means 'the sum of ', B = to the benefits to society and C = the costs to society.

A problem arises from using this equation in its raw form. When we measure costs and benefits, some happen immediately, and some happen at some future date. People would prefer to have money today than in the future. This is because £100 today is worth more than a promise of £100 in 10 years since it can earn interest in the intervening period. Therefore future values must be adjusted to give present values. This is known as discounting and the rate used to discount is generally related to the long-term interest rate. The formula for finding a present value is :

$$\frac{B_t}{(1+r)^t}$$

where B_t = the benefit in year t and r = the discount rate.

Thus incorporating discounting techniques to the formula for social acceptability for projects gives :

$$\frac{B_t}{(1+r)^t} > \frac{C_t}{(1+r)^t}$$

Where C_t is the benefit in year *t*.

There is considerable debate amongst environmental economists about the use of discount rates since, if environmental damage resulting from a project results in the distant future, then its effects are minimized in cost-benefit analysis by discounting. It is felt by some that this attributes too little significance to, for example, the potential damage caused by storing nuclear waste.

Pricing the Environment

It is relatively straightforward for firms to perform private cost-benefit analysis and determine a profit-maximizing level of output. The costs of inputs are readily available and selling prices can be gauged from scanning the competition, from historical data and, ultimately, are determined in the market. There are thus some firm figures which inform production levels.

However when we move into the arena of external costs and benefits we encounter the problem of missing markets and thus find pricing difficult. We can easily calculate the costs of aircraft use in terms of fuel, staffing and depreciation, but how do we measure the cost of aircraft noise? We clearly need to address this problem if we are to use cost-benefit analysis to determine a level of economic development which maximizes total private and social profitability.

Several methods have been developed by environmental economists to impute value for unpriced goods or services and these are now explained.

Willingness to Pay (WTP) Method

Here survey techniques are used to find out how much households are willing to pay for the preservation of an environmental asset—for example, a piece of woodland threatened by a road development. The survey can include people who are currently visiting the asset and those who do not visit it but care about it. The total valuation of the asset can then be found by multiplying the average WTP by the number of people who enjoy the asset.

The main difficulty of using the WTP method is whether respondents reply to the hypothetical WTP question in the same way as they would if faced with actual payment.

Hedonistic Pricing Method (HPM)

Hedonistic Pricing Values environmental resources by considering their effect on the prices of goods or services that have readily observable market prices. House prices are a convenient yardstick for this exercise.

House prices are affected by a number of factors—condition, number of rooms, central heating, garden size and nearness to transport and shops. They are also affected by environmental factors, for example prices will be depressed by the presence of aircraft noise and increased by the presence of a park. HPM involves the collection of data recording price, and the presence or absence of all the salient determinants of price. Once a price can be established to reflect the non-environmental factors (number of rooms, etc.) Then the effects of the environmental factor under analysis (*e.g.* aircraft noise) can be attributed to variations in the price of houses with otherwise similar characteristics. An imputed cost can then be attributed for aircraft noise nuisance.

Difficulties involved with HPM mainly centre around the large number of differences that occur between houses, and the changes in other factors such as interest rates during data collection.

Travel Cost Method (TCM)

The assumption behind this method of environmental assets valuation is that there is a relationship between the travel costs that a visitor has incurred to visit a tourism or recreational site and their valuation of that site. The attraction of this method is that travel costs for visitors by car are readily measurable as they consist mainly of petrol costs. A survey records the distance visitors travelled to the site, and technical details about their car. From this, travel costs are calculated. This is then compared to the number of visits the individual makes per year to the site.

Figure 13.1 illustrates a typical scatter diagram which might result from plotting travel costs against number of visits, after adjusting for other factors such as income differences. A typically shaped demand curve DO relates the price of visiting the site (measured by travel costs) to the demand (The number of visits per year.) A total value of the site for recreational use can be obtained from this information.

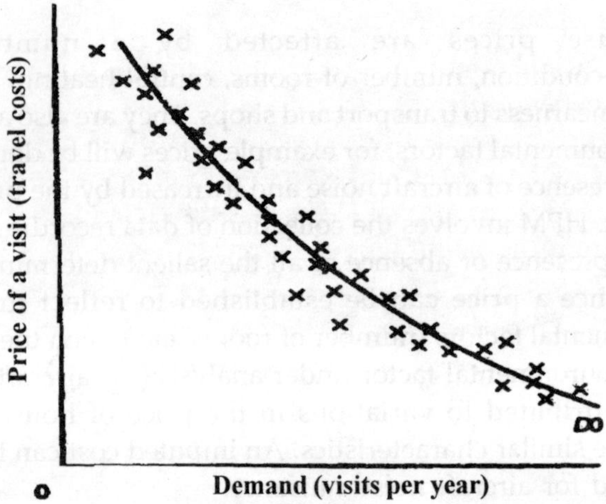

Fig. 13.1. Use of travel cost method to construct a demand curve for a tourism/recreational site.

There are however problems which arise in using TCM. First travelling involves use of time which represents an additional cost for many people. Second, some people may arrive on bicycle or on foot and thus register no travel cost, even though their actual valuation of the site may be positive. Third, people may combine visiting the site with other activities on the same journey and it is difficult to unscramble the contribution of travel costs to each.

Dose-Response Method

This valuation method depends upon the availability of data linking the effects of pollution to a response in, for example, human health, or crop production. The effects of sewage pollution in the sea could be measured in terms of medical resources needed to remedy pollution-induced sickness, and loss of earnings.

Replacement Cost Technique

This might offer a way of measuring some of the environmental effects of acid rain. For example, the cost of restoration of buildings damaged by such pollution could be measured and thus the cost of acid-rain pollution measured.

Mitigation Behaviour Method

Some pollution effects result in households undertaking defensive expenditure which can be measured in the market. The existence of aircraft noise pollution, for example, may lead households to fit double glazing to mitigate its effects. This defensive expenditure can be summed to find costs incurred from the pollution.

Privatization of Free-Access Resources

Since free-access resources are often overused (for example the sea as a waste sink), privatization of such resources is sometimes advocated. In such a case use of the resources (*e.g.* sewage disposal) would have to be bought and thus a price would be charged for a hitherto free service. The price would fluctuate, like all market prices, to reflect the demand and supply of the service.

Controlling Environmental Damage

The first step towards controlling environmental damage and promoting sustainability is understanding the environmental impacts of economic activity. The next step is the measurement of external costs and benefits in monetary terms, as described in the previous section. This then raises the question of how such information can be used to provide a socially optimum use of resources in the economy (one that considers wider environmental effects than that produced from actions based solely on free market prices).

There are several possible solutions raining from ownership, to direct regulation and market-based incentives.

Ownership

There is little incentive for an organization in the private sector to consider cost-benefit analysis when appraising a project. It will, instead, attempt to satisfy its shareholders by seeking to maximize profits. However, in principle a public sector organization has an incentive to consider social costs and benefits, since external costs will fall upon the electorate. The actual way in which public sector organizations approach externalities will in practice depend upon the demands of the government.

Voluntary sector organizations may have aims and objectives which encompass consideration of the full social costs and benefits. Exhibit 13.2, describing National Trust conservation work, illustrates this.

Direct Regulation

Direct regulation methods, sometimes known as command and control (CAC), involve the government setting environmental standards. These might take the form of water quality standards or planning regulations. They can be divided into preventive controls and retrospective controls. By and large the preventive controls are more effective.

Exhibit 13.2. Issues

As a major conservation charity, the Trust does its utmost to practise what it preaches : it therefore aims to minimise adverse effects of its activities on the environment. Surveys of sewage and farm-waste discharges were largely completed in 1993, and innovative ways of treating waste and of minimising it in the first place are being brought in.

The Trust also committed itself to reducing its energy consumption and to producing full Environmental Impact Assessments for all proposals exploiting renewable energy.

Source : The National Trust; The Year in Brief 1993-4.

Planning permission is a preventive control seeking to stop developments that do not meet planning guidelines. Planning guidelines are devised to ensure that developments consider wider environmental issues and impacts. Enforcement is relatively straightforward since building may not commence without the necessary permission. This type of control is criticized for its bureaucratic nature and the extra costs that are generated.

Retrospective controls include the setting of environmental control targets, after the externality-producing project has been commissioned. These include limits to aircraft and other noise, and water quality levels. Litter laws and penalties also fall under this category. Critics argue that such control methods themselves use considerable resources in monitoring and policing the limits, and that non-compliance rates can be high. Figure 13.2 in the next section compares their effectiveness with green taxes.

Market-Based Incentives

The idea behind market-based incentives is to incorporate externalities into existing market prices so as to cause producers to adapt their behaviour accordingly. It follows the polluter pays principle (PPP) adopted by the OECD in 1972 as its key economic instrument for environmental policy.

The key to PPP is the adjustment of market prices so that firms pay the full and true costs of externalities or environmental degradation. Thus, instead of the environment being separate and external to the free market, the two are integrated, and market prices signal not just private costs and benefits but full social costs and benefits.

The main ways of implementing the PPP include deposit-refund schemes, marketable permits, product charges and emission charges.

Deposit-Refund Schemes

This is a scheme for encouraging recycling, as in bottle deposits, or in minimizing dumping, as in supermarket trolley schemes. If you dump your trolley you lose your deposit.

Marketable Permits

Permits are issued allowing a given level of pollution. For example, the total number of noise units for aircraft could be stipulated for a particular airport. These permits are then tradable. Supporters of this system stress its flexibility. Some aircraft operators can reduce noise pollution more cheaply than others. They can do so and sell permits to those who find it expensive to reduce noise pollution. Thus the total amount of pollution is limited, but how it is achieved is likely to involve flexibility and lowest costs.

Product Charges

This involves charges on goods or services which casue externalities in production, use or disposal. One of the economic justifications for taxes on alcohol is to reduce consumption and thus minimize externalities in use (being drunk and disorderly). It is interesting to speculate whether scenes such as those described in exhibit 13.3 are less common in countries such as Norway and Sweden where there are much higher alcohol taxes.

Emission Charges

These are taxes on the emission of air, noise, water and solid waste pollution. Figure 13.2 compares the operation of an environmental tax with a direct environmental control.

Exhibit 13.3. Emergency : Britons having Fun—Sandra Barwick

It was New Year's Eve, out the mood was not exactly festive in the accident and emergency department of St. Thomas's Hospital. 'We don't normally have vomit bowls laid out at reception,' sighed the assistant director, Susan White, 'but those are what we are going to need.' The first casualty arrived, at 11.25, prone on his trolley, visible only in patches : large hairy legs, a pair of immobile trainers, some vomit-speckled hair. 'He's had a combination of beer, champagne and something else' said the ambulanceman, deadpan. 'We think he's Spanish.' A faint cry of 'Waaaa-aaaa' came from the trolley as it was wheeled away.

At midnight, the chimes of Big Ben came over the television. In they came, one after the other, bound to their trolleys. Almost all were men in their late teens or early 20s, in dirty jeans over which they had vomited. Outside the minor surgeries department a line of men sat or lay : punchmarks embedded on their cheeks, bottles broken on their heads, noses broken, lips cut. One had been bitten, one had had a cigarette stubbed out on his eye.

'Happy New Year,' the ambulanceman said with ironic detachment to their prone charges.

Source : The Independent, 2 January 1993 (adapted).

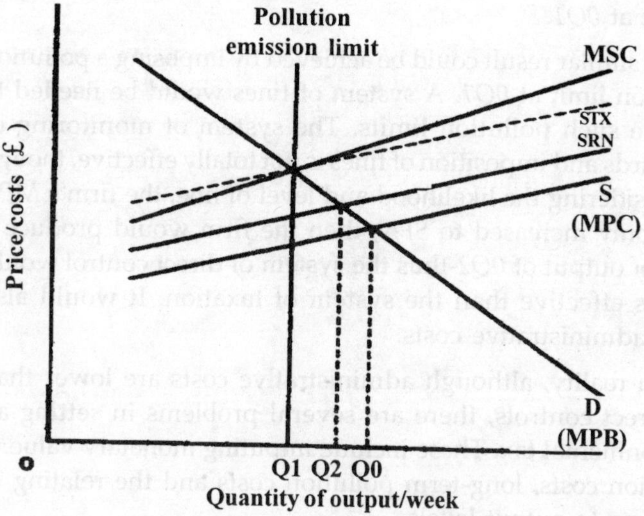

Fig. 13.2. Comparison of taxation and direct environmental control. See text for details.

D represents the demand curve and marginal private benefit for a product. *S* represents the supply curve and marginal private costs of production. Profit-maximizing firms will continue to produce where the price paid for extra sales (indicated by the demand curve) is greater than the extra costs of production (marginal private cost). They will thus produce a level of output of *0Q0*.

However, in this example, production causes pollution, and external costs. Adding these to marginal private costs generates the marginal social cost curve *MSC*. The socially optimum level of output is now found at *0Q1* since production should be increased at all points where marginal private benefit (MPB; indicated by how much consumers are willing to pay for extra units of the good) exceeds marginal social cost.

The imposition of a pollution tax is designed to make the firm internalize the previously external costs of pollution and integrate environmental considerations. A pollution tax which raised the marginal private costs curve (*S* or *MPC*) to *STX* would cause the firm's private profit-maximizing level of output to coincide with the social profit-maximizing level of output at *0Q1*.

A similar result could be achieved by imposing a pollution emission limit at *0Q1*. A system of fines would be needed to enforce such pollution limits. The system of monitoring of standards and imposition of fines is not totally effective, though If, considering the likelihood and level of fine, the firm's *MPC* were only increased to *SFN*, then the firm would produce a level of output of *0Q2*-thus the system of direct control would be less effective than the system of taxation. It would also incur administrative costs.

In reality, although administrative costs are lower than for direct controls, there are several problems in setting an environmental tax. These include imputing monetary value to pollution costs, long-term pollution costs and the relating of pollution to output levels.

A further criticism of environmental taxes and environmental charging is their regressive nature, in that their effects will hit the poor proportionately more than the rich. In theory this problem might be addressed by compensating the poor by income tax adjustments.

Green Consumers

Leisure and tourism consumers themselves have power to change the environmental effects of goods and services by purchasing those which are environmentally friendly. In order to do this they first need raised consciousness about the environmental effects of their purchases. Special-interest groups such as Friends of the Earth are an important source of consumer education in this respect.

Second consumers need more information supplied with goods and services about their environmental effects. Such 'ecolabelling' has gained ground in areas such as detergents but has yet to be widely adopted in key leisure and tourism products.

The power of the individual is also spreading from the

high street to the stock exchange as ethical investors ask questions about environmental impacts when considering share purchases.

Policy Shapers

Government environmental policy and thus its deployment of direct controls and market-based incentives is informed by a wide range of sources. The government itself will have a general political agenda which it wishes to pursue. Its own government departments, particularly the Department of Heritage, the Department of Transport, Regions and the Environment, are an important source of ideas. Publicly funded quangos such as the Sports Council, English Heritage and the Countryside Commission add to the picture. The leisure and tourism industry itself will lobby government either via individual firms or through trade associations such as the British Hospitality Association. Finally there is a range of voluntary associations and interest groups which generally focus on a particular issue. Examples include Tourism Concern, the Council for the Protection of Rural England and the Ramblers Association.

Firms' Environmental Policies

Increasingly, individual firms are appointing environmental managers, compiling environmental policies and conducting environmental audits and action plans. There are several motives for this. First, anticipation of government controls may save money in the long run or even preclude their need. Second environmental action leads to savings on input costs. Finally an improved market image may result.

Leadership in this area has come from the CBI and the World Travel and Tourism Council (WTTC), both of which have published guidelines. The key WTTC guidelines are listed in exhibit 13.4.

Organizations such as BA produce a regular environmental reports setting and monitoring targets for :

Exhibit 13.4. World Travel and Tourism Council Environmental Guidelines

Environmental improvement programmes should be systematic and comprehensive. They should aim to :

- identity and continue to reduce environmental impact, paying particular attention to new projects
- pay due regard to environmental concerns in design, planning, construction and implementation
- be sensitive to conservation of environmentally protected or threatened areas, species and scenic aesthetics, achieving landscape enhancement where possible
- practice energy conservation
- reduce and recycle waste
- practice fresh-water management and control sewage disposal
- control and diminish air emissions and pollutants
- monitor, control, and reduce noise levels
- control and reduce environmentally unfriendly products, such as asbestos, CFCs, pesticides and toxic, corrosive, infectious, explosive or flammable materials
- respect and support historic or religious objects and sites
- exercise due regard for the interests of local populations, including their history, traditions and culture and future development
- consider environmental issues as a key factor in the overall development of travel and tourism destinations

Source : World Travel and Tourism Environmental Research Centre, 1994.

- noise
- emissions
- waste
- congestion
- tourism and conservation

Finally, environmental impact assessment (EIA) has become an EU requirement for some projects.

Review of Key Terms

- Sustainable development = development which can endure over the long run.
- Intergenerational equity = ensuring future generations do not inherit less capital than the current one.
- Natural capital = raw materials and the natural environment.
- Regenerative capacity = limit to harvesting of renewable resource whilst maintaining stock level.
- Cost—benefit analysis = comparison of full social costs and benefits of a project.
- Discounting = adjusting future monetary values to present monetary values.
- Willingness to pay (WTP) method = discovery of what people would be prepared to pay for a currently unpriced resource.
- Hedonistic pricing method (HPM) = imputing a price for an environmental externality by determining its effects on other prices.
- Travel cost method (TCM) = imputing the value of a site by measuring the cost of travel to it.
- Dose-response method = measuring effects of pollution in monetary terms.
- Replacement cost technique = measuring costs of pollution by calculating restoration costs.

- Mitigation behaviour method = increasing costs of pollution by counting defective expenditure.
- Command and control (CAC) = direct regulations, *e.g.* water quality regulations.
- Market-based incentives = adjusting prices to reflect external costs.
- Polluter pays principle (PPP) = polluter pays the full cost of pollution effects.

Data Questions

Task 19.1 A real adventure (and so cheap) : 'sustainable tourism' gives little back to the Third World – Rupert Gordon Walker

We wait on a path in the Hinku Valley as another weather-battered group creaks towards us from Mera, one of Nepal's 20, 000 ft (about 6000m) trekking mountains. Their strained, peeling faces contrast with their porters' clear complexions and bored expressions. One scabby Lancastrian in hi-tech gear gasps through windcracked lips, 'It's amazing. But now I'm shattered ; I'm emotionally and physically drained. 'Another mumbles that he will be back to 'conquer it next time', while 20 over-burdened, under-clad porters rush past, anxious that nothing should interrupt their journey home to the comfort of a wood fire. It is just as well they hurried away, as they might not have cared for the parting word of one of our number. 'They have to learn,' he said. 'They can't keep chopping down trees.' His remarks epitomised one of the chief ambiguities in what has come to be known as 'sustainable tourism' – tourism that, according to its proponents, should do minimal harm to the environment and tries to put something back.

The campaign for 'sustainable tourism' is a branch that sprouted from the 1987 report of the UN-sponsored World Commission on Environment and Development. The report, Our Common Future, extends the most recent hand-hold for those who feel, with Ruskin, fear and loathing for the 'plague wind' of industrialization.

Organizations like Tourism Concern, founded in 1988, are in the vanguard of a movement that derides so-called 'eco-tourism'—tourism to wilderness areas—as a marketing gimmick used by travel companies. 'Sustainable tourism' which aspires to put something back into underdeveloped countries, appears to be having little effect.

While World Tourist Organisation figures show a 17 per cent shift towards the Third World as the holiday-maker's preferred destination between 1980 and 1989, this increase has not hard the predicted effect. If you ignore unquantifiable 'trickle-down' benefits, the Third World's share of receipts from tourism has actually fallen by 4 per cent.

This paradox is explained by a feature of such tourism that is depressingly evident to anyone who has endured the affronted whine of the professional on sabbatical when 'overcharged' for a taxi trip to the Giza pyramids that costs less than his Tube fare to work. You cannot help suspecting that the campaign for 'sustainable tourism' is little more than a rationalised desire to keep the Third World a cheap place to visit.

It is an inescapable fact that the notion of 'sustainable tourism' is riddled with internal conflicts. Its adherents tend to assume that the interests of the local communities coincide with their own desire to preserve such regions, whereas the local communities might actually prefer their national government's development schemes. It also tends to forget that by trying to preserve the colourful backwardness that supports their image of primitive arcadia, it may also be maintaining hideous levels of poverty and deep social injustices. In other words, 'sustainable tourism' may fail to make either an economic or a moral contribution to the regions it says it wants to help.

In paper commissioned by the World Wide Fund for Nature called Beyond the Green Horizon (1992), Tourism Concern pleads for what we all yearn for when faced with wear and tear on our favourite landscape : the preservation of the status quo through restraint and positive conservation policies. It also insists that local people must determine whether their own backyard should receive visitors at all, and then reap the economic benefits if they do.

The alternative to preservation does not have to be sex tours to Manila, but nor should it be the creation of parks for Western interest groups that designate indigenous communities as 'guardiane of nature and local customs'.

Self-indulgence is not the least of the faults of the self-righteous. In Banos, Ecuador, a 25-year-old Australian globe-trekker consults his Lonely Planet guide book. He eats muesli in a bed-and-breakfast run by a young ex-advertising couple from London, while New Age music hums from the CD player. He turns to a man who has recommended a cheap local guide for a jungle trip. 'It says he kills animals.' 'He has to, there aren't any cafes out there.' 'I don't care. I'm not impressed.

Source : The Independent, 13 August, 1993.

Questions :

1. What definition of sustainable tourism is given in the article? How does it compare to the Brudtland definition of sustainability? Does the Nepal trek fulfil the conditions for sustainable tourism?
2. Is the 'chopping down of tress of logical sherpas sustainable? If not, why does it occur?
3. 'You cannot help suspecting that the campaign for 'sustainable tourism' is little more than a rationalized desire to keep the Third World a cheap place to visit.' Is this a just criticism or misunderstanding of sustainable tourism?
4. What problems of valuation of the natural environment might arise if cost-benefit analysis were used to judge between 'preserving colourful backwardness' of a tourism destination or providing industrial development?

Task 13.2 Environment : Under Deafening Skies

Residents of the tiny village of Longford barely flinch any more. Living within a few hundred yards of one of Heathrow's two runways, they have become accustomed to the deafening roar of transatlantic jumbos as they heave themselves into the skies. Lunchtime conversation under umbrellas outside the White Horse stops involuntarily every few minutes to allow the ear-splitting din to die down. The plane passes, chatter resumes...for a moment.

'You get used to it,' the locals shrug philosophically. Many work or have worked at the airport. They have learned to rely for their sanity on the hours of relative peace when Heathrow switches its operations to the south runway. Until then, those at home tend to spend most of the time locked behind double glazing.

It might seem bad now, but with a dramatic increase in the number of passengers forecast by the aviation industry and consequent expansion plans, environmentalists are fearful of what lies ahead. At Heathrow, already the world's busiest international airport, the BAA has lodged a formal planning application for a massive fifth terminal costing £900m, which will double the airport's annual capacity to nearly 80 million passengers.

Clusters of opposition groups have mushroomed around the country's main airports to fight the expansion plans. The argument they have to counter is the creation of much-needed jobs and the economic shot-in-the-arm which the aviation industry claims they would bring.

Rita Pearce, who has lived in Longford for 23 years and worked for Pan-American at Heathrow for 16, now believes enough is enough. The pollution has already taken its toll on her family's health, she says—she has had pleurisy five times in 2 years and her two daughters have developed asthma—and she believes increased air traffic and the introduction of night flights from October will make life there unbearable. 'It's going to be absolute hell' she said.

If planning permission for the fifth terminal is granted, in addition to the main terminal building with up to three satellites, there are plans for three giant car parks, with access provided by a new spur road from the M25 spanning the Colne Valley Park, described by Friends of the Earth as a unique river valley in the capital, important for wildlife and recreation. The plans also assume the M25 will be widened to 14 lanes in the Stainse area to the south-west. The sewage works, meanwhile, occupying the site of the proposed T5, would have to be shifted on to green belt land to the north-west of the airport.

Families in the area don't believe reassurances that T5 will not require a third runway. A report last week suggested the BA had drawn up plans for a new Heathrow runway to the south of the existing two.

Source : Guardian, 23 July 1993 (adapted).

Questions :

1 Draw up a list of private and social costs and benefits of the development of T5.

2 In what ways could you attempt to measure the monetary value of the costs and benefits?

3 Under what economic circumstances should the T5 development go ahead?

Task 13.3 Show Them the Way to go Dome

January 1999's Transport Retort (the magazine of Transport 2000) reported on transport plans for the expected 70, 000 daily visitors to the Millennium Dome in Greenwich, London. These include a tube link, satellite park-and-ride schemes, and car access only for orange badge holders. The government has promised a car-free event. However it is estimated that 25 per cent of visitors will make part of their journey by car or taxi. This means about one and a half million car journeys assuming two people to a car. Greenwich already suffers from poor air quality—during 1997, ozone, nitrogen dioxide and particulates were higher than international health guidelines on at least twenty days—and the Dome will make things worse. This is especially serious for the 20 per cent of children who have asthma and the 10 per cent of adults who are unable to work because of a long-term respiratory illness. Public opinion has forced a reduction in inner-city park-and-ride schemes because they increase local congestion and pollution and arguably contribute to car dependency. However, a 1000-car site is still planned at Woolwich just across the river. In addition, traffic is likely to increase because of the new Sainsbury's (1400-car park) and the Millennium Eco-village (paradoxically including a 1423-car park). Greenwich council admit that many people may try to leave their cars just outside the mile-and-a-half parking exclusion zone.

In the mid-1990s, various organization devised methodologies for measuring some of the external effects of road transport in the United Kingdom. The figures for air and noise pollution were approximately £20, 000 million and £3000 million respectively, congestion costs about £19 000 million and the cost of death and injuries about £3000m depending on the valuation put on a life.

Transport Retort in July 1998 listed other impacts of road transport including :

- Stress for travellers and residents.
- Loss of green space for roads and parking.
- Worsening health for increasingly car-dependent people (sedentary lifestyles in place of walking and cycling).
- Loss of independent mobility of children, senior citizens and non-car-owners because of deteriorating public transport.

Other external costs include the cost of providing street lighting and the associated light pollution, long term damage to buildings through vibration, and the deaths each year of about one million domestic and wild animals.

Sources : compiled by Nigel North from :

Transport Retort, January 1999, 'Dome Alone'.

Transport Retort, July 1998, diagram 'quantified health effects of traffic are only the tip of the iceberg'.

Blue Print 5, 'The True Costs of Road Transport' Maddison, Pearce et al., (1996) Earthscan.

Royal Commission Report, (1995), Transport and the Environment, Oxford University Press.

How Vehicle Pollution Affects our Health, Ashden Trust, 1994.

Questions :

1. What are externalities? List the external costs of raod transport mentioned in the article.
2. In the estimates of external costs, each of the 3600 lives lost annually is valued at about £700 000. Some international studies argue that this figure should be closer to £2 million. 'With this new figure calculate the total measured external costs of road transport for the United Kingdom.
3. The special taxation (petrol duty and vehicle excise duty) paid by motorists is estimated at £26 000 million for 1998-1999. Comment on the argument that motorists pay too much tax.
4. The article lists some impacts which are not measured. Suggest ways to attempt to measure those external effects.
5. What practical policies would you suggest to persuade visitors to the Dome to leave their cars at home?

Task 13.4 WTTC Environmental Guidelines

Refer to WTTC guidelines listed in exhibit 13.4.

Questions :

1. What incentives and disincentives are there for firms to adopt these guidelines?
2. Use the guidelines to evaluate critically the

environmental friendliness of a named organization in the leisure and tourism sector.

Task 13.5

Table 13.1 illustrates some of the possible economic benefits and costs of leisure and tourism. Critically review the comprehensiveness of the table and use it as a basis to analyse the effects of two leisure or tourism developments.

Table 13.1

Leisure and Tourism Costs and Benefits

Benefits	*Costs*
Satisfaction of wants	Distortion of local prices
Employment	Satisfaction of some wants at the expense of others
Foreign exchange earnings	Imports
Technology transfer	Congestion
Improved health	Aesthetic degradation
Better understanding of things	Pollution
Regeneration in depressed areas	Resource depletion
Engine for economic growth	Erosion
Source of profit	Loss of natural environment
	Loss of local control of resources

14 Integrated Case Studies

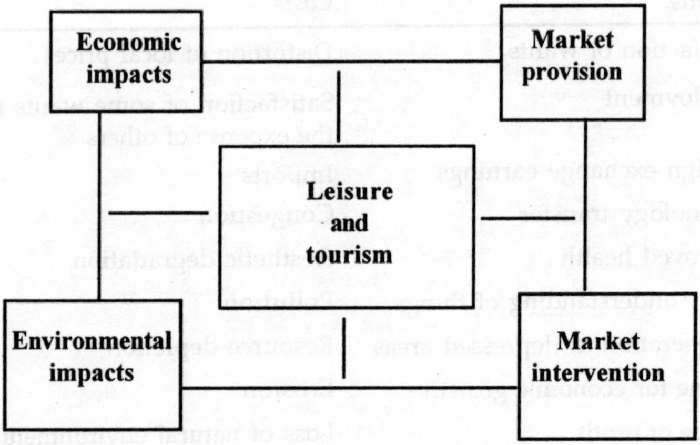

Objectives

The objectives of the case studies in this chapter are to analyse economic features and developments in the leisure and tourism sector which cut across chapter headings. This is shown in Figure 14.1.

Case 1

Is Ecotourism Sustainable Costa Rica—too Successful for its Own Good

A three-hour boat trip through a maze of jungle-lined canals takes us from the town of Moln, on the Caribbean coast of Costa Rica, to Tortuguero, 'the turtle region'. As we drift through the sinuous turns of the waterways, our guide points

	Case 1	*Case 2*	*Case 3*	*Case 4*
CH1	X		X	
CH2		X	X	
CH3		X		
CH4		X		X
CH5		X		
CH6		X	X	
CH7	X	X	X	X
CH8		X		X
CH9		X	X	
CH10		X		
CH11		X		
CH12		X		
CH13			X	
CH14	X	X		X
CH15	X		X	
CH16		X		
CH17	X	X	X	X
CH18	X	X		X
CH19	X	X		X

Fig. 14.1 Matrix of chapter subjects in case studies.

out monkeys, snakes, caimans, mud turtles and dozens of different birds. A real-life amusement park with awesome jungle life! The hamlet of Tortuguero has two churches, three bars, two souvenir shops and is the headquarters of the Caribbean Conservation Corporation (CCC). The organization runs the Tortuguero National History Museum and works with researchers and paying volunteers to monitor sea turtle activity and bird populations. The CCC was active in instigating the creation of Tortuguero National Park to protect the endangered species of sea turtles poached for their shells, meat and eggs—a rumoured aphrodisiac. Our nocturnal visit to witness the fascinating natural ritual of turtle nesting has to be arranged with a certified local guide. No memorabilia pictures allowed since flashlights deter turtles from nesting. Our guide explains : 'Before the park was created in 1973, people used to live by hunting the turtles. Now most locals have some sort of part-time or seasonal job to provide services for tourists and permanent researchers. Some people still resent imposed restrictions on hunting and farming but the new generation has a vested interest in conservation'.

In Tortuguero, we stay at Tortuga Lodge owned by Costa Rica Expeditions, one of the country's most renowned ecotourism operators. They have installed a solar energy system and water-saving fixtures with the help of a local energy-efficiency expert. The operator also implements a local programme in Tortuguero whereby all the lodges and hotels used in their tours donate a dollar per participant to the local community. The project has helped fund improvements to the school and the installation of a water distribution system. Impressive trip so far. But, mosquitoes are voracious and sharks patrol local waters. The journey back to the Capital, San Jose, will be by single-engine charter since Tortuguero is inaccessible by road. A 12 kg baggage restriction is imposed for all passengers to ensure safety and to save on costs.

Along with Belize, Costa Rica is the most renowned ecotourism destination of Latin America. International scientists and biologists were the first to take an interest in the country's immense biodiversity and played a significant role in promoting environmental conservation. While Costa Rica covers a mere 0.03 per cent of the planet's surface, it has over 5 per cent of all life forms on earth. Today, 27 per cent of the territory is under some form of protection—either as National Parks, Wildlife Refuges or Biological Reserves. The first ecotourism initiatives launched by private enterprises capitalized on the expanding park system to entice foreign tourists. Tourism arrivals grew at an average annual rate of 15 per cent between 1990 and 1994, well above the global tourism average. In spite of a sharp drop in growth (3 per cent) in 1996, the country, which is roughly the size of Wales, attracts some 792 000 visitors annually. Critics fear that its popularity will lead to its downfall. The new conservation challenge is to control the crowds that flock to the rainforest. 'On national holidays, we've had hundreds of people entering the park' says a ranger at Manuel Antonio Natural Park. 'The noise people make while walking along the paths puts enormous psychological pressure on some animals. We've had to close the area on Mondays to give the animals a rest. Now there's talk of closing it on Tuesdays too.'

In the Monteverde Reserve administrators have set a 100 visitors-a-day ceiling to preserve ecological integrity. Environmentalists have campaigned against paved road access to the protected areas in order to control numbers. Many of the parks require four-wheel drives to reach them and some can only be accessed by boat or on foot. Most parks still lack visitor centres and trails are not always marked. However, in a controversial step in 1994 park entrance fees for foreigners rose from US$1 to an unrealistic US$15 causing uproar among ecotourists. Subsequently the 'Green Pass' was introduced allowing entrance to five national parks at 50 per cent of the official price. 'We've got to focus on the type of visitor we want to attract', adds the ranger. 'Do we really want the day-tripper culture up here? Maybe they'd better stay in their enclaves. Some scientists here would even claim that if so-called ecotourists were really concerned about the rainforest, they'd support conservation organizations from home rather than invading sensitive ecosystems.'

In 1502, on his fourth and last voyage to the New World, Christopher Columbus reached the Caribbean shores of Central America and met natives wearing heavy golden necklaces. Believing he had found the mythical 'Eldorado' he named area 'Costa Rica', the rich coast. The land, however, did not yield any gold and remained one of he poorest colonies of the Spanish Empire. Introduced in the 1820s, coffee became the main generator of foreign exchange boosting Costa Rica's economic development. Owing to a slump in market prices, coffee export earings dropped to third place (US$ 245.4 million),in 1990 overtaken by bananas (US$ 315 million) and tourism (US$ 275 million), in first and second places respectively. Since 1993 tourism has established itself as the largest earner of foreign exchange totalling US$ 688.6 million in 1996, which accounts for 23.4 per cent of all export revenue. Costa Rica may have found its new 'Eldorado'. It is today one of the most prosperous and stable countries of Central America. Tourism receipts represent 8.9 per cent of GDP (1994) and the industry is reported to be the most important sector for employment, generating over 60,000 direct jobs and a similar number of indirect ones.

In spite of increases in export earnings, economic growth fell from 4.5 per cent in 1994 to around 1.5 per cent 1996. The country is under constant pressure from the International Monetary Fund and the Inter-American Development Bank to reduce its fiscal deficit and repay its foreign debt. The Government response to increase revenues included a 1 per cent levy on company assets, the raising of import tariffs and a 50 per cent rise in the national sales tax – from 10 per cent to 15 per cent. This increase, added to the 5 per cent tax on air transport, the 3 per cent levy on hotel accommodation (to finance the Costa Rican Institute of Tourism) and the 10 per cent service charge, makes the national tourism product an expensive and uncompetitive option.

Battles often rage in Costa Rica over land use. Until the tourism boom deforestation was seen as the means to economic development. Large companies, often foreign multinationals, are still involved in logging tropical rainforests for their precious hardwoods, mining, large-scale cattle raising and the exploitation of banana plantations. The practice of pesticide spraying of bananas constitutes not only a major environmental problem but also a health hazard for plantation workers who are said to suffer from pesticide poisoning. The growth of the population, expected to reach 4 million in 2000, has led to increasing encroachments upon the rainforest for subsistence farming.

Advocates for tourism development argue that its economic significance has prevented further destruction of the forest. When tourists visits parks and reserves they are sending positive messages to the government and they are paying for the conservation of Costa Rica's natural and wildlife resources' exclaims out guide from Costa Rica Expeditions. 'We use local businesses whenever possible and invest in the training of local guides. That way the dollars stay in the country and everyone benefits.

In 1995, at the Berlin Climate Change Summit, Costa Rica's President, Jose Maria Figueres, took the issue one step further by suggesting, along with other world nations, that industrialized countries should finance conservation projects such as reforestation in developing countries as the cost of saving the planet should be shared by all.

Source : Anne Aichroth.

Questions :

1. Explain differences in the concepts of ecotourism and sustainable tourism drawing examples from the article. To what extent is ecotourism sustainable?
2. Discuss and evaluate arguments for and against each of the following :
   - The extension of the road system to remote natural reserves.
   - The increase in park entrance fees.
   - The taxation of tourist facilities.
3. Assess the overall costs and benefits of tourism for Costa Rica's economy and environment.
4. What opportunity costs are incurred through agricultural and industrial use of the land?
5. Comment upon the President of Costa Rica's request at the 1995 Climate Change Summit in Berlin.

Case 2

The Economic Impacts of Football

The English Premier league continues to flourish. It had a combined turnover of £464 millions in 1996-1997 and is the richest in the world. Its nearest rival, Italy's Serie A, had a turnover of £377 million. It is growing at a remarkable rate of 37 per cent per annum and average profits per club stand at £4.3 million. The two star performers in the Premiership were Manchester United with a turnover of £88 million followed by Newcastle United with a turnover of £41 million.

Organizations

A number of UK football clubs are now public limited companies and their share prices appear in stock exchange listings. These clubs include Manchester United and Tottenham Hotspur. Public limited company (pic) status means that giving value to shareholders becomes a prime consideration for clubs. The period between 1994 and 1996 was a particularly good one, for football share prices when Manchester United's shares rose from £1.30 to £4.80 and Tottenham's from 70p to £4.80. The financial figures for Manchester United, shown in the Table 20.1, give some reasons for this rise in share values. Newcastle United was floated on the stock exchange in April 1997. The flotation helped to raise capital to pay for their new 80,000-seater stadium. Although its shares are now quoted on the stock exchange, Sir John Hall and his family still own the majority shareholdering in the club through their company, Cameron Hall Developments Ltd.

Table 14.1

Financial Profile of Manchester United pic, 1993-1997

Year ended 31 July	*1993*	*1994*	*1995*	*1996*	*1997*
Turnover £000s	25177	43815	60622	53316	87939
Operating profit £000s	7392	10999	15649	14167	26201
Per-tax profit £000s	4202	10776	20014	15399	27577

Source : Annual Company Reports and Account.

Elsewhere in Europe, Italian Serie A teams are planning to float, with Lazio favourite to be the first. A number of Dutch, German and Scandinavian clubs are also planning to float and capitalize on the growing popularity of the game.

The soccer business, like any other, is subject to take-overs and mergers. In 1997, Olympic Marseille, one of the top French clubs bought Adidas, the German sports company. In 1998, Rupert Murdoch's News Corporation (owners of BskyB, a major provider of football TV coverage) made a take-over bid for Manchester United whose share prices had fallen to £2.20. This represents a form of vertical integration where the owner of supply channels would also own a service to be supplied. As such the government has to rule whether this is in the public interest. Similar vertical integration has occurred in Mexico where the TV company Televisa owns the America, Necaxa, and Atlante football clubs and TV Azteca owns Atletico Morelia and Veracruz. Problems that can arise from these arrangements include manipulation of publicity, arrangements for match times, and using tactics unfavourable to competing clubs.

In addition to this vertical integration there are moves by UK clubs to integrate horizontally with foreign sides. This can create synergies, and achieve economies of scale. Everton, Tranmere Rovers and Manchester City have all invested in Irish clubs. These can then be used to nurture new and young players and make their squads broader and more flexible.

Ticket Prices

Ticket sales are of prime importance and typically account for 40-50 per cent of a club's revenue. Ticket prices pose an interesting economic problem for clubs : they are governed by the underlying supply of and demand for seats. On the supply side, the necessity for Premiership clubs to move to all-seating stadia as a result of Taylor Report has in many cases limited supply. The supply curve for seats is totally inelastic at the capacity level of the stadium. Demand for seats is strong owing to the continued high profile of the Premier League. For popular clubs with limited capacity this means that there is often excess demand for tickets. For example, Premier League and FA Cup champions (1997-1998) Arsenal have a maximum capacity of 38 000 at their home ground at Highbury in North London. Their matches are regularly sold out. Indeed their European Champions League (1998-1999) matches which were held at Wembley sold at a capacity of 73 000. This is an indication of potential demand.

Football clubs are unique and therefore competition is limited. Adam Brown, who sits on the government's Football Task Force, argues that 'clubs should each be regarded as monopolies and regulated accordingly'. He adds : 'You can't "buy" Manchester United from anywhere else can you?' There is potential to increase prices so as to equate demand with supply and increase sales revenue. Indeed, average ticket prices in the Premiership rose £13.25 in 1996 to £15.45 in 1997, an increase of 16.6 per cent during a period when inflation in general was only 3.6 per cent. However, there is still excess demand for tickets at many clubs. Currently the excess demand for Arsenal tickets is managed by membership schemes, first come first served allocation and operation of ticket touts in the illicit market.

Other Income Sources

The other major source of income of clubs is from TV sponsorship. Premiership income has been substantially bolstered fromby income from television deals. A four-year contract with BSkyB worth £693 million was signed in 1997-1998, which provides for extra payments for overseas rights after 1998-1999. At the international level, the rights for the 2002 World Cup TV coverage have been sold by FIFA to a German company for $2.2 billion. Mintel estimate that about 25 per cent of spectators at matches buy a programme at an average price of £1.50. Merchandising and sponsorship also add to income. Manchester United's main sponsors, the electrical goods company Sharp, currently (1999) pay the club £2 million per year. United also has an additional group of eight sponsors. United seeks to exploit its brand in innovative ways. For example, it has formed a new joint venture company with Countryside Leisure Management to build a 100-bed hotel next to its Old Trafford stadium. The club will receive a fee for every guest.

Catering is not yet well developed in most clubs. The quality of food and drink sold in most grounds is poor with a predominance of burgers, hot dogs and pies sold at stand-up bars in consumer-unfriendly conditions. In 1997-1998, catering is estimated to generate an average revenue of £1.50 per head for 40 per cent of the crowd. The potential for increased revenue here is considerable as supporters currently spend large sums on food and drink before and after matches outside the ground.

Costs

Wage inflation has been notable in the Premier League. Wages rose in 1995-1996 by 34 per cent and again by 35 per cent in 1996-1997. The Bosman ruling that allows players freedom of movement when their contracts have expired has helped to inflate wages and transfer fees for players still under contract stood at £240 million in 1996-1997.

International Trade

Football can affect a country's balance of payments on the import side and the export side. In terms of imports, transfers to the English premier league totalled £100 million in 1996-1997 and reached such a value in 1998 that for the first time the Office for National Statistics is to include them in UK balance of payments accounts. Jaap Stam set the record with a £10.5 million signing from PSV Eindhoven to Manchester United, and overall £70 million of soccer imports took place between June and August of 1998. Table 14.2 records some of the key transfers.

Signing international stars is a key strategy in maintaining performance which in turn improves the export potential of soccer. This is illustrated by the fact that Manchester United is developing plans to exploit its brand globally. It has a target to open 150 United shops around the world before 2002. To achieve its aim it has established a new subsidiary, Manchester

United International, and is employing design consultants specializing in leisure brands to plan the stores. Its first shops have already opened at airports in Dublin, Copenhagen and Hong Kong, selling merchandise such as replica kits, memorabilia and videos.

Table 14.2

Premiership Signings from Overseas, 1998

Player	*Signed from*	*Signed to*	*Price (£m)*
Jaap Stam	PSV Eindhoven	Manchester United	10.5
Pierluigi Casiraghi	Lazio	Chelsea	5.4
Dietmar Hamman	Bayern Munich	Newcastle	5.0
Marcel Desailly	AC Milan	Chelsea	4.6
Jesper Blomqvist	Parma	Manchester United	4.4
Olivier Dacourt	Strasbourg	Everton	3.8
Vegard Heggam	Rosenborg	Liverpool	3.5

Ironically, this expansion programme was launched in 1998 which was a poor year for merchandise sales that were down from £29 million to £24 million. However, the United chairman, Professor Sir Roland Smith, put this down to two short-term problems—the club is about to change its strip and the poor financial situation in Asia has affected exports. He reported that market research carried out by the club had indicated good medium-term prospects for the venture.

Summary of opportunities and threats facing clubs.

- Consumer spending on football remains strong.
- Demand for tickets strong at top end of game.
- Virtual fans.
- Season ticket holders.
- Restricted capacities at grounds.
- Take-overs and mergers.
- Secondary revenue : merchandising, catering etc.
- Players' wages and transfer fees.

- BSkyB rights.
- Divide between premier league and the rest is growing.
- Exploitation of consumers by clubs.
- Importance of financial results for plcs.
- High fixed costs for some clubs.
- Importance of staying at the top.

Sources : Deloitte and Touche (1998), *Annual Review of Football Finance.*

Mintel (1998), *The Football Report.*

Sir Norman Chester Centre for Football Research (1998), *Premier League Survey.*

Colman's Football Food Guide (1998)

Fletcher Research (1998), *How to Make Money out of Football.*

Newspapers : The *Guardian and The Times.*

Questions :

1. Compile a list of economic impacts of football and comment on their measurement. Are there any negative impacts of football?
2. Discuss the issues surrounding ticket prices for Premiership matches, and evaluate different approaches to pricing and ticket allocation.
3. Conduct an opportunities and threats analysis on a named football club.
4. Evaluate the advantage and disadvantages of the flotation of Newcastle United to its various stakeholders.
5. Use economic analysis to explain wages of footballers compared to those of stewards. Is there an economic case for controlling wages?
6. Prepare a time series chart of share prices for a named club. Account for the movements in share prices.

7. What kind of take-over was the purchase of Olympic Marseille by Adidas? Evaluate the move from the point of view of consumer interests and those of Adidas.
8. What evidence is there to support the view that football clubs are a monopoly? Should this be seen as a problem?

Case 3

Cuba : sun, sand, sex and sea – a sustainable route to rising GNP?

Cuba's centrally planned economy has recently gone through a period of extreme difficulty as illustrated in Figure 14.2, and chronicled by Avella and Mills (1996 : 56) :

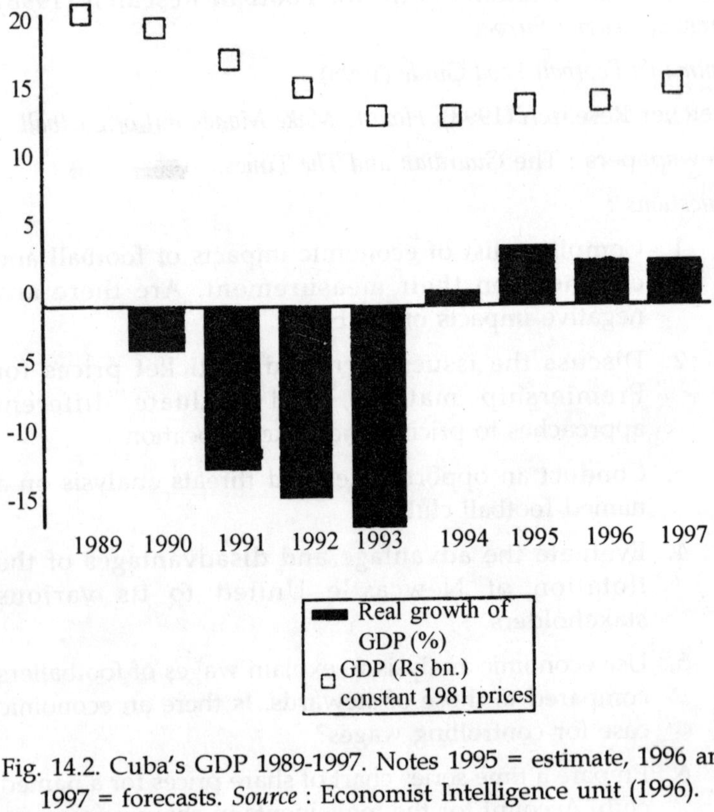

Fig. 14.2. Cuba's GDP 1989-1997. Notes 1995 = estimate, 1996 and 1997 = forecasts. *Source* : Economist Intelligence unit (1996).

The Gross Social Product has declined by 46% in five years because of reduced international trade, particularly in respect of sugar exports..... The island's factories are producing at only 30% capacity.....

Most of these difficulties may be traced back to the collapse of the former soviet Union in 1991 which led to the annual loss of :

...US$6 billion in economic aid, $1 billion in military assistance, 10 million tons of oil, and $6 billion worth of imported goods. [Cuba] also lost its major trading partner, and now had to sell its sugar at a fair market value.

Perrottet and Biondi, 1995 : 60–1

It is these factors which led Fidel Castro to introduce, in 1990, 'a special period in peacetime', a period of intense economic austerity which still persists. The passing of the Helms-Burton Act in 1996 has added to economic difficulties with a tightening of US-led economic sanctions against Cuba.

Perhaps the most vivid illustration of Cuba's economic collapse was the 1994 *balseros* (rafters) exodus which hit the international headlines. Thousands of *balseros* deployed inner tubes and makeshift rafts in an attempt to find economic salvation in Miami. It is not hard for the visitor to Cuba to see how this 'special period' translates into everyday living. A significant part of the fishing fleet remains in the harbour through lack of fuel. Many houses remain unfinished through lack of building materials. The fabric of the city of Havana is falling apart. The average salary is 170 pesos a month rising to 400 pesos for a teacher and 500 pesos for a doctor. But there is a chronic shortage of basic groceries—from soap and toothpaste to cooking oil, and so the local currency—the peso is virtually worthless. There is little in the peso stores that isn't rationed. The huge motorways that span the island are virtually empty.

Against this backdrop of economic hardship, tourism has emerged as a key source of economic growth and regeneration. Figure 14.3 illustrates tourism's growing importance for foreign currency earnings. While the top four export earners for Cuba in 1989 were sugar, nickel, shellfish and tobacco, by 1994, tourism earnings had surpassed those of sugar which have been hit by a combination of poor harvests and the loss of guaranteed prices in the markets of the former Soviet Union.

Table 14.3 illustrates tourist arrivals between 1990 and 1995. It can be seen that there has been a dramatic growth in tourism arrivals which roughly doubled between 1990 and 1994. The estimated arrivals for 1996 are 930, 000. (Casals, 1996), and there are ambitious plans for the future :

The country is not yet satisfied with the growth rate, number of visitors or the amount of businesses, although these are coming close to the projections for the year 2000, when Cuba must receive between 2.3 to 2.5 million tourists, contributing some three billion dollars to the Cuban economy.

Casals, 1996 :14

Table 14.3

Cuba : Tourist Arrivals and Gross Revenue

Year	*Tourist arrivals (000s)*	*Gross revenue % growth*	*$ million*
1990	327	3.8	243
1991	415	26.7	387
1992	455	9.7	567
1993	544	19.5	720
1994	617	13.5	850
1995	738	19.6	1100

Source : Economist Intelligence Unit (1996).

Tourism development and tourism strategy .

Cuba's tourism industry currently spans the following types of tourism :

- Medical.
- Cultural and heritage.
- Sex.

- Socialism.
- Beach-resort.
- Conference and business.
- Special interest.

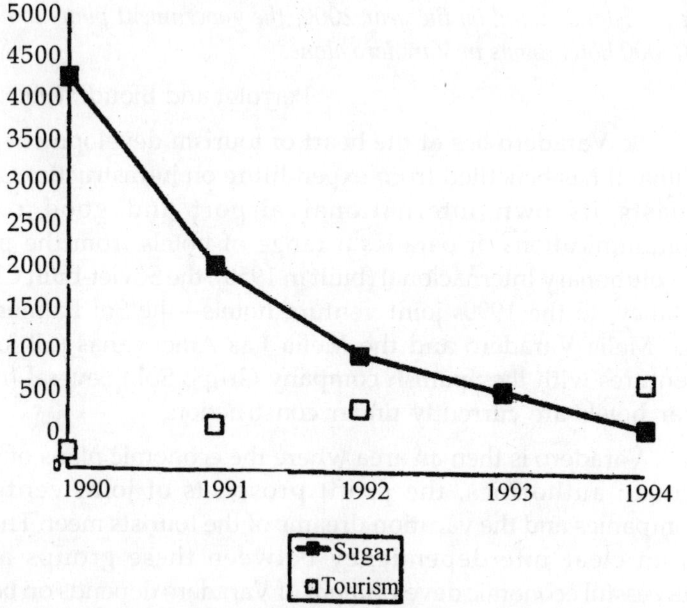

Fig. 14.3. Cuba's foreign earnings from sugar and tourism ($ millions). *Note* : 1994 = estimate. *Source* : Economist intelligence Unit (1995).

Of these, cultural and heritage and beach resort tourism are the most important, although dollar desperation means that prostitution is endemic and sex tourism permeates may of the categories. Cultural and heritage tourism is focused on the two major sites of Havana and Trinidad. Their attraction is underlined by the fact that Havana was designated by UNESCO in 1982 world cultural heritage status, and Trinidad, a UNESCO world heritage site in 1988.

Cuba has a number of beach resorts including Santa Lucia, Cayo Coco, Guadalavaca, Ancon and Cayo Largo, but its principal beach resort is Varadero. Varadero is a 45 km narrow peninsula with over 20 km of beaches. It is situated on the north of the island, about 80 km east of Havana. Its prime importance in terms of tourism is illustrated by the following :

By 1994 there were over 22, 000.... tourist quality hotel rooms in the island....and by the year 2000, the government plans to have 30, 000 hotel rooms in Varadero alone.

Perrotet and Biondi, 1995 : 71

So Varadero lies at the heart of tourism development for Cuba. It has benefited from-expenditure on infrastructure and boasts its own international airport and good road communications. It parades a range of hotels from the pre-revolutionary Internacional (built in 1950), the Soviet-built Club Atabey, to the 1990s joint venture hotels—the Sol Palmeras, the Melia Varadero and the Melia Las Americanas (all joint ventures with the Spanish company Grupo Sol.) Several five-star hotels are currently under construction.

Varadero is then an area where the economic plans of the Cuban authorities, the profit prospects of joint venture companies and the vacation dreams of the tourists meet. There is an clear interdependency between these groups and successful economic development of Varaderó depends on both demand and supply side factors. On the supply side the availability of capital to expand capacity and improve resort infrastructure is crucial. Hence the importance of joint ventures, and the potency of the Helms—Burton Act to deter such ventures. Recent reports (Economist Intelligence Unit, 1996) suggest a mixed reaction to Helms—Burton. A $400 million investment from Canadian Wally Berkoff has recently been announced, and Sol Melia intend to retain their Cuban interests. On the other hand two Spanish companies—Paradores Nacionales de Turismo and Hoteles Occidentales—have postponed investment decisions.

Another issue on the supply side, a problem common to socialist countries, is their lack of service culture (Burns, 1995) and consequential difficulties in delivering services to a high quality. Finally on the supply side, Cuban destinations must vie with other Caribbean destinations who are also competing strongly for the tourist dollar. This mix of factors (undeveloped resort infrastructure, uneven service and strong competition) points up the strategy currently being pursued by the Cuban authorities as a low-price/ limited value-added one (Kotler, 1988; Bowman; 1992; Tribe, 1997).

We therefore now turn our attention to the demand side to discover how well this policy is received by tourists. In particular, do they allow for the relatively low price of the destination in their overall evaluation of their holiday experience? Tribe and Snaith (1998) found that in reality holiday-makers do not expect Varadero to be any different from other Caribbean destinations such as Mustique, or Antigua or Barbados. As a result of their high expectations, the product they are offered in resorts such as Varadero is often unsatisfactory for them.

Now this has potentially serious consequences for Cuba's tourism, and general economic policy. Emphasis hitherto has been on beds, beds, beds. This is a narrow supply side policy. It is narrow because the supply-side requires a more general attention to resort development. Tribe and Snaith (1998) suggest that items requiring urgent attention which emerge from their survey are :

- Restaurant provision.
- Bar provision.
- Nightlife provision.
- Shopping facilities.
- Hotel meal provision.
- Prices in Varadero.
- Access to Cuban heritage and culture.
- Industrial pollution.
- Service quality.

Then there is the question of prostitution to which the authorities maintain an ambivalent attitude.

In conclusion, tourism represents a key strand in Cuba's economic renewal but many brochures and NTO materials give a very carefully selected view of Varadero, and significant aspects are left out in the presentation of the destination. This leads to significant critical gaps between expectations and realizations for holidaymakers to Varadero. Current marketing of Varadero is therefore unsustainable, and this threatens the longer-term economic prospects. The routes to sustainable marketing (in the economic sense) are either to upgrade reality towards publicity or to downgrade publicity towards reality.

Thus one route to closing these gaps is to make brochures for Varadero more honest. Although, 'a stone's throw from the beach' is no longer used in brochures to describe treks of more than a kilometre, partial views and accounts of destinations are still common and result in dissatisfaction. The other route is to transform Varadero as a destination. There are already signs of this in Varadero which has embarked upon a programme of five-star hotel construction. But the creation of enclaves within an enclave is not a substitute for balanced development of the resort. Considerable development of infrastructure is required to support the stock of economy hotels.

Questions :

1. What economic problems is Cuba facing and to what extent can tourism assist in solving these problems?
2. What are the strengths and weaknesses of Cuba as a holiday destination?
3. What are the opportunities and threats facing Cuba as a holiday destination?
4. Varadero is then an area where the economic plans of the Cuban authorities, the profit prospects of joint venture companies and the vacation dreams of the tourists meet.' Explain what is meant by this statement and what conflicts exist between these parties.

5. What are the key environmental impacts of tourism to Cuba?
6. Assess the relative merits of a tourism development programme for Cuba based on :
   - Central planning.
   - Private enterprise.
   - Mixed ventures.
7. 'Multinational enterprises are the key to Cuban development.' Critically evaluate this statement.

References

1. Avella, A. and Mills, A. (1996) : Tourism in Cuba in the 1990s : back to the future, *Tourism Management*, **17(1)**.
2. Bowman, C. (1992) : Charting Competitive Strategy. In : Faulkner, D. and Johnson, G. (eds.), *The Challenge of Strategic Management*, London, Kogan Page.
3. Burns, P. (1996) : Hotel management training in Eastern Europe : Challenges for Romania, *Progress in Tourism and Hospitality Research*, **1(1)** : pp. 53-62.
4. Calder, S. and Hatchwell, E. (1993) : *Travellers Survival Kit : Cuba*, Oxford, Vacation Work.
5. Calder, S. and Wheat, S. (1995) : Travel : Why do you think they're called operators?, *Independent Newspaper*, 2 September, London.
6. Casals, R. (1996) : Increased participation by foreign capital, *Granma International*, 5 June, p. 14, Havana.
7. Economist Intelligence Unit (1995) : Country *Report : Cuba, Dominican Republic, Haiti, Puerto Rico*, Second Quarter, London, Economist Publications.
8. Economist Intelligence Unit (1996) : Country *Report : Cuba, Dominican Republic, Haiti, Puerto Rico*, Third Quarter, London, Economist Publications.
9. Hall, D. (1992) : Tourism development in Cuba. In : Harrison, D. (ed.), *Tourism and the Less Developed Countries*, London, Belhaven Press.
10. Hatchwell, E. and Calder, S. (1995) : Cuba in Focus : *A guide*

to the people, politics and culture, London, Latin America Bureau.

11. Katz, I. (1995) : Travel : Cuba, *Guardian*, London, 1 July, p.42.
12. Kotler, P. (1988), *Marketing Management,* Hemel Hempstead, Prentice-Hall.
13. *Observer* (1994) : Game for a fistful of dollars, 26 June.
14. Perrotet, T. and Biondi, J. (eds.), (1995) : *Insight Guides* : Cuba, Hong Kong, APA Publications.
15. Pollard, J. and Rodriguez, R. (1993) : Tourism and Torremolinos, *Tourism Management,* August, pp. 247-58.
16. Poon, A. (1993) : *Tourism, Technology and Competitive Strategies,* Oxford, CAB International.
17. Ryan, C. (1995) : *Researching Tourism Satisfaction,* London, Routledge.
18. Tribe, J. (1997) : *Corporate Strategy for Tourism,* London, International Thomson Business Press.
19. Tribe, J. and Snaith, T. (1998) : From SERVQUAL to HOLSAT; holiday satisfaction in Cuba, *Tourism Management,* **19(1)**.

Case 4

Tourism : A Taxing Business

The following extracts reveal different attitudes to taxes on tourism.

1. Tourism Taxation

Taxes on the tourism industry can stifle growth if they are not equitable and applied after careful consultation between fiscal authorities and the tourism sector, according to a report, *Tourism Taxation,* prepared by the WTO. Graham Wason from management consultants Deloitte Touch who prepared the report says 'Governments have realized that taxing tourism is an easy way to gain extra revenue without upsetting their own voters and the industry is very concerned about the upward trend'. He identified 40 different types of taxes levied on the tourism industry throughout the world and noted that tax rates were increasing. 'It is not realistic to say we don't want to be taxed. If we didn't pay taxes there would be no money for improving airports or roads or to invest in necessary social services, but it is important that tourism is not unfairly taxed.'

The report notes that charges for entry and exit visas are among the worst taxes on tourism with some countries such as the Marshall Islands charging $20 to enter the country and another $20 to leave. Consultant Oliver Bennet suggests 'It is much better to encourage people to come into the country and then to tax them on consumption while they are there.' Other problems noted are when governments change taxes without giving tour operators sufficient time to incorporate the changes into their pricing structures.

Euro MP Petrus Cornelissen urged the EU to give tourism priority treatment because of its ability to create new jobs. He particularly criticized plans to scrap duty-free shopping in 1999 which threatened the jobs of 100 000 people employed directly or indirectly in the sector. He said "Tax-free shops are not just a bonus for travellers, they are a major source of revenue for the airport authorities, enabling airport fees to be kept at lower levels.

Source : WTO Press Release.

2. Taxing the Seychelles

The government of the Seychelles has imposed a $100 environmental tax on tourists payable on arrival at the airport. The tax is being imposed in order to limit visitor numbers and provide funds for environmental projects. In 1998 about 130 000 tourists a year visited the island and the government wants to encourage an upper limit of 180 000 so as not to overcrowd the beaches. The tax is also part of a strategy to maintain the upmarket image for the island.

Keith Betton of the Association of British Travel Agents thinks that the tax is a bad idea. 'The bottom end of the market is very price sensitive. This could send people to other holiday destinations like Mauritius'.

Source : The Guardian.

3. Enough is Enough

More than 75 groups in 23 countries are protesting today (6 November 1998) as part of Friends of the Earth Europe's *Right Price for Air Travel* campaign. They are calling on governments and the European Union to introduce a kerosene tax for all flights with the EU as well as emissions-related charges and stricter noise and emissions around airports.

Air travel is the fasters-growing source of greenhouse gas emissions. It is responsible for about 7 per cent of global warming, including 3 per cent of global carbon dioxide emissions. Yet a 50-year-old international agreement means airlines pay no duty on the fuel they use, whereas motorists and long-distance coach operators have to pay over 40 pence per litre. Even train companies pay 3 pence per litre for their diesel. Roger Higman, Friends of the Earth's senior transport campaigner, said : 'Flying is the most polluting form of transport there is. Yet airlines pay no duty on the fuel they use and therefore have little incentive to conserve fuel or control their emissions. The tax exemption gives airlines an unfair advantage over other forms of transport, encouraging people to travel in the least environmentally friendly way. The Chancellor...must back European moves to end this loophole by taxing airlines for the fuel they use'.

Source : Friends of the Earth Press Release, 6 November 1998.

4. Different Accounts of Aircraft Pollution

Pat Malone :

- 'Aircraft emissions are not covered by international agreements seeking to limit emissions of greenhouse gases. At the Kyoto environmental summit last year they were specifically exempted because negotiators could not agree on how to pin responsibility on individual nations.'
- 'Aircraft burn 3 per cent of all fossil fuels used on earth, and their turbines produce between 1.5 billion and 2.2 billion tones of CO_2 every year.'

- 'Passenger jets may be responsible for as much as 10 per cent of all greenhouse gas emissions—according to some estimates—with their pollution being injected directly into the upper atmosphere as a kind of "intravenous fix" for global warming.'

Source : The Observer, 8 November 1998.

Pierre Jeanniot, Director-General, International Air Transport Association :

- 'Allow me to correct some of Pat Malone's assertions on air pollution (News, 8 November) : "Aircraft produce between 1.5 and 2.2 billion tones of CO_2 every year". The true figure is closer to 0.5 billion tonnes, that is, 2.5 per cent of the world total from the burning of fossil fuels.'
- 'Passenger jets may be responsible for as much as 10 per cent of all greenhouse gas (GHG) emissions.' Carbon dioxide emissions from air traffic contribute about 1.5 per cent of man-made annual input to global warming. Cumulative emissions of exhaust gases from air traffic are thought to be around 3 per cent.

Source : Letter to the *Observer*, 22 November 1998.

Questions :

1. What kinds of taxes are imposed on tourism?
2. Explain the relationship between demerit goods, merit goods, public goods, taxation and tourism.
3. Why is elasticity of demand an important consideration in setting tax levels.
4. Evaluate the case for scrapping duty free tax concessions.
5. What are the arguments for and against taxation of aviation fuel?
6. What factors should determine the amount of tax imposed on aviation fuel.
7. In what ways could taxes on tourism be used to

maximize employment and minimize environmental damage?

8. Compare taxation with other instruments for achieving environmental improvements in the leisure and tourism sector.

9. Why is it important to accurately assess the environmental impacts of air travel? Why do disagreements such as those noted above make life difficult for economists?